LIFE GOING FORWARD IN
America

— PART 3 —

BILL FLYNN

ISBN 978-1-0980-4467-1 (paperback)
ISBN 978-1-0980-4468-8 (digital)

Christian Faith Publishing, Inc.
832 Park Avenue
Meadville, PA 16335
www.christianfaithpublishing.com

Printed in the United States of America

In memory of Ronald Wayne Samartino, January 28, 1969, to December 26, 2006.

*Ronny Samartino, age twelve, at The Rockpile south of
Wildwood Crest, New Jersey, learning how to surf*

CONTENTS

PREFACE

It has been fourteen years since I self-published the book *Pure Power*. The readers of *Pure Power* have encouraged me to write in more detail about certain topics, my adventures and my experiences in life. It pleases me to know part 1 and part 2 have given people hope, encouragement, and a sense of peace. I received many letters from readers, and part 3 answers some of their concerns. In chapter 1, I have written about my walks. It ended after I walked two thousand miles along back roads through eleven states. My thanks go out to everyone who encouraged me and supported the purpose of promoting individual peace and nonviolence in schools. By naming people, schools, chamber of commerce's, newspapers, and businesses, I hope they will see I appreciate their support. An event of violence and hatred ended "Journey for Peace." For the first time, I am telling the story publicly in this book. Time needed to go by before I could make it public because of the threats and attempts made by a certain hate group. I could not put family members in danger. By ending the walk, the threats stopped. The chapter titled "Journey for Peace" includes this story. My walking proved to be successful despite the acts of violence against me. I will not be silenced! This book is about purpose, so I am putting it out and encouraging students to read it. As you will see, part 3 is different than the previous writings. I have tried to broaden my works and cover more topics. This book, in total, is the most important works of my life. It will still be around long after I am gone. This is a good thing!

CHAPTER I

Journey for Peace

The first official steps I took on "Journey for Peace" was in front of the Stratton, Maine Post Office after mailing a letter off to my parents letting them know the walk began the morning of May 15, 1997. Stratton is a village within the town of Eustis, Maine. This is why you may see me refer to my hometown in Maine as Eustis/ Stratton. I lived there from December 1989 to May 1997 when I literally walked out of town. For the next two years, my time was occupied with walking or working for short periods to keep financing my walking.

"Me at Stratton Post Office on 5/15/97 looking South"

One mile down the road, I stopped at our local eatery, Mainely Yours, where a group of local people joined me for breakfast. After an hour of joking and having a fun time, everyone cheered me on, and six women and two men joined me for the first day's walk. We walked along the shoulder of Route 27 until we reached Sugarloaf Mountain Resort which is home of the world-known Sugarloaf USA Ski Mountain. We walked despite a chilly light rain and a long upward climb followed by an even longer decent along Route 27 South. We even had an adult cow moose cross the road just ahead of us where the Appalachian Trail crosses the narrow two-lane highway. Sighting of moose is common in this region of Maine. I remember that day a day of laughter, jokes, and genuine friendships. When we reached the entrance to Sugarloaf USA, we had a picture taken of us wet, happy walkers.

"First day of Journey for Grace. Fellow hikers for the day"
From left: Bill, Bill, Pam, Clair, Linda, Debbi, IZA,
Kathy, Jean First Day of a Long Journey

We parted with mixed feelings of joy and sadness. I knew the journey would continue without having these supportive people by my side, but I knew they would be with me in spirit every step of the way. I then walked up the access road to the base area of Sugarloaf where I stayed the night in a comfortable unit, compliments of the management at the resort. Sugarloaf Resort is a first-class resort, so I sure was treated. I slept really good that night!

The second day was both eventful and encouraging. While walking down the access road to get back onto Route 27, several of the resort's personnel joined me and filmed me walking so they could record and feature my walk on their world wide website. It was the first major media report concerning "Journey for Peace." Then as I turned back onto Route 27 South, the entire student body and teachers of Carrabassett Valley Academy of Carrabassett Valley, Maine, were awaiting to greet me. They totally surprised me! They were grouped along the side of the road to welcome and encourage me. The academy is one of the best schools in the United States for students interested in progressing toward the Olympics. The academy has plenty of success stories. Look them up!

I did not expect to see anyone that morning. I will always remember those students and teachers. They were full of questions about the journey, so I spent quite a bit of time speaking with them. We talked right there alongside the road within an area of grass in front of the school. A few of the questions I remember were: "Aren't you worried about being alone along the roads?"; "What inspires you to attempt such a venture?"; "How can we follow your progress?" They were very concerned about what they could do as individuals to promote nonviolence in schools and personal peace in their lives. I gave them my best thoughts and answers which came from the heart. I learned from them, and they listened to me. The one thing I can say is that those students of teenage years already knew what respect and courtesy is all about. Thank you, CVA of Carrabassett Valley, Maine!

Later in the day, the temperature dropped quickly, and the wind grew to over thirty miles an hour. It snowed. It was May 16! I knew it could happen since this is the mountain region of Maine. My body felt the cold. My hands felt frozen even though I was exerting plenty of energy by walking at a brisk pace and carrying a fifty-five-pound backpack. I stopped at a small rest area south of the valley and bundled up. The extra clothing that I had packed for the first part of the walk came in handy and warmed my body.

The Message I Carried

Whenever I spoke to students, I read them a prepared message I wrote for the walk. This is the message I gave and offered throughout the walk. Here is what I wrote and spoke about.

The message I wish to give involves six points:

1. Respect
2. Simplicity
3. Knowledge
4. Hope
5. Communication
6. Truth

Respect: involves your thoughts and your actions. Respect of God, yourself, others, and of the environment is key to understanding peace. Respect does not stand alone but leads the way to limiting violence.

Knowledge: is a progression of life! Each society throughout history has (and still does) taught their young so they can survive on their own after adolescence. A good education and an understanding of basic values and principles promote nonviolence. Knowledge is gained by schooling, by learning from mistakes, and by experiences we all encounter during our everyday life.

Hope: is what keeps a person going when things get tough. With hope, we can dream, we can set goals, and we can cope better with sufferings or hardships. Help those who seem hopeless, and it will lift your spirit when they turn toward hope. A person without hope is more likely to hurt themselves or others. Rescuing someone from hopelessness is a step toward promoting nonviolence. It may even be a leap!

Communication: Between students, teachers, administrators, law enforcement, and especially parents is essential to limiting violence in school. Communication between students is essential to preventing a deadly and horrible event. Students know the most when it comes to what other students discuss or complain about. If just one student knows about a plan to shoot or harm those at their school, communication becomes a responsibility.

Truth: leads to trust and trust leads to peace. Young people see the value of trust than most adults do. This is my opinion based on experience. The ability to listen and then to answer with truth is a sign of a strong person. Society today lacks truth. It is time to turn the pages of time and value truth again. Today's students can direct society back to truth if they demand the truth more often and expose the untruths. Truth, justice, and compassion are needed to keep society in balance.

This was the only written message I carried with me on the journey. Because I was usually introduced to the student bodies as being a martial arts instructor and a writer, they listened more intently to the things I spoke about. I took questions at every school I spoke at. If I didn't have an answer to a question, I would tell them so. I spoke "from the heart" which connected with students. Whether it was a first grade or a senior class, they were interested in my purpose and my method of getting the message out. With school shootings increasing and the news media reporting more about school violence during that period of time, I felt compelled to continue walking and to speak at any school I was asked to visit. By the third day of "Journey for Peace," we knew that over five hundred students were following my progress. This surely kept hope alive with me. I will mention this one thing because there are those who have questioned if I profited financially by speaking at schools. I never received a penny for my time with the students. I didn't even consider being paid. If they or their parents bought my book, *Pure Power*, it was not at the schools. Besides, every penny I received from the sales of the book went toward the expenses of the walk. Even my original cost of having one thousand books printed went toward my walks. I need to explain this because many people have a hard time understanding that *purpose* has more value than money. Dollars were needed, but my focus was on the message first. I am questioned often about the things I do or the things I have done. This is fine. I realize it is hard for people living within a materialistic world to believe a person can put purpose before profit. I also understand the questioning because our world is littered with scam artists, dishonest people, and those befitting financially within the charity world. Along the journey, I was answering the skeptics, but the majority of people I saw were trying to benefit society, so they voiced their encouragement to me or sent letters to my mailbox as I walked.

Now back to the walks. I learned a lesson along Route 27. Because the road is heavily crowned and the shoulders of the road follow the crown, my heels blistered along the sides of both feet. By the time I arrived in Kingfield, my feet were blistered badly. At Kingfield, Maine, I stayed at the Inn on Winter's Hill which is a bed-and-breakfast establishment. The owners had previously offered me a free stay, so I took them up on their friendly offer. The first thing I did after being shown to my room was address my blister problems. After seeing how bad my heels were, I knew I would need an extra day to heal somewhat. I also knew my stash of moleskin would be coming in handy. Moleskin is a hiker's savior when it comes to blisters. Without the moleskin, I would do severe damage to the areas already hurting from the skin being off. When I was ready to resume the journey, I would put moleskin over the entire area affected and leave it on until it fell off on its own. The moleskin I put on in Kingfield remained on my feet for several days. Without the moleskin on, you have to wait for your skin to heal again. Experienced hikers know what I mean. Hiking along the sides of roads is quite different than hiking trails in the woods or up mountain sides. Your feet are on a slant because of the road's curvature, so the pressure to the sides of your heels are greater than if you are walking "level" footed. Plus, my backpack weighed fifty-five pounds because of the extra clothing and gear I needed while still in the mountain region of Maine.

Kingfield, Maine, was a good stop. I had visited and spoken to the students at Kingfield Elementary School several weeks before starting the journey, so it was comforting to me when several of them wished me luck as they spotted me walking through town. Students at Stratton Elementary School, Kingfield Elementary School, Rangeley Lakes Regional School, Carrabassett Valley Academy, and my own students at Neko-Ashi Dojo in Eustis were now tracking the progress of the journey. Information was going out on Sugarloaf's website, local newspapers, and through Julie Bolduc's website in Stratton, Maine. Julie volunteered to use her site so students everywhere could get periodic updates and an occasional photo concerning the walks. The farther I walked, the more school students and teachers joined with following me via the Internet. I knew of two schools that had put up a map of the United States and used thumbtacks to show the route I had covered as I progressed. It is a good way of learning geography, I guess.

Sensei (teacher) Ron Perkins, Sensei Tom Lemont, and Sensei Mike Butler took over the teaching at Neko-Ashi Dojo before I left Eustis. There were over forty students learning the art of USA-GOJU Karate in Eustis. Every sensei taught for free so the youth of the area could learn an art without worrying about being able to afford it. I founded the dojo with the help of the town's governing body. The first class was held in January 1990 with a handful of students. I congratulate the people of Eustis/Stratton, the Selectmen, and my Black Belts for continuing a great program. Ron Perkins's two sons also helped to teach. They began learning at the age of seven in the early 1990s. Billy Perkins and Bobby Perkins each attained the second-degree black belt level under my teaching with the approval of Sensei Edward Verycken, now tenth-degree black belt and the head of USA-GOJU Karate. I no longer teach due to a serious fall in construction in 2003. That story will come later. Mike Butler and his son Derek were the first two black belts in Eustis history. The same night of their test, Mike's other son Davin passed his purple belt test. This was on July 7, 1996. USA-GOJU Karate was founded by Peter Urban in 1964. He formed the American GOJU Karate Association which continues today.

After two nights in Kingfield and a lot of care to my blistering heels, I put on the moleskin and set out toward Farmington, Maine. Halfway to Farmington, I camped in the woods for the night. I found a clear spot in the woods about a hundred yards from the road. I had no campfire and therefore no heat. I slept in a bivy shelter which was waterproof and wind resistant. A bivy shelter is a one-person tent which holds you, your sleeping bag, and affords you enough room to turn over in your sleep. It is lightweight and strong with a sealed floor of Gore-Tex material. Where your head is, there is a screen for ventilation. A storm flap covers this if needed.

I had a good night's sleep. Just before sunrise, I was awakened by an old porcupine sniffing my face through the screen. I could not figure out what it was at first, being still groggy and half asleep. When it backed up a little, I saw it was a large porcupine with grayish black hair and its spines were upright. I prayed it would keep moving away. It slowly did. You can imagine how relieved I felt! I don't ever want to be nose to nose with an old porcupine again. He turned around, gave me one final look, then disappeared into the forest's undergrowth.

A heavy frost covered the bivy shelter, so I lay awake until the sun rose and warmed the tents outside. An hour after sunrise, I was back on Route 27 south. Every four to five miles, I stopped to check my feet. I felt pain while walking, but you just have to live with it and see it through. When I reached Farmington, Maine, I was out of the higher elevations, and the temperatures were warmer. Jean Demers from Eustis had volunteered to drive down and meet me when I arrived in Farmington. I phoned Jean after settling into a single unit at the Mount Blue Motel. He was taking my cold weather clothing and gear back with him to Eustis and store it for me. This lightened my pack to forty-five pounds, according to how much water and food I carried. Ten pounds less weight along with a less crown in the roads would be a blessing. Thank you, Jean, again.

While staying in Farmington, I did a book signing at the Mr. Paperback bookstore. About thirty people showed up to purchase *Pure Power* and to listen to the ideas I had concerning "Journey for Peace." Every book sold helped me finance the walk. The owners of Mount Blue Motel ordered ten copies of *Pure Power*, and they gave me a low price on the motel rent. I was learning how people believe in purpose. By hearing their words, accepting their kindness, and seeing their desire for peace in everyday life, it comforted me. I did have the skeptics no matter where I went, but they were few in number and were overshadowed by the interest people had with the good things in life.

While in Farmington, I took time to write a fictional story relating to the school shootings which seemed to be increasing since the tragedy at Columbine High in Jefferson County, Colorado. The continuing shootings affected all of us. I wrote this because we all had questions about the *why* of these acts. This is a young girl's situation. It is fiction.

Senseless Harm

"Why me? I never called him any names or teased him. Why am I laying here in pain and not able to move? He knows me! We have classes together. I lent him my pen yesterday. Why did he have to shoot me? What has made him so mean?

"Oh no! He is shooting again. I guess it isn't just me. Sounds like he is in the gym area. Someone please stop him!

When will someone find me and get me help? I can't take this pain much longer! I wish I could move 'cause I know I'm losing blood somewhere. I hear them running. Why don't they see me? There's another shot! He must be farther away by the sound of it. Or is it that I am fading? Is this where I spend the last minutes of my life? God, please, I am only sixteen! There is so much I haven't done, so much I've dreamed of doing. I must be fading. It's getting so quiet, and I can't keep my eyes open. I don't feel the pain now, but I know I'm hurt bad. This can't be real. Maybe I am dreaming. Yeah right, that's it. I'll wake up and find myself in study class. I've seen too many news reports about school shootings, and now they are in my dreams. Yeah, I am just dreaming.

"Who is shaking me? Oh, it is you, Robin. My eyes may be blurred, but you are such a welcome sight! Thanks for waking me from that terrible dream. Robin, don't you hear me? Why are you crying? I can feel your tears falling onto my face, but why can't I hear any sounds? I can't move! It isn't a dream. I am dying! I wish you could hear me, Robin. I love you. Good-bye, my twin."

After two days in Farmington, Maine, I resumed walking. It felt good to have a lighter backpack and to wear clean clothes again. About a half mile outside of Farmington, I stood and looked back to see the mountains I had walked from. From the spot I stood, I could see most of Farmington. The city is a college town with no high-rise buildings. A division of the University of Maine is there, and there is a lot of history associated with the city itself. While looking back, a familiar truck pulled off the road near me. It was Stephen Philbrick from Oquossoc, Maine. It was great to see Steve. We talked for quite a while. He is the kind of person you can trust with your life if needed. Steve and his two sons, Tyler and Quinn, came to the karate dojo for several years. This was how I got to know the three as friends. Steve and his wife own Bald Mountain Camps in Oquossoc, Maine. The camps are a gem of Maine which have been in their family for generations. After finishing my journey, I visited them a few times. They are good people living a good Mainer's life!

Several miles later, I left Route 27 and picked up Route 4 South. The roadside was mostly level now and easier to walk. My feet could heal much faster now. Most of the journey would be spontaneous now. I would not know where my nights would be spent or even if I could stay at campgrounds. It is quite an adventure and a bit scary not knowing the territory you are walking into.

The days were long. With walking alone, it gets boring unless there are people you meet and share stories with. One thought came to me after leaving Farmington and having a successful book signing at the Mr. Paperback bookstore. I will try my best to recall it now after thirteen years and six months of my "life going forward." I thought, *How is it I cannot get a publisher when the people who read* Pure Power *tell me it is a good book with a strong message? And I am willing to walk across the United States to promote the theme of* Pure Power— *peace.* Before starting the journey, I wrote query letters to over one hundred publishers. Every response was a polite no. I also wrote to thirty or more corporations in hopes of receiving a few sponsors to help me finance the walk and my visits to schools. Again, I received polite nos. I believe the reason for rejection was because I am not a celebrity and I am not well known. Public figures and celebrities also have publicists and agents. I am one person with a very limited bank account. The funding for "Journey for Peace" came primarily from my savings, book sales, and people's donations which were small yet greatly appreciated. Hope stayed alive because of the people I spoke with along the way. Encouragement came daily. Concern about living peaceful lives seemed to be shared by everyone I came in contact with. "Journey for Peace" still has purpose. This is why I am writing about it, the people involved and the places I walked through.

The next town I came to was Jay-Livermore, Maine. They have a large wood and pulp mill there which keeps the city alive because of the jobs the mill provides. As I entered Jay-Livermore, Maine, my walking miles totaled seventy-one. My strength had increased, and my feet were healing. I stayed the night just south of town. The following day led me to Turner, Maine, where I left Route 4 and started west on Route 117. I trekked eighteen miles that day and found a great camping spot at Martin Stream Campgrounds. The best part of my stay was a potluck dinner shared by over forty "regulars" who camped there. I was invited to share the various home-cooked meals they had, and I enjoyed every dish I tried. It rained that night and into the morning. Since the people at Martin Stream Campgrounds were so nice to be with, I decided to stay another day.

The next two towns were South Paris and Norway, Maine. I walked over Streaked Mountain with blackflies swarming around me. This was their time of the year to appear in mass. I was prepared! I had one pair of long pants and a net jacket to cover my upper body and head. The net jacket protects you from the scores of bites you might receive. It keeps the biting bugs from getting into your eyes, your hair, and even your nose. When they swarm around you, it is like a small cloud of biting flies. Without protection, you can go a little crazy. In some areas of the eastern United States, people put up with "gnats" which are very similar to the blackflies of Maine and New Hampshire. A blackfly eats a very tiny piece of your skin. This is the bite. You won't feel the bite until later when it becomes itchy. When the blackflies are biting, the fish follow suit, or so they say.

After Norway, I walked to Bridgton, Maine, where C.C. Hamilton and her mother put me up in a small cabin along the shoreline of Highland Lake. When I woke the next morning, I experienced a great view from the cabin. The early morning sun shined across the lake's surface. The lake's water lay still and looked like a mirror. The trees along the far side of the lake were reflected by the still water. Far in the distance, I could see Mount Washington with snow still covering its higher elevations. I was in Maine, looking at a mountain in New Hampshire. It was a great distance away, yet it looked impressive. Mount Washington is the highest mountain in the northeastern United States. It is a site for weather research which is done year-round at its summit laboratory.

Right in front of the cabin, I saw an occasional fish rising to the surface, feeding on bugs. Talk about peace. This sure was the place and the morning to experience it. Bridgton, Maine, is one beautiful place!

The blisters on both of my heels were healed now, and skin had grown back in the areas where they were most damaged. My right knee had swollen, but it was feeling much better because of a neo-prene covering I wore for about five days while walking. After leaving Bridgton, I rarely had to use moleskin again, and my knee felt strong after the swelling ceased and went away. My leg muscles grew stronger, my pace quickened, and my body weight lessoned. The nights became warmer as I headed southwest. The days were comfortable with the temperatures averaging in the seventy to eighty-degree levels.

Sebago Lake Region is a popular summer spot in Maine. Lucky for me, I walked through this area just before the season started. I bought an unusual postcard in a small coffee shop. I mailed it to my parents who got a kick out of it. The card shows a highway directional sign made of wooden arrows. The arrows point the way to Norway, Paris, Denmark, Naples, Sweden, Poland, Mexico, Peru, and China. These are all small cities in Maine.

In East Sebago, Maine, I stayed for a night at the Rockcraft Retreat Center. David Brown overheard me talking with a few locals about the journey while we sat at the counter of a small eatery, having coffee and sandwiches. After leaving the local establishment, David approached me and offered me a place to stay the night. The retreat wasn't open yet, but he told me I could stay in the Carriage House which had nine bunk beds, a bathroom, and a television. He gave me directions how to get there, and I took him up on his generous offer. Two miles down the road (Route 117-107S), I met him there, and he showed me around the retreat. I had walked sixteen miles that day, so a warm shower and a comfortable bed felt great. With having a television to watch, I was able to catch up on the news. My usual way of knowing what was going on in the world was reading a newspaper each day. The Carriage House is where groups stay while having their retreats. The center is right on Sebago Lake, and the grounds are surrounded by woods. The main house on the property was once the owner's mansion. I am not sure if it was the surroundings or the good spirits the center had which caused me to write a short story that night, but here it is.

Heaven Revealed

I awoke inspired as the morning sun warmed the forest surrounding my cabin. The pond out front lay still, as mist floated above its surface. Today will be the day I shall write about heaven!

Spirit Mountain rose high above my peaceful home in Maine. By noon, I had climbed to its summit and settled myself on the peak where I could look down at the pond and the wooded valley I call home. Very few people visit this land where moose, black bears, deer, and various other creatures roam free. It is the very nature of the surroundings which lead me to write and to contemplate upon that which is most important. So as I sit cross-legged on the peak of Spirit Mountain, inspiration begins, and my pen begins to follow.

Heaven is where God is and where our spirits will be forever because of His blessings. With our physical death, our spirit (soul) leaves the body and joins a spiritual community within the universe. God's kingdom has music, appealing scents, comfort, and total security. Time is no longer measured since heaven is eternal. Pain does not exist. Sleep is not needed. Our nourishment is love, not water and food. There is no evil in heaven. It is exiled to hell. Jesus greets us with open arms, and He opens our spiritual eyes to truth and knowledge no human is allowed to see. We celebrate with those who have come before us, and we give all the glory to God, our Father.

Heaven is a state of joy and peace. Violence does not exist. There is no fear, no anxieties, no greed or jealousy, no vanity. God frees us from suffering and from sin when He welcomes us into His home. Heaven is freedom, happiness, eternal love, and an existence without flaw. Because Jesus Christ died on the cross and resurrected three days later, we can enter heaven. God is our Judge, our Creator, and our Father. As I look out from atop the mountain, I hope He will allow you and me to live forever with Him in heaven! My time on earth is brief, but it has such a tremendous purpose. Which path leads to heaven? It is the path Jesus Christ showed us.

The walk continued by traveling (on foot) through Gorham, Maine, then Westbrook which is not far from the first big city on the journey—Portland, Maine. I was now one hundred and seventy miles into the walk. I felt excited about reaching Portland because I knew there would be a package awaiting me at the post office there. Mom had sent a "mail drop" to me, marked general delivery, which contained letters from people, the mail being forwarded to my parents from my PO Box in Stratton, Maine, and cookies she had baked. Mom also put in my favorite snacks, marshmallow treats she made at my request.

I arrived in Portland during the early morning hours. It was June 1, 1997. I booked two nights at the Saint James Place, which is a hotel. I needed some time to get my package, read the mail, do my laundry, and watch a movie or two. I had phoned Mom from Harrison, Maine, to set up the mail drop. Harrison is just outside of Bridgton, Maine. I was informed there were quite a few letters, so I was anxious to read them and to see what various people would say in their letters.

After checking into my room, I went to the post office. There were two packages awaiting me. My sister, Colleen, had also sent me a package which included the e-mails she received from people and a report on how many books had been ordered since I began the walk on May 15, 1997. The book sales were not promising. Most every bookstore I had visited along the way did not order books even though the managers told me they would. There is a saying I use a lot. It is, "Promises, promises." The e-mails from people were comforting and encouraged me to keep at it. I felt very disappointed about the bookstore owners and managers not ordering books. Many of them had told me they would be ordering five to ten books. I had figured about two to three hundred books would have sold, but only fifty books were sold, and they were to people I had met along the way who contacted my sister.

Being in a large city made me realize the journey would be costly at times. I prefer to camp at campgrounds or state parks because the costs are much less and the social atmosphere is good. It is my belief that people are more defensive in areas having large numbers of people. In these areas, people tend to be less friendly, and they keep more to themselves and to the people they know. I do not blame them because it is safer to be with people who you know. But I do not like the atmosphere of cities. I can only imagine what people were thinking when they saw me walking through their cities carrying a big backpack on my back and carrying a walking stick. Believe me, I received a ton of curious looks and comments! The most common were: "Are you running away from home?"; "Are you lost?"; and "The woods are that way." (pointing out of town); "Did you just get out of prison?" I took all their comments by returning a smile and giving them a friendly nod.

Because of the numerous newspaper articles written about the walk, I was not always a stranger. When I received a friendly shout or wave from people driving by me along the road, I figured they had read one of the articles about "Journey for Peace." The further I walked, the more "word of mouth" carried the details about me.

Before leaving Portland, Maine, I packed a box with items I could do without now that hot weather was becoming the norm. The one pair of long pants, a long-sleeved cotton pullover, two pairs of socks, and a few other items were put into the box. I mailed it to my parents whom I would visit later along the route I planned. I needed to reduce the weight of the pack so more water could be carried. With hotter days, my intake of water increased and kept me from dehydrating.

I left Portland, Maine, on June third. The first newspaper reporter to actually walk along with me as he interviewed was Arron Smith, a reporter for the *York County Coast Star* out of Kennebunk, Maine. I had previously walked through Saco, Biddeford, and

Kennebunk. Aaron caught me near the border of Wells and North Berwick, Maine. We were on Route 9, close to the New Hampshire/Maine border. We walked over a mile together as Aaron asked me a variety of questions. Because of always being on the move, I hardly ever got to read the articles people wrote, so I asked Aaron if he would send the article to my dad. Dad was keeping a journal for me. He put all the postcards I sent, newspaper articles sent to him, and letters people wrote into a binder. Thanks to Dad, I am now able to write about the journey without totally relying on memory. Aaron's article arrived at my parents' house, just as dozens of others did while I was walking. The article was about a thousand words, and it included a picture of me along the side of Route 9. Here is a quote which I remember well: "Flynn said the scent of the sea was the first thing he noticed when he walked into Wells. 'I could smell the ocean, so I knew I was close,' said Flynn."

When I entered Wells, Maine, my two-hundredth mile was reached. The news covering "Journey for Peace" was always behind me because I was alone in planning and communication. I did not carry a cell phone. I used calling cards to call my brother-in-law, Dave Kettering, to give him reports of the progress. He would then e-mail Julie Bolduc, in Stratton, so she could post it on her website. Basically, I received newspaper coverage by stopping in at any news office I walked by. Radio coverage was received in the same way. Some of the people I met along the way would call in and tell reporters about the journey. More than a few times, I was surprised by seeing a reporter pull up alongside the road ahead of me and ask for an interview. It all helped to get the message out. The journey was spontaneous. Because of this, I was not able to speak at schools in most towns because it would have to be approved by the school planning boards. The Catholic schools were easy to speak at. I simply went to see the Monsignor at a parish, and his approval had me speaking in their classrooms or student assemblies. I usually spent a half an hour with a monsignor explaining the purpose of "Journey for Peace," showed him the references I carried with me and my book *Pure Power*. I was never turned down by any monsignor or priest.

Private schools have less "red tape" and don't have to be "politically correct."

After going through Berwick, Maine, I got a bit lost. I was trying to get to Rochester, New Hampshire, but I ended up in Dover, New Hampshire. When you get turned around on foot, it isn't easy. It is not like traveling in a car, if you know what I mean. Going miles in the wrong direction does not help your progress. After twenty-one miles of walking that day, I had to rent a motel room in the city. There were no camping spots for quite a distance, and I was tired. After talking with the motel manager, I found out I had walked to far north. He gave me directions to follow the next day, which would lead me out of Dover and back onto Route 9 West. When you are walking the roadside, you cannot walk along some major highways, interstate highways, and various bridges. This causes pedestrian longer routes to follow. I was learning the realities of walking across country as I progressed.

Outside of Rochester, New Hampshire, the walk took me along the North River for miles. I camped at a small campground where the ticks seemed to be everywhere. Inside the camp shower room, I removed at least a dozen ticks from my body. I sprayed the inside of the bivy shelter to keep the ticks away from me while sleeping. It worked. The camp didn't have a store, so in the morning, I walked six miles before having breakfast because I didn't prepare myself the day before. When you don't have food and you are on foot, it is water that fills you and keeps you going. I had run out of the coffee bags I usually used for morning coffees, so when I eventually reached a small general store which served breakfast, it felt good! I ordered a large meal and had a double dose of coffee.

That night, I stayed in Northwood Narrows, New Hampshire, after covering fifteen to eighteen miles along Route 202. It is amazing how many antique stores there are along the roads of Southern New Hampshire. The roads are flat with good, solid shoulders, so the trekking was easy. The soles of the boots I started with were worn down, so I bought a pair of sneakers and discarded the boots. Efforts of getting a shoe or sneaker sponsor were fruitless even though I was receiving much newspaper coverage. Their name brand could have received quite a bit of advertising. Oh well!

The next day brought me to the State Capital, Concord, New Hampshire. It is an impressive city with great political history. Most of the people along Main Street were dressed in business suits or fine clothing. I really stood out walking along the avenue, carrying a backpack and wearing shorts, a T-shirt, and sneakers. I received quite a few curious stares. With being curious myself, looking at the Capital Building and the numerous political headquarters buildings I walked right by the turn, I should have made in town to put me back onto Route 9 West. A mile later, I asked a person how I could find the road to Route 9. He gave me directions which would take me through a college campus and then back onto Route 9. It turned out to be a long day of walking, but I was thrilled to have seen the Capital Building where so much news is covered during the presidential primaries every four years. On June 19, I walked into the rural town of Hillsboro, New Hampshire, where the local people treated me great. I spent the night at the 1830 House Motel, where Brenda and George Hanson offered me a room at no cost after learning of the purpose of "Journey for Peace." They even set up an interview for me with the local newspaper, *The Messenger*. Floyd Henderson, from *The Messenger*, interviewed me and took pictures of me with my backpack on, in front of The Corner Store where we had breakfast (the following morning) with some of the locals. I enjoyed those fine people who knew how to laugh and "spin a few yarns" (tell stories). Floyd's article came out on June 23, 1997. Brenda Hanson mailed a copy of it to my dad. I hope everyone in Hillsboro is doing fine. You have a nice place to live.

I started out again after a restful stay at the 1830 House Motel with a full stomach, after a hearty breakfast at The Corner Store. Fog kept visibility low for several hours, yet the temperature felt comfortable. It was at seventy degrees with no breeze. For any readers who have never been to New Hampshire, I recommend you take a tour sometime and drive around on the back roads to see all the structures, homes, monuments, and antique stores which are full of American history. Because of a slow pace, I was able to stop and read the many sign markers along the roadside, which explain the significance of particular places. On top of these metal signs is the seal of the state of New Hampshire. Here is one example of a particular sign I read that day.

"In 1772, the people called Methodist held their first religious meeting in this state, on the James Robertson farm, 1.2 miles from here, on Christian Street, with Phillip Embury as the preacher. On June 20, 1803, Francis Asbury spoke here using as his text: 'Let us run with patience the race that is set before us.'"

A Civil War Monument alongside of Route 9 in Sullivan Center, New Hampshire, is across the road from a small general store I had stopped at to buy some food and fluids. The monument is about fifteen feet high and set on a mound surrounded by a wood rail fence. It is the first Civil War marker in New Hampshire to be raised and dedicated. It was erected in 1867 by the Ladies Aid Society. I am guessing it was hand built. It resembles our Washington Monument, in Washington DC, yet it was built earlier.

Near Stoddard, New Hampshire, there is another historic marker right off the shoulder of Route 9. Lucky for me and others, we are able to see the actual bridge still intact but not used for years. It is the Stone Arch Bridge. It was used by horsemen and wagons crossing a small shallow river, which still runs under it. The stones (arch stones) were shaped by experts and placed together without the use of mortar. It was built during the early nineteenth century through this forested area. As I sat looking at the unique structure, I pictured the people back then crossing the bridge on their horses or wagons. It was most likely one of the main routes of travel. It is truly an architectural wonder. And it has stood the test of time and environmental wear.

I am getting ahead of myself, but since I am writing about historic markers, I wish to tell you about the one marker which both educated me and brought a strong sense of sadness to me. A lone historic marker in New York State will always be in my memory. It is along a back road. I didn't have a camera, and I didn't make a note about the location of this marker, but I am sure it can be found because the state sets these markers and they have records concerning their markers.

Until reading this marker, I was not aware that slaves were used to farmlands in New York State. The landowner (back then) owned a prominent estate and used his slaves to work his farm. Not far from this marker is where the slaves lived, in small, one-story houses, set away from the landowner's mansion. The slaves were given the spot near the marker to bury their dead. Originally, it was a ravine near a gravel road. Now it is a hill about thirty feet high and the size of half a football field. There are no burial markers because the dead were buried atop each other, in wooden coffins, built by their fellow slaves. I sat looking at the hill, now covered by bushes and small trees. I felt extremely sad. I wondered how many people must have been buried there and just how many years this site was used by the African slaves, forced to work their entire lives for someone else's gain. If you sit at that spot, I am sure you will sense a feeling of theirs spirits crying out to you. I felt it! The only other time I experienced a feeling of having spirits around me was when I entered the Alamo at San Antonio, Texas, if you know what I mean. I am not comparing what occurred at both of these places. I am explaining the feeling I sensed about a certain spiritual presence. I sat and prayed at the burial site before continuing to walk. I am sure the landowner's family had their own cemetery with markers and monuments for people to see their names and years of life. If this "hill" gets national attention someday, I am sure many people will travel to say a prayer there. It is good the state of New York erected a historic marker at the spot, so a person like myself can learn about the souls buried there.

Three Hundred Miles

Upon entering Keen, New Hampshire, I had walked three hundred miles from Eustis, Maine. My legs were solid, I weighed twenty pounds less, and temperatures were warm, and my pace averaged four miles an hour. Book sales were just not happening. I was busy walking, and bookstore owners would not carry *Pure Power* because I did not have a distributor. As a result, the financing for the walk was coming from my savings. This concerned me deeply because I knew my savings could not carry me across the country. I did not give up hope! I knew when I started the journey it would not be easy and that the purpose of the walk was stronger than material things. I knew (and still know) the feeling of peace as an individual, so if I could spread the feeling to other people, then the journey was worth the effort. I spoke with many people along the way who were curious about the journey. Along the roadsides, at campgrounds, in rest areas, or simply sitting at a park bench, I conversed with people of all ages and backgrounds. A question I was asked repeatedly was, "How does a person come to know personal peace?" The answer was generally like this: first, you must get to know yourself. You need to know your faults, your values, your likes and dislikes. You need to question your life. What is your purpose for living? I believe everyone has a purpose, no matter how small or how big. You need to have humility and live by principles. Faith in God is essential. Without God, we cannot have or know peace because He gives us hope and love. A person of peace knows forgiveness. Forgiving yourself then righting your wrongs is important. We all must accept the fact that we make mistakes and others make mistakes. Trying to correct our mistakes is hard at times, but working toward leading a better life is fruitful and rewarding. We can forgive others if we forgive ourselves. I can forgive, but I usually do not forget because I do not wish mistakes to be repeated. Avoiding negative people and negative things is a big part of how I live. Being with positive thinking people who enjoy life is where I wish to be. Having a sense of humor is important in enjoying each day. Having a good laugh with people strengthens personal peace and is good for our health. Music is another good thing. Since the beginning of humans, music has been there. It is the food and nourishment of the soul. There are lyrics which follow a different path, but generally, music is good for everyone. To know personal peace, we must do without certain things: envy, guilt, hate, greed, selfishness, violence, to mention a few. Knowing peace is not easily obtained. To know peace is a tremendous blessing. I do not always have peace, yet I do know peace. Others can bring violence to me or to you. There are things in life we cannot control. These people can only steal our "inner peace" if we allow them to. The "inner peace" we have is because of our faith. We could (anyone of us) die a violent death, but the life after death is peaceful. With the knowledge that Jesus is with me every step I take in life, good or bad, brings me peace. His love is unconditional. We need such love because we all have faults.

This book is a goal for me to having a purpose in my life. Explaining my thoughts, ideas, and philosophy is personal yet shared because I want the readers to understand me. I do not wish to ever preach to people. I wish to share. This is why I titled this book *Life Going Forward*. We are not sure how long we will live. I see this book as an extension of my life since it will be around many years after I am gone. Peace is a powerful thing! It influences people when they see how good it is. Peace brings prosperity and better health. It brings neighbors and even countries together. It is good!

About a mile west of Keene, New Hampshire, I met Shawna Sevigny, a staff writer for *The Sunday Sentinel* of Keene. She did her interview alongside Route 9. Steve Hooper took a few pictures. Shawna informed me *The Sunday Sentinel* is read by close to or over one million people. Her article, along with a picture taken by Steve, came out on June 15, 1997. I was in Vermont by then. Shawna sent a copy to my dad. It is in the collection of articles Dad kept for me. She wrote a good and honest report about myself, *Pure Power*, and the journey.

Between Keene, New Hampshire, and Brattleboro, Vermont, my heels began to ache and feel tender. They became so sore, I stopped at a fire station to see if any paramedics were on duty. I was in luck. Two paramedics were on duty, and they checked both of my heels. They told me my heels were probably bruised from the constant pounding they were receiving from walking on hard surfaces. They convinced me to give my heels a rest for a week or more. If I continued to walk, my heels would only get worse, and I did not need that. I decided to catch a bus out of Brattleboro, Vermont, to visit my parents in North Wildwood, New Jersey, for about ten days. I figured to do a few book signings while there and maybe even get some advanced publicity done to spur the book sales. I had shipped a few cases of books to my parents before I began walking, so I had plenty of books to generate some funds.

It turned out to be a very positive decision. I got to see my parents, my brother Jack, and my brother Dennis after eight months of not seeing them. I did a book signing at North Wildwood's Annual Italian Festival and sold over thirty copies of *Pure Power*. I got to swim and to surf at the beach. My heels got better, and I visited some of my close friends again. The *Cape May County Herald* and the *Wildwood Leader* newspapers each published articles about "Journey for Peace." Johnathan Maslow of the *Herald* wrote the article for the *Herald*, which came out in their July 2, 1997, copy. Michelle Montgomery, staff writer, wrote the article for the *Wildwood Leader*, which came out on June 25, 1997. I think most newspapers have their past articles available to people via the Internet. This is why I am putting the dates of various stories written. Michelle Montgomery and Jonathan Maslow each wrote a long and comprehensive article, which helped in informing people of my efforts. I grew up in North Wildwood, New Jersey, which is in Cape May County, so their articles reached a lot of people I know from the area.

After ten days, I returned to Brattleboro, Vermont, by bus to resume walking. My heels felt good. I stopped by the fire station to thank the paramedics. They were happy to see my heels had gotten better, and they wished me a safe journey. To put in perspective, the time involved with walking the roads compared to driving a vehicle, I will use Brattleboro and North Wildwood as an example. It takes me seven hours to drive my pickup truck, from Brattleboro, Vermont to North Wildwood, New Jersey. In July 1997, it took me twenty-seven days to walk from Brattleboro, Vermont, to North Wildwood, New Jersey. There is a lot involved when traveling on foot, as you can see.

Vermont is known for its many covered bridges. Many are historic, and some are still in use. One is the Creamery Bridge in Brattleboro. It has 1879 marked on it, and the bridge is still in use. It has been restored over the years, and it looks to be well maintained. The structure appeared to be made of mostly wood, like most of the covered bridges I saw in New England. I was told, Vermont has more covered bridges still in use than all the other New England states combined. The many covered bridges I saw along the walk were single lane and built across small rivers or streams. They are all unique and historically interesting to see. They remind us of the more simplistic era of our country's history.

The walk across Vermont is short on miles but not easy. I had two mountains to walk over. Hogback Mountain was my first climb. I have been there several times before while on skiing trips, but I was driving a vehicle then. The climb up didn't bother my legs because of the shape my leg muscles were in. As with most climbs, the reward is at the top where you can see for miles. There is a lone building right at the top of Hogback Mountain. It is the Vermont Country Market. From their deck, you have a spectacular view of forests, smaller mountains, and a few rooftops visible among the trees. They claim you can see one hundred miles on a clear day from the market's deck. When I was there, it was a cloudy day, yet I could still see many miles beyond Hogback.

Woodford Mountain was the other climb I made along Route 9, in Vermont. I will always remember the long descent I had. This was the longest descent of the walk. The western side of Woodford Mountain seemed like an endless descent. My calf muscles and ankle tendons were all sore by the time I reached the bottom elevation. I had only walked thirteen miles that day, but it felt like much more. That night, I stayed at a hiker's hostel. There were several hikers staying the night there also. We conversed for hours about a multitude of topics. The hostel supplies you with a bed, a warm shower, and a kitchen. It only cost me ten dollars for the night. Everyone sleeps in the same room, which had about twenty single beds. The bathrooms are shared, yet everyone keeps them clean. The living room is where we all gathered at night to share stories and news. Conversation is what happens! It is quite common among hikers to converse for hours. The hikers I met were hiking the Long Trail, which connects with the Appalachian Trail.

Because of the heat during the days, more water is needed to be carried to keep my strength up. The average temperatures were now in the high eighties and low nineties with humidity levels at eighty percent. Along Route 9, I came to where the Long Trail is. I camped near the trail that night, alongside a stream. It was a great place to rest for the night. There was a clean "open air' bathroom which is a luxury when you are hiking.

The last miles in Vermont took me through Bennington, Vermont. Bennington is a very unique place. Walking along Route 9, you can see homes marked with historic plaques dating back into the 1700s and early 1800s. These homes are in terrific shape and seemed to be lived in. The Bennington Battle Monument is located in the city. It stands three hundred and six feet tall. The battle of Bennington was fought on August 16, 1777. The Green Mountain Boys were victorious over the British. I didn't take the time to walk out to the monument, but I could see it clearly from Route 9 just outside of town. I did visit the Bennington Museum since it is located in town along the route I walked. It has a huge source of Revolutionary War history.

Later that day, July 5, 1997, I crossed into New York State. This marked over four hundred miles of walking since leaving Eustis, Maine. I began walking south along Route 7 and Route 22 South. I purchased a travel road map to use through the state. I needed to stay clear of any big cities and to walk along roads which are less populated. On July 6, I camped at a family owned and run campground along Route 7. It is in Petersburg, New York. The campground was inexpensive, clean, and—best of all—safe. New York State is very large. It has vast forestlands, mountains, lakes, rivers, and apple farms. On one really hot day, as I walked along, I stopped at one. There was a sign which read, "Cold Apple Cider Inside." Because it was not the picking season, the large building was full of pallets with several forklifts parked inside. The person I spoke with told me that when the apples are picked later in the season, the warehouse and yard is bustling with workers, trucks, and apples galore! I bought half a gallon of their cold apple cider then sat outside, in the shade, to enjoy the New York cider. The temperature was ninety-six degrees. I had walked about fifteen miles since morning. When I say that cold apple cider was the best drink I ever enjoyed, I mean it!

The route south, in New York State, took me through the Hudson Valley, then southwest toward Unionville, New York, where

I crossed the border into New Jersey. The walk in New York was quite an adventure. I survived two major storms, extremely hot and humid weather and went through an area of one small city controlled by a gang.

The first storm hit an area during the day of July 7, 1997. I was near New Lebanon, New York, at the time. I had stopped at a roadside ice-cream store and treated myself to a large banana-split ice cream with a lot of toppings. A young couple sat with me. They were curious about me having a backpack, so I explained to them about the journey. They warned me about tornado warnings for our area. They were traveling by motorcycle. The sky around us was bright blue and very clear. Without hearing weather reports on the radio or television, you would never guess bad weather was coming our way. We conversed for a while, wished each other luck, and went our separate ways. The banana split and a quart of ice water hit the spot!

After the stop, it was an uphill climb for about a mile and a half. Reaching the top, I turned to look back and saw a frightening sky about two to three miles away. I knew it was a bad one! The color of the clouds was blueish green and dark. There was a definite line contrasting against the clear blue sky above me. Fierce lightning strikes were hitting the earth below those clouds. There were no buildings near me; only open farmland. I searched for somewhere to ride the storm out. There was a deep ravine near the road. It was probably there to control runoff from the snow melting after winter. I found a spot to sit in the ravine, which I hoped would protect me in case of a tornado. Within fifteen minutes, the storm hit my area. I sat covered by my rain poncho. Darkness came, even though it was about three o'clock in the afternoon. I huddled down as the sound of a freight train going by, wised by. There were no trains anywhere near! Later, I learned from people in the area that a small tornado did come through without doing much damage because its path covered mostly farm fields. Three other tornados hit the area between me and Kingston, New York. I saw a lot of damage done by one of them as I walked around a small village the following day. I had to detour because of electric lines laying on the ground, debris being cleaned up, and trees toppled onto the Main Street.

The second storm happened while I was camping for the night at a campground near Walden, New York. I had pitched my bivy shelter on a small hill. There was a picnic area with a shelter, right at the base of the grass covered hill where people could eat and associate with other campers. The storm hit during the night, as I slept comfortably in the small, yet dry, bivy shelter. In the morning, I saw the flooded campers below. I then realized my spot had been the best spot in the campground even though I was without electric, water, or a picnic table. Sometimes, the cheaper sites are the better sites. After having breakfast at their camp store, I packed my gear and walked out. I felt sorry for the many campers whose tents had blown over and were soaked by rain. Some tents had four to six inches of water around them. I am sure those people had a sleepless night.

My adventure in the gang area was scary but without incident. Two undercover policemen warned me ahead of time about a section of a small city I was approaching. They stopped me about a mile from the city. They had heard about my walk from other law enforcement people, and they wanted to make sure I could safely walk thru their area. I will not name the city because it would not be fair to all the other people living there. They told me to make it through the gang area during daylight hours and to stay on the sidewalk. "Don't talk to anyone. Don't respond to anyone. Keep your eyes looking forward and keep a steady pace. We will be watching your back, from our vehicle, in case anything happens. You should be okay, but we will be there. You'll have a quarter of a mile to walk through their area." I thanked them, then we talked for a while about the martial arts and law enforcement.

As I walked within the gang's neighborhood, I knew it was a rough bunch hanging out there. Graffito covered every wall, every door, and even on vehicles parked there. I saw about forty young people who appeared to be gang members, as I walked along. Several of them made comments about me carrying a backpack, but I ignored their comments and kept to my pace. By not initiating anything, by not appearing to be a victim, and by keeping to myself, as I walked past them, they let me continue on without any problems. I am sure that if I showed them any disrespect at all or even a slight glance of displeasure, I would have had serious problems. I knew it was their territory, and I was simply passing through. I am glad the two undercover cops advised me on how to go through that area. They knew how this particular gang thinks, so their advice helped. With other gangs, I may not have been able to walk through their turf. Along the journey, I had to make several detours around certain area because of this.

My favorite place while going through New York State was New Paltz, New York. This is not far from where "Woodstock" happened. I had almost gone to Woodstock, but I couldn't get off from work, so I stayed home. I was going to ride my motorcycle to get there and back. Who knows how Woodstock might have changed my life. I was about seventeen at that time, and I was not too mature in my thinking. At the same time, I may have had a really fun time. No one knew at the time just how big the event would be. All we knew was a lot of good musicians were going to be there. Woodstock was the biggest musical occurrence our generation had. The people who went there experienced a historic event. Oh well, I stayed home and worked.

The thing I liked about New Paltz, New York, is that many of the storeowners in the older section of town are original Woodstocker's, who never left the area after the festival ended. One such owner contacted David Olson, who wrote for the *Times Herald-Record* of Middleton, New York. I met with David while in New Paltz, and he interviewed me. His article came out on July 10, 1997, the day I walked into Middleton after walking fifty-five miles after leaving New Paltz. Between New Paltz and Middleton, I went the wrong way (again) for about five miles. With help from local people, I was directed in the right direction after becoming confused and *lost*. The last day of walking toward Middleton was extremely hot and humid. I covered twenty-three miles and drank water throughout the day. The temperatures were ranging into the nineties and near the one-hundred-degree mark. I took a motel room on July 10 to get a needed rest and a break from the heat. To enjoy the comfort of a morning breakfast at their restaurant felt really, really good!

On July 12, I came into Unionville, New York. The Appalachian Trail is only a mile or so from this small town. There is a hostel where hikers, coming off the trail, stay. They leave the trail to buy supplies, receive mail drops and relax at a place where they can shower, do laundry, and eat a meal at a diner or restaurant. This is a luxury for every long-distance hiker after they have rough it for days out on the trail. The hostel charged me five dollars to stay the night. I enjoyed the company of four hikers who had just come off the trail to spend a few nights in town. The three women and one male started walking the trail (AT) in Georgia. They were planning to finish the entire trail which ends in Maine. We talked for several hours that evening. I was familiar with the Appalachian Trail, in Maine, so I informed them about what to expect. The four hikers had one story after another about their experiences since beginning the trail. You could tell their bond of friendship was strong, by the way they kidded each other and joked around. Ask any person who has hiked the Appalachian Trail, from end to end, and they will tell you, "The four hikers are family." I have a great respect for those hikers who have done the AT, from Georgia to Maine, or vice versa. On average, it takes four to five months to complete the entire trail.

The next day, I crossed the New Jersey/New York border while walking along Route 284 south. Sussex, New Jersey, was my goal for that day. The following day was the hottest day yet! Midday temperatures went over one hundred degrees with very high humidity. I walked eighteen miles, drank water constantly, and sweated up a storm. Upon entering Newton, New Jersey, late in the day, I headed to Swartswood State Park to camp at their camping site section. It proved to be quite an exciting night! Just after dark, I was laying inside of my bivy shelter with the tent screen up over my head. The site was located near a wooded area. There was a large grass area where I lay. The neighbors were busy cooking their supper on barbecues some twenty yards away. The sun had set hours earlier. The campground was lighted only by the lanterns or campfires at people's sites. It was a peaceful and calm night. I had eaten earlier. Tired from walking in the intense heat, I was now ready for a long sleep. My head rested on a folded T-shirt which was my pillow for the night.

I thought I could hear something coming toward me. I focused on the sound, which was actually more of a vibration on the ground than a noise. Whatever it was, it came closer and closer and then suddenly stopped. When I heard it sniffing me and my shelter, I realized there was a bear within inches of me! I lay perfectly still. My food was hanging from a tree branch far enough away from my shelter, so there was no food for him (or her) to have where I lay. The bear's breath stunk. The sooner the bear would leave, the better. It did. I saw its large silhouette move away from me then crossing the dirt road and moving toward another part of the campground. I fell asleep within minutes of the bear leaving. I was really tired, and the bear was not interested in me. It was exploring the area for an easy meal, and people had food at their campsites. Many hours later, my neighbors woke me, and most everyone else within the state park camping area. They were all in their suburban vehicle honking the horn, screaming and terrified as the large black bear knocked over their barbecue, ate food from their coolers, then tore their large tent down. This went on for about an hour, until the bear left, waddling off into the forest. I fell back asleep. The next morning, I learned the bear had ravaged several sites. My neighbors estimated the bear to be around three hundred pounds or more. The family had stayed inside their vehicle until daylight, fearing the bear would return. They said they were worried about me, but they were afraid to exit their vehicle. I told them about a bear sniffing me and my shelter and that the bear was only looking for food. I was not on the menu because their food supplies were too easy to get to. That morning, Park Rangers were questioning people about the bear. Other Rangers were out looking for the bear (or bears) so they could relocate the unwanted guest. At the parks, every camper is prewarned about black bears roaming through the parks. Because these bears are not hunted by hunters, they have no fear of humans. Where bears are hunted, you are lucky to even spot a bear because they avoid humans. This is common knowledge to most outdoorsmen. If humans are feared by an animal, humans will rarely be attacked. Bears will eat almost anything. If there is garbage or food supplies left around, they will want it. It is only natural.

The heat wave we were all experiencing continued. The destination for the day was Hope, New Jersey, but first, I walked back into Newton to do an interview with the *New Jersey Herald* newspaper, which has their offices in the center of town. The news editor assigned Kathy Stevens, Herald Staff Writer, to the story about "Journey for Peace." Her article came out on July 20, 1997, in the *New Jersey Sunday Herald*. Kathy included a photo of me standing in Newton. She mailed a copy of the article to my father who included it into his collection.

It was fourteen miles to Hope, New Jersey, along Route 519, then another three miles out to Jenny Jump State Forrest, which has campsites. In Hope, there is a church with a cemetery next to it. I think it is Saint John's Church, which is a historic place. I took a picture of one particular grave marker, bordered by an iron fence. It is where John Hart is buried. He is one of the signers of our Declaration of Independence, signed on July 4, 1776. The church is within Hope Village.

Jenny Jump State Forrest had such a bad bear problem that I was the only camper in the park that night. I didn't have much of a choice. I was on foot, tired and hot. It was the middle of July, a clear blue sky above, a clean and well-maintained park with modern bathhouses, yet there was no one around. Two bears visited me just before dark. They kept their distance, but I knew they wanted the hoagie I was eating. I gathered my things then walked down a hill to one of the bathhouses, which had a deck around it. The building appeared to be brand new. It was constructed of concrete, and it had steel doors! I put my things inside then watched the two bears who were coming slowly toward the bathhouse. I stood outside on the deck yet ready to dart inside if the bears came too close. They appeared to be several years old and about two hundred pounds or more. They stood about twenty yards from me, as we eyed each other. They seemed to be more curious than they were threatening. With the temperature being over one hundred degrees, they were not very energetic. I spoke to them to see what kind of response they would give. The sound of my voice did not faze the two black bears a bit. They simply stood on "all fours" and looked at me. They must have gotten a whiff of the trash in two large dumpsters, across the dirt road, because that was where they went. For about an hour, they made quite a mess pulling trash and garbage from the dumpsters. After they left, I never saw the two black bears again. I slept on the deck that night alone yet peaceful under a sky full of brilliant stars.

Somewhere between Hope, New Jersey, and Oxford, New Jersey, a deer tick had gotten onto my leg and infected me on the calf muscle. The dreaded red circle about an inch in diameter appeared, but I could not see the tick. I was hoping the tick's head wasn't still under my skin. I stopped at a fire station where the guys examined the infected area with a magnifying glass. The head was not there, which was good news. The bad news was I had symptoms of contracting Lyme disease from the tick's visit. I had a slight fever, aching joints (especially my wrists and elbows), and my energy level was dropping. I figured I should get a motel room for a few days. If the infected area got any worse, I would have to see a doctor.

The one little tick put me under for over forty-eight hours! Those big bears didn't bother me, but a tick the size of a gnat gave me a high fever, put my equilibrium out of sync, and caused aches to my joints. After two full days in bed, my system began to feel better. I drank water, but I could not eat. My system was busy fighting off the Lyme inflection. Luckily, I recovered on the third day. The motel owners were concerned about me, and they checked on me each day. The fever broke, and I began to feel hungry. I took a shower then went outside. I spoke with the owners who were happy to see me outside again. They directed me to a diner next door, where I ate some soup and bread. The color in my face returned to normal, and my energy level felt stronger even though I was still feeling weak.

The town I was in was Washington, New Jersey, in Warren County. This is where our family lived until I was eight years old. I felt anxious about seeing the town again, so I took two more nights at the motel. I went to see our old house, on Youmans Avenue. It looked so much smaller than what I had remembered it to be. I went up to Main Street where all the stores are. While there, I stopped into the Babbling Book bookstore and spoke to the owner, Ami Mazzata. She ordered ten copies of *Pure Power* so she could sell them in her store. If every bookstore owner or manager was like Ami, "Journey for Peace" could have been financed a lot easier.

The movie theater we went to, as kids, was still there. I took a picture of the Washington Twin Cinema for memory sake. My brothers and I saw many a movie there. Mom and Dad allowed us to go to the Saturday Matinees quite often. Dwight Pulieri was often with us. His mom is Alice Pulieri, who still lives in Washington (2012). She is our honorary aunt and was a best friend of my parents. Aunt Alice has never forgotten our birthdays. Every year, my three brothers and my sister receive a card and note from her.

I stopped at the Warren Reporter to see if I could get a news story about the journey. Lucas Rivera wrote a lengthy article, which appeared on the front page of the *Warren Reporter* on Saturday, August 2, 1997. Barbara K. Longley took a photo showing me walking along Main Street. Lucas comically compared me to Forrest Gump. His long article covered a lot of bases with a fair amount of information about the walk and of me revisiting my old hometown. I enjoyed reading his article, when it arrived at my parent's house, while I was taking a break from walking to work at a job so my funds could be increased. Lucas Rivera is a very good writer!

Feeling strong enough to resume walking the roadsides again, I set out on Route 31 south toward Clinton, New Jersey, then to Flemington, New Jersey. The most miles I walked in one day was on July 19, 1997. With temperatures reaching nine-eight degrees and the humidity being eighty percent, I covered twenty-eight miles. Arriving in Flemington, I felt tired and ready for a good night's sleep. Without any camping areas nearby, I had to rent a motel room again. Staying at motels was killing me financially, but when you are in heavily populated areas and on foot, there is not much of a choice if you want to be safe at night. During the journey, I met quite a few people who were homeless, who sleep under bridges, in parks, abandoned properties or anywhere they could hide from being seen. They were of all ages, and they come from a variety of backgrounds. Life is hard at times, and some of these people I met were experiencing the hardest time of their lives. Whatever the problems they were having, it was a tough life. For them, it was a time in their lives without a job, money, or a place they could call home. It is not always because of drug use, alcohol, or mental problems. Hard times come to good people sometimes, and if money runs out, where are you? Knowing how unsafe the streets can be at night, I used my hard-earned money to stay safe during the walk. I felt safer camping at campgrounds than I did being in a city environment. I witnessed many young people without a place to stay. For many of them, it was no fault of their own. They simply had no one to help them. For others, it was because of bad choices they make. It is reality! Homelessness is degrading and extremely unsafe. It is tough. It is not a peaceful life. It is not a secure life. It is not a comfortable life. Hopelessness is common. America is a wealthy country, yet we have people suffering from hunger, and we have young people without shelter. Luckily, we have concerned people who dedicate their time and energies toward helping people to get a fresh start again. If you read the stories and work done by the Covenant House, in New York City, you may be able to understand the plight of these young people better.

Walking into Trenton, New Jersey, the state capital, I found myself lost within a maze of streets, avenues, and highways. All the way through the city, I asked people for directions. I will admit it, I was lost! When Route 206 appeared (magically), I knew where I was. I was in the southern part of Trenton and entering Bordentown, New Jersey. From this point on, I did not need maps or directions because during my younger years, I rode a 750cc BMW motorcycle all through southern New Jersey. Bordentown was always a "turning around" point whenever I rode a good distance.

Forrest Fires in the Pinelands

At Vincentown, New Jersey, people warned me about forest fires occurring within and around the Pinelands. The Pinelands is a vast area within the southern portion of the state. Wharton State Forest is a large portion of the Pinelands. My route took me right through this forested section of New Jersey. I bought a bicycle with knobbed tires to have with me in case I needed to get through an area faster than I could walk. It was not very hard to walk the bike along with me. I simply held the center of the handle bars and walked the bike right next to me. By switching sides every now and then, my arms didn't get sore. After Vincentown are small towns such as Beaverville, Red Lion, Leisuretowne, Hampton Lakes, Indian Mills, and Atsion. Near Atsion, I camped for the night. The smell of smoke was all around, yet I had not seen any fires yet.

The following day was when fires threatened my progress. Whenever I came to an area burning, I biked along the roadside until I passed it safely. It was a slow burning fire. The underbrush was burning, but the trees were not. Only the trunks of the pine trees were getting scorched, along the region I was traveling. If there had been any wind, I would not have been able to go through the heavily forested lands. The most serious burning section I went through was about four miles of flame and smoke. I biked on the road, most of the four miles, since there were virtually no vehicles traveling the roads. After making it beyond the flames and burning underbrush, I walked again. There was a trucker's diner just south of where the fires were. I stopped there to refresh myself with cold iced tea and a few cheeseburgers. The food, drinks, and especially the friendly people at the diner made my day!

I camped within the Wharton State Forest for a second night of having nature all around me. The Pinelands is commonly referred to as the "Pine Barrens" by the people living in South Jersey. It consists of over one hundred square miles of protected forests, cranberry bogs (farms), cedar swamps, and farmlands. The Mullica River flows right through the region. The river begins at the Delaware River, then across the state, emptying into the Great Bay which flows into the Atlantic Ocean. During the nineteen seventies and eighties, I enjoyed hiking, camping, canoeing, hunting, and riding my motorcycle within the Pinelands region. The most popular site, where many people visit during the warmer seasons, is Batsto Historic Village. The scout troop I was with made numerous trips throughout the Pine Barrens. Troop #185 of North Wildwood, New Jersey, hiked the Batona Trail during February each year. We spent five days and four nights camping and hiking so the boys could experience backpacking from campsite to campsite during the cold of winter. They all earned their camping, cooking, and some earned their hiking merit badges by doing the trip. They were awarded the Fifty-Mile Award also. The Batona Trail is marked and goes right past Batsto Village.

Hammonton, New Jersey, was my next stop. Hammonton is a city built within some of the best farmlands in the state. The crops grown around Hammonton feed millions of people. I remember one enormous field with lines and lines of asparagus plants. The varieties of plants grown in the Hammonton area make their region popular with people who enjoy buying crops at roadside farm markets. I walked along Route 206, then onto Route 54, which took me right to the Main Street of Hammonton. The huge trees in their residential area are some of the oldest trees found in the state. Some trees have trunks measuring four to five feet in diameter. The heights of the trees tower over the well-kept houses which appear to be very old yet solidly built.

The *Record-Journal* newspaper did a story about the walk. Their office is in Hammonton. Frank Scussa wrote the article then mailed it to my dad. As I entered Hammonton, New Jersey, the miles walked were six hundred and fifty miles from Eustis/Stratton, Maine. My body seemed void of any fat. My calf and thigh muscles had grown. The heat of summer wasn't bothering me as long as I kept drinking water all day long.

The walk from Hammonton to Vineland and then to Port Elizabeth were the two wettest days since beginning the walk. It rained steadily for two days and two nights. Because of the Gore-Tex cover on my backpack, the things inside stayed dry. I was soaked while walking, but because of the warm temperatures, I never felt chilled. The aggravating thing about walking in the rain is your feet get sore because your skin gets soft and uncomfortable inside wet footgear. I went barefooted at night but had to wear my sneakers during the day in order to walk the twenty plus miles I covered each day. The sneakers were sopping wet for almost three days! On July 25, 1997, I reached the Cedar Lake Campgrounds near Belleplain State Forrest. This was where I dried off good! After taking a hot shower, washed and dried my sneaks by using their clothes dryer, I felt good again. My campsite was located right on the Cedar Lake shoreline. I had a few guests that night. We shared a couple of hours of friendly conversation and laughter. It was a good night!

The following day was special. I followed the backroads from Cedar Lake to Route 47 South. The destination was to the Wienberger's house, along Route 47. Willie Wienberger was a classmate at Wildwood Catholic High School (class of 1971). His wife Lynn and his two daughters, Kori and Keely, were awaiting my arrival. I had called them from the campground to let them know I was on my way. The Wienberger family are special friends. I visited them regularly over the years, and they visited me several times after I moved to Maine in 1989. Willie and I were great friends throughout high school and beyond. He passed away several years ago. He fought a tough fight with Lynn, Kori, and Keely always there caring for him. We all miss his fun spirit and his love for life! I spent the night with Willie, Lynn, Kori, and Keely. We enjoyed a feast for supper then spent the time talking about "Journey for Peace." Kori was one of the biggest fans of the journey. She even walked with me from Cape May, New Jersey, to the Delaware Lewis Ferry. This was when I visited Kori and Keely's school to speak at Star of the Sea Elementary School in Cape May. After speaking to the students there, Kori walked with me to become one of the actual participants of the "Journey for Peace."

I realize I am jumping ahead here, but I want to keep the story about the Weinbergers in one spot as a tribute to William Wienberger.

North Wildwood Homecoming

On the morning of July 28, 1997, I was greeted at the bridge entering my hometown of North Wildwood, New Jersey. Mayor Aldo Palombo, along with members of the city council, greeted me with a police escort. Mom and my brother Dennis, along with Mom's neighbor Elaine, were there also. Dad was not feeling well enough to be there, but I saw him later at the house. It was a happy experience to see the city leaders take time out of their busy schedule to become a part of "Journey for Peace." Mayor Palombo handed me a letter he had prepared. It reads:

> The city of North Wildwood takes pride in acknowledging your unbelievable commitment to walk across the USA from east to west.
>
> Having known you most of your life, I believe that you will accomplish this monumental task.
>
> Courage, discipline, and faith in God will give you inspiration to meet your needs.
>
> On behalf of the city of North Wildwood, I want to wish you well and good luck!
>
> Sincerely,
> Mayor Aldo A. Palombo

The sun shone on all of us that beautiful morning at the shore. Mom showed them all up, though. She was the only one to walk over to the high bridge, and she was the oldest person there. When we got to the top of the bridge and we could see most of the island from the bay side, she said, "Now I know why they all drove across the bridge." We laughed then proceeded down to where Dennis and Elaine were waiting for us at Mom's van. Now that I was in Wildwood, I would take a long break from walking to find work. I needed to replenish the funds so the journey could go on. I had completed 703 miles on foot, with a backpack, walking the secondary roads from Eustis, Maine, to North Wildwood, New Jersey. It took a bit of time and effort.

Ten Weeks in Wildwood

I found a job at Morey's Pier on the Boardwalk. It is a family amusement pier which runs from the boardwalk toward the ocean. I worked as a mechanic who helps maintain the safety and operations of various rides on the pier. When I wasn't working, I was surfing the waves with boards my old surfing buddies lent me. Surfing was always my favorite hobby and art.

For the readers who have never seen a boardwalk along the ocean, I will describe it. A boardwalk like ours is built along the ocean's beachfront so people can walk along without getting sand in their shoes. The elevated boardwalk allows the ocean to flow under it during a storm tide or even an exceptionally high tide. The Wildwood Boardwalk is about 2.8 miles long and the width of a two-lane road. The landside has stores built along it with access ramps at every street end. The "walk" itself is supported by concrete pillars then wood beams which act as joists to create a walkway. Basically, the deck of a boardwalk is built similar to how on outside deck is built on a house. Our boardwalk is elevated about ten feet above the beach. The beach side of the boardwalk is mostly open so everyone can view the beach and ocean. I wrote short stories about the Wildwood beach and boardwalk in November 1999.

I Am the Boardwalk

Please allow me to boast. I have survived one hundred years, and I am still standing strong. I was here before you were born, and I'll be here long after you go. When I first appeared, people rode horses and traveled by train. I sat level to the beach and was vulnerable to every storm. Later, I was raised and even moved a few times. I remember the ocean's cool water used to flow under me at high tide and fisherman even cast from my deck.

I have never been off the island, yet I've seen every fashion the world has offered, heard every language there is to hear, and I've been walked on by more humans than any other wooden structure on earth. I am famous, yes! Songs are sung about me, stories are written, and I am photographed all the time. But I see my success by the children's excitement, laughter, and sheer joy of being on me. I am their wooden playground full of sounds, lights, rides, food, and toys. Admit it, adults, even most of you have succumbed to my allure. It is ironic, though, because of you I am here and because of me you are here. It is a friendship built on fun, romance, and money. By the way, do you realize how any coins have dropped through my cracks all these years? The kids knew. I've watched generation after generation of them scooping up the treasures under me.

My enemy is less active these days, but fire has tried and tried to destroy me. Do you remember the storm of '62? Waves rolled over me and pounded my deck. My neighbor, the sea, tried hard to drag me away. Despite the fires, storms, and even decay, I still stand strong and invite the world. Will I still stand one hundred years from now? Will I be moved, or will I look the same? I am more than a structure. I am a landmark unique in this world. China has its wall, France has its tower, and the Wildwoods have me, the Boardwalk.

I Am the Beach

Yes, you know me well. My white sand and wet shoreline is your playground by the sea. I can honestly say I've seen every configuration of a human foot there is and every degree of sunburn or tan possible. Nowhere on earth can you see sandcastles built and decorated with such imagination and patience. Give a child a bucket and shovel, then set them free. I'm the best babysitter there is!

I have grown wider as my neighbor recedes eastward. Where you lay your blanket now, there were once fish swimming overhead and clam boats dredging back and forth. Many years ago, I was located where you now have concrete, asphalt, and buildings. I am larger now than ever before. Be careful, though. The locals have a saying, "What the sea gives, the sea can take away." I am similar to the girls and their bathing suits. Years ago, I was covered, and today, I am almost bare.

It is fun observing you humans. You are so predictable. If it is hot and sunny, you all come visit me. When it rains, you desert me. As the sun sets, you walk off talking about dinner and the boardwalk. As darkness blankets me, the young couples appear, walking hand in hand. Wow, the stories I could tell! I've got to admit, it's a pretty romantic place. A starlit sky, the moon rays dancing across the ocean, a gentle breeze with the music of the waves serenading you simply spells romance.

There is another local saying, "I am the beach! I am the queen of the Wildwoods."

Along with working and surfing while in North Wildwood, I was able to organize letters people had sent me, photos I took, and read the newspaper articles Dad had organized in a large binder. I sent correspondence out to various people, and I sent a letter to Julie Bolduc in Maine who posted it on her website which many of the school students were following. Julie added this information onto her website plus put in a personal note.

A Special Note from Me (Julie)

"This is a very inspirational book which I have read (*Pure Power*). It really moved me. That is why I have put this page on my website for free. Also Bill is a good friend of the family. I believe in what he is doing."

I thanked Julie many times for the help she provided. Without her site, the school children could not have followed my progress. And as you will read later, the governor of Kentucky would not have had the material about my message to put throughout his state's school system. Thank you again, Julie!

Book Signings

During the ten weeks in Wildwood, New Jersey, I did four book signing vents. Atlantic Books, located on the Boardwalk, hosted me for two separate signings. Morey's Pier allowed me to do an afternoon signing in August. The Catanoso Family allowed me to do a similar book signing on their amusement pier called Dinosaur Beach. The biggest even was signing books at the Annual Irish Festival held in North Wildwood. Channel 40 News interviewed me and included their interview on their six o'clock report out of Atlantic City, New Jersey. This was on September 10, 1997, just prior to me continuing the journey.

The Press of Atlantic City ran a newspaper article on September 10, 1997. Debra Rich wrote the article titled "The Power of Walking." The *Cape May County Herald* did numerous articles. The *Wildwood Leader* newspaper also covered the walk at various times. The newspaper that covered the journey the most was the *Irregular* out of Kingfield, Maine. Their articles and photographs began with my planning of the "Journey for Peace," the work stops, the visits I made to Sugarloaf USA Ski Resort, school visits, and even articles after my walking was done. Their communications to the people in the Wester Maine Mountain Region of Maine kept the people there abreast of my progress. Thanks go to Heidi Murphy, Bob Gray, and Scott Thistle who wrote the very first article on "Journey for Peace." The article was titled "Eustis Man Begins Trek for Peace." The *Irregular* can be accessed at www.theirregular.com.

Walk Continues

On September 22, 1997, I walked out of Wildwood through Wildwood Crest, New Jersey, and was joined by Kori Wienberger at her school in Cape May. We walked to North Cape May where the Cape May Lewes Ferry is. The only way over to Delaware was by taking the ferry across the Delaware Bay to Lewes, Delaware (or swim). That night, I camped at Cape Henlopen State Park which is only a mile from the ferry landing. My campsite was terrific! I could see the Delaware Bay and the Atlantic Ocean at the same time. Temperatures were mild, and the stars shone bright in the sky that night. I have to say, it was the favorite camp spot of the entire journey. There were plenty of fishermen and women fishing, camping and having a fun time there. I will definitely return there. One of the men fishing told me about a trail through the dunes which would bring me to the Rehobeth Beach without walking the roads. I followed his advice the next morning, and he was right. It wasn't a short walk, but it was a good venture along the beachfront dunes. When I arrived in Rehobeth Beach, Delaware, I made my way to the Rehobeth Beach-Dewey Beach Chamber of Commerce where Carol Everhart was the executive director of the chamber. She set up an interview with the Cape Gazette to help get the journey's message out about nonviolence in the schools and on how to realize individual peace. The article came out on October 10, 1997.

The next campground was on the Indian River across from a small Coast Guard Base and right on the inlet flowing in from the Atlantic Ocean. During our earlier years, we surfers camped there many times to surf the waves at Rehobeth Beach, Dewey Beach, and the jetties at Indian River Outlet. While walking through Bethany Beach, Delaware, Kerin Magill interviewed me and wrote an article titled "Karate Teacher Walking to California to Promote Peace." She wrote for the *Wave Newspaper* in Bethany Beach. Kerin must have been into the martial arts because she focused on my experiences within the art and the philosophies of the art of karate. Kerin wrote an interesting article.

The walk in Delaware took less than four days. I arrived at Ocean City, Maryland, on September 25, 1997. I found a place to stay after leaving Ocean City's south end. In Snow Hill, Maryland (where I spent a night), there is a local restaurant which had an all-you-can-eat special for Maryland crabs. Little to say, I feasted! Maryland is known for their crab meals.

Pocomoke City, Maryland, was the next city on the journey. I camped at Pocomoke River State Forest and Park which is just south of the city. It was off-season, so there were very few people there. The restrooms were clean modern and had showers and heat. They also had coin operated washers and dryers which enabled me to have clean clothes again. Pocomoke is another spot I will revisit someday. The park has a lot of acreage with a river traveling through plenty of forestland. Camping there is a safe, which is a plus when you are alone and on foot. This is important (safety) because you don't know most of the areas you are walking through. You don't know who you can trust. You don't know what to expect. I found humans to be more a threat to my safety than the fires, tornadoes, animals, snakes, snow and ice, heat or tough terrain, and physical exertions I encountered. Most people are good, and many of the ones I met encouraged me, but there are those along the roads who you must be very careful around. I had to be aware of the dangers along the roads, the streets, and the territories I walked through. When I spoke to students at the various schools I visited, one of the things I said to them was, "Do not follow my example by walking alone, especially across the country without support and a group to be with. Whether you bike or walk, always be with a group." Having a purpose in life, doing good for other's sake, and believing in Jesus Christ kept me walking. I know I will not do it again alone. It is just too dangerous in today's environment. When I found a comfortable and safe place for a night's stay, it was golden. Later on within this book, you will see I speak from experience about the dangers some people caused me. I have always enjoyed having adventures. I am not done having adventures. If God allows me, I have a great one planned.

While walking on Route 13 heading south, my route plan unraveled when I discovered I could not cross over to the mainland of Virginia by using the Smith Pass Ferry. It was a seasonal passage only, and the season was over until the next summer. I decided to stay on Route 13 and see if I could catch a ride across the Chesapeake Bay Bridge and Tunnel. The Delmarva Peninsula is a great area to walk through, bike, or simply to be at. I can now say, "Yeah, I walked the Delmarva Peninsula." Another good spot to camp is at Cherrystone Family Camping and RV Resort in Cheriton, Virginia. I stayed two nights there because I needed a good rest, and this was a good place to do it. I could see the Chesapeake Bay from my tent site. I swam in their pool and purchased food at their general store. There were many people around me at the campsite to converse with. Socializing is an easy thing to do at campgrounds. Several people offered to give me a ride across the Chesapeake Bay Bridge and Tunnel, but I had to decline because I had to cover the distance to the bridge on foot and then seek a ride. I wanted to walk every mile I could because it was a walk, a journey on foot. Only Jesus can walk on water, so when I got to the bridge and tunnel, I would cross over like every other human does—in a vehicle.

After a good rest at the campground, I returned to Route 13 South. After the first ten miles, I took a break along the road. While sitting near an empty building in a business part of small town, a recreational vehicle pulled into the lot next to the vacant store. My sneakers and socks were off my feet so I could get some air to them. My socks were draped over my backpack so they could dry in the sun while I sat resting. The man who was driving the RV came over to me, and he asked if I needed a ride. I explained to him I was on a walking journey and declined his offer with a courteous "thank you." He persisted by saying, "I made room for you and your backpack in my camper. I'll take you anywhere you want."

My "street smarts" kicked in. I looked at the man and told him, "No."

I watched his face, and I paid more attention his tone of voice as he repeated, "But I made room for you. You need some help, and I am offering it to you."

I smiled and remained sitting as I looked right into his eyes. "I do not need help, sir. I have been doing pretty good walking, and I have a goal to complete." The tone of his voice and his eyes told me he had sinister motives. He looked to be in his thirties. He reminded me of a yuppie type of person. Since there were a lot of cars going by and because we were very visible to everyone, I did not worry much about him doing anything. I had already observed his attire to see if he could have been concealing a gun. He looked clean (meaning no gun). The third time he persisted to sway me into his RV, I stood up, looked him in the face, and said, "You can leave now. Thank you, but no, thank you." He seemed very disappointed, but he did go back to his vehicle. As he started to pull away, he stopped, rolled down his window, and said, "God must be your copilot." I thought about his last comment to me long after he had driven away—northbound. My guess is that no good would have happened if I had taken the ride. Like I said many times, there are people out there who are just not safe to be around. Even though this guy wore expensive casual wear, drove a recreational camper worth fifty to sixth thousand dollars, and acted like a Good Samaritan, my girl told me to watch out and be careful. I did.

Kiptopeke, Virginia, is right before the Chesapeake Bay Bridge and Tunnel. A state trooper told me where I could be picked up by a bus which would take me across. He made a few calls from his car then told me I was all set. "Wait over there, and a bus will pick you up within the hour." I thanked him, and he wished me luck. Every law-enforcement person I met from Eustis, Maine, to this spot in Kiptopeke, Virginia, was supportive of my efforts and watched my back along the roads. Because of the newspaper articles being put out about "Journey for Peace," most of the state troopers already knew about me. Many took time to pull over alongside the roads to talk with me. They are more aware of the violence going on every day than we civilians are. School violence and school shootings were in the news.

I am jumping ahead of myself, but I think this is an appropriate place to put these letters from Paul E. Patton, governor of Kentucky, and Wilmer S. Cody, commissioner of Kentucky Department of Education. Because of the tragic school shooting in their state, I informed them about my walk and what I was telling the students about having less violence.

On January 5, 1998, Governor Paul E. Patton wrote: "Thank you for sharing the information about your 'Journey for Peace.' I appreciate your efforts to promote peace at home and school. I have forwarded your letter to Wilmer S. Cody, commissioner of education, so that he may share your information with his staff."

On January 12, 1998, Commissioner Wilmer S. Cody wrote: "Thank you for sharing information about your 'Journey for Peace.' I commend you and your efforts in promoting peace at school and at home. Our recent experience in Kentucky has certainly heightened our awareness that students need to find peaceful ways of resolving their problems. I will share the information about your journey with staff in the office of communications so that it may be included in publications that are distributed to schools. They can also include your website as a contact point for the schools which have Internet access. Again, thank you for your concern. I wish you the best as you continue your journey."

Because of the governor's concern and the commissioner's actions, the message of my journey was reaching millions of students, teachers, parents, and administrators across Kentucky which was a state I was not going to journey through. At least my words made the journey to Kentucky and the good people there.

Across the Bay

When you cross over the Chesapeake Bay heading south, there is the First Landing Seashore State Park where you can camp. It is on Route 60 which runs along the bay and then the Atlantic Ocean. It is "basic" camping. There is nothing fancy about it, but the surroundings are priceless. My site was within the sand dunes and close to the showers and restrooms. The bay was only a minute's walk away. A ten-minute walk away is Fort Story and the Old Cape Henry Memorial. Even though the camping spot was east of the bridge, I camped there. My route would now be west. In that direction, there are three major cities. With city walking comes motel expenses.

Camping at state parks cost me an average of ten to fourteen dollars a night. As long as I could shower and be safe for the night was just fine. Besides, when you camp at places like state parks or family campgrounds, you are able to communicate with people better. Motels do not lend to meeting people. You rent your room, go to eat, then retire for the night within your room watching television. With camping, you set up your site, get a good shower, walk around the area meeting people, and maybe sit around a small campfire. People tend to invite you to have conversations around their fires or you invite them to your site for friendly talks. The atmosphere is usually laid-back and civil with the various sound of nature around you. Laughter is as common as the birds in the trees.

City Walking

Virginia Beach, Norfolk, Portsmouth, Chesapeake, and Suffolk are five large cities I had to trek through as I started due west for the first time. The area is full of military personnel and activities. The United States Navy is very evident within the area because of the ports and waterways. Camp Pendlelon is at Virginia Beach right next to the Oceana Naval Air Station. I saw plenty of our nation's jets in the sky while I was walking. The locals told me they practice taking off and landing on a regular basis. The area is an important place for our Navy, and the area has a tremendous historical value to our nation. It is the gateway into the Chesapeake Bay which meets the Atlantic Ocean. The Chesapeake Bay goes all the way up to Baltimore, Maryland. The Potomac River outlets into the Chesapeake Bay. The Potomac River flows through Washington DC, our nation's capital. The lands around the Chesapeake Bay are teeming with historical sites, parks, monuments, and museums concerning the great events and people who helped shape and define the United States. Its history goes back to the original colonies and to the Native Americans who were here before the European settlers arrived. Fishing, clamming, and crabbing have always been a huge source of food for the region and is still an important industry. My diet is usually seafood whenever I am around the Chesapeake.

The walk took me through the cities. To be honest, I did not enjoy being on foot within the cities. I prefer the quiet backroads or the roads going through small towns and villages. A person with a large backpack on is out of place within the cities. Who else had a forty-pound backpack carrying a tent, sleeping bag, and other gear? You know what I mean? People along the sidewalks and roadways stared at me. I was not in my environment!

Time of Decision

Somewhere in Suffolk along Route 58, which is also known as Military Highway, I took a motel room for the night. I had covered nine hundred miles of walking up to this point. Worries about how far I could continue walking with the money I had left and the fact that most campgrounds were closing for the fall caused me to think hard about what I should do. I had to be realistic about my circumstances. My decision was to take a break from walking and return to Eustis, Maine, where I knew I could find a job at Sugarloaf Ski Mountain for the winter. I could return to Suffolk, Virginia, in the spring to continue walking. By taking a break for the winter, I could write to more corporations, show them my progress, and maybe, maybe get a few sponsors to help finance the almost three thousand miles ahead of me.

I caught a bus from Suffolk, Virginia, to Philadelphia, Pennsylvania. From there, I caught a bus to Portland, Maine. When I arrived in Portland, Jean Demers of Stratton, Maine, came and got me. He took me back to Eustis/Stratton, Maine. I was greeted warmly when arriving back to my hometown of eight years. I found work at Sugarloaf Ski Mountain with the help of the management there. During the months of November, December, January, February, and March, I worked the late shift from 4:00 p.m. to 1:00 a.m. six days a week. I hitchhiked to and from work. In all that time, I received rides to and from work. It is a seven-mile trip each way. The people of the area were a great help to me! There was only one morning when I had to walk the distance after getting off work. It was one-thirty in the morning. We had already received a foot of snow, and it was not letting up. The only vehicles on the road were the snowplows. I walked the access road down from the mountain and onto Route 27 north keeping a keen eye out for the snowplows. When I saw them coming, I hurriedly climbed over the snowbank and got out of their way. Visibility was poor, and they had a job to do. I made sure I was out of their way! It took me two hours to get back to the apartment I was renting in Stratton. Needless to say, I slept soundly that morning.

During those five months, I corresponded quite a bit with people who had written letters to me while I was walking. My sister sent me a package of letters, and my parents mailed me the letters sent to their address. Congressman John E. Baldwin and his staff were following my progress from the start. He was a member of the United States Congress, representing the Second District of Maine. He became the governor of Maine a few years after my journey was done. Because of his letters and continued interest of what I was doing, I kept him and his staff posted. I thanked him for his continuous moral support. Without the encouragement from him, his staff, and the many other people who were sending me letters, I would have had doubts about my efforts. I never doubted the purpose of the journey, yet I worried because I was unable to find sponsors to help cover finances.

In January 1998, US Congressman Tom Allen of Maine sent me a letter and informed me he and his staff were following my progress on Julie Boldwin's website. From his letter to me, I could tell he supported the message I was transmitting to the students following the journey. Letters of support kept coming in and this spurred me on. Here are a few of the other leaders of cities, states, and schools who sent me encouragement. I will include a sentence from each.

Christine Todd Whitman, governor of New Jersey: "You can be proud of the hard work and stamina what have carried you thus far on your cross-country trek from Maine to California."

Angus S. King Jr., governor of Maine: "The message you are communicating is one of the most valuable a child can ever learn."

Christopher J. Whyte, director of scheduling for Governor James S. Gilmore III of the Commonwealth of Virginia: "Thank you for your letter inviting Jim Gilmore to 'walk a mile' with you during your 'Journey for Peace' through Virginia in late March."

Frank R. Lautenberg, US senator of New Jersey: "It's a great display of initiative and determination, and I am proud that you chose to make New Jersey a stop along the way."

Carol A. Everhart, executive director Rehoboth Beach-Dewey Beach Chamber of Commerce: "How exciting that you chose the Rehoboth Beach-Dewey Beach Chamber of Commerce as a stop off on your incredible 'Journey for Peace.' If we had known you were planning to rest your weary feet at our doorstop, we would certainly have had some sort of gala welcome or at least some Epsom salts and a soothing foot bath!"

Kaileigh A. Tara, mayor of Lewiston, Maine: "Thank you for your dedication and commitment to a cause that affects us all. I am sure that your experience has afforded you the gift of a very unique perspective of our world."

Sharon Hicks, scheduler for Governor Mike Huckabee of Arkansas: "Thanks for your recent scheduling request inviting Governor Huckabee to walk an Arkansas mile with you during your 'Journey for Peace' in the Natural State" (March 24, 1998).

Stephen C. Philbrick, owner Bald Mountain Camps in Oquossoc, Maine: "Tyler and Quinn certainly enjoyed your talk at their school."

Sue B. Wood, PBS affiliate in Richmond, Virginia: "We are interested in doing a feature on his trip through Virginia for our weekly television program." This was sent to my sister while I was out-of-touch along the road and almost across the state of Virginia.

Tom Allen, US congressman of Maine, First District: "Best of luck on your journey. I know you will see many interesting places and share your message with people along the way" (January 28, 1998). These are a few of the letters I received, and they were all much longer, but I took a short part of each so you can see their interest. The letters which came in from students, parents, teachers, and others were more personal. I decided not to print any of those because they are not public figures. Basically, the letters I received told me I was on the right path. Violence in the schools and at home is not a trivial matter. Before starting the journey and while I was actually on the journey, school violence was in the news and being talked about at every school board meeting. The Columbine tragedy in Jefferson County, Colorado, shocked our nation! It also made me think about what I could do as an average citizen to help prevent more tragedies like that from happening. One of the thoughts I continuously held on to throughout the walk came from an Appalachian Trail hiker I met. His words were, "Ordinary people do extraordinary things kept me walking during the tough times. I am an ordinary person. I was trying to do an extraordinary thing."

Starting Up Again

Feeling anxious to resume my walk, I thanked everyone I worked with at Sugarloaf USA Ski Resort. A special thanks go to Warren Cook and John Diller who helped me get the job. The owner, Les Otten, had a check sent to me for two hundred and fifty dollars. This made Sugarloaf USA the first corporate sponsor of "Journey for Peace!"

I packed my backpack. It was late March. The temperatures in Virginia were mild, and the camping areas there would soon be open again. People were still skiing at Sugarloaf, but then that is Maine. I bid so long to the students at Neko-Ashi Dojo in Stratton where Ron Perkins, Tom Lemont, Rusty Fearon, and some of my other black belt students were keeping the nonprofit USA-GOJO Karate School going. It had felt good to teach classes again!

After many hours riding buses and waiting for transfers at bus terminals, I arrived in Wildwood, New Jersey, to visit with my parents. Two days later, I was back on the buses heading south to Suffolk, Virginia, to resume walking where I had left off. The first thing I did when getting to Suffolk was to buy a bicycle to have with me on the walk. Having a bike enabled me to peddle to campsites or campgrounds which were usually two to four miles off the roads I walked. This time, I put luggage carriers on the back of the bike so I could carry more water with me. It was no problem walking the bike next to me as I walked along. Having more water sure helped me!

On April 8, 1998, *The Virginian-Pilot* newspaper put out a story about "Journey for Peace." Lind McNath, staff writer for the *Pilot*, had interviewed me while I was in Suffolk, Virginia. She wrote a great piece which reached several hundreds of thousands of readers. While I was walking along Route 58, not far from Franklin, Virginia, a policeman in his patrol vehicle stopped to talk with me. He showed me the article and gave it to me to read. We talked for about ten minutes. When he got a call on his radio, he bid me farewell and sped off. It makes a person feel good to know the people in law enforcement support what you are doing. He made my day!

The walk across Virginia, heading due west, is a long, long way. I am changing the format now in how I have been writing about the journey because of the dramatic events I am about to relate. Because I do not wish to put blame on any small town or region I was in while some very bad things were occurring, I will only say that I was nearing the foothills of the Appalachian Mountains and just near the North Carolina border with Virginia. Here is my account of the events that changed "Journey for Peace." Writing about the three days of stress, violence, and hate thrown at me back then is not easy. It has been almost fourteen years ago, yet I remember the people, the circumstances, and the disappointment I felt like it was only yesterday. I enjoy writing, but writing about this is not fun.

The morning temperature was mild. I wore only a T-shirt, shorts, cotton socks, and sneakers. Visibility was low because the clouds were just above the forested area surrounding the back road I was trekking along. The air sat still. Every now and then, a car or truck passed by as I walked the large shoulder of the road. I felt relaxed, comfortable, and it was enjoyable being in that country setting.

Hearing a vehicle coming toward me from behind, I paid no attention to it until it quickly slowed down as it approached. I turned and looked to my left. Suddenly, a blast came from the passenger side of the van. The blast's concussion set me back a bit. I thought for sure I was hit! I looked down at my chest and stomach to see if I was hit. Then I ripped off my backpack thinking maybe the bullet had hit it. Meanwhile, the van had sped away, tearing down the road. With all the commotion and sudden surprise, I didn't get the license plate number, but I did get a view of the van which was reddish in color. I stood for a few minutes trying to comprehend what had just occurred. Then I realized they could come back. I ran into the woods, went west for several hundred yards, then found a spot where I could view the road yet not be seen. I stayed there for an hour without seeing the van again. The map I carried showed a small town about a mile or two west of me, so I decided to get there as fast as I could peddle the bike I was walking. When I reached the town, I began walking again. There were people around, and the town had a small business section. Just outside of their main street area I found a motel. The owner allowed me to check in early since it wasn't a busy day for them. I didn't say a word to him about what had happened. I needed to think.

With over twenty-five years of experience in hunting and target shooting, the sound of the blast resembled that of my old .45 caliber handgun. The question in my head was, why? I did not hear any laughter or a voice yelling to me. If it were a couple of young punks getting their kicks, I probably would have heard something from them. It seemed eerie. A van slows down, someone takes a shot at me from only yards away, then they speed off without a sound or a clue to why they wanted me harmed. It sure was weird. I tried to relax inside the motel room. I watched television and snacked heavily that day. After hours of thinking about what had happened, I decided to go on with the walk early the next morning. I would walk along the side of the road facing the traffic so I could see what was coming toward me. I checked the map and set a goal of twenty-five miles which would get me to a rather large town. If nothing else happened, then I could figure it was just a couple of crazies out joy riding and being uncivilized. There are plenty of these characters along the roads. In New York State, I had some young kids swinging baseball bats at me as they drove by. Luckily, they missed!

The next day was uneventful. I walked along the road, stopped at a general store for lunch, went through two small communities, and then came to a tourist spot late in the day. I took another motel room for the night just to be on the safe side. I felt relieved and slept good that night. The road I walked along the next day was divided because the westbound side sat higher up than the eastbound lanes. For days, the terrain had been hilly since my walk was nearing the Appalachian Mountain foothills.

It was near noon when an eastbound pickup truck stopped alongside the road below from where I was. I could see two men in the back of the truck, the driver and a passenger inside the cab. One of the men in the back of the truck pointed at me and yelled, "There he is!" The passenger got out of the truck, but the driver stayed in his seat, just looking up at me from his position. They had a rifle hanging on a gun rack against the pickup's rear window. The rifle remained there the whole time they were there. They were yelling at me. I have never before felt such hate in people's voices. They called me names I care not to repeat because their words deserve not to be repeated. I knew the situation was very dangerous for me. When I heard one of them yell, "We missed you the other day," I knew for sure I was in trouble. I did not respond to them at all. I simply stood tall and listened to their words. Because of the distance and the elevation divide between us, I was safe for the moment. To those four young, white males with shaved heads, I was the target of their hate. I learned later on why they wanted to do harm to me and why they wanted me to end my journey. At the time, I was mentally ready to defend myself if they had come up the embankment toward me. Luckily, they stayed below throwing their verbal threats and hateful words at me. Then came the words which knocked me out. The driver stepped out of the truck and yelled, "You have twenty-four hours to end your walk. We know where your family lives! The only reason you are still alive is because you are white!" They all gave me the raised arm salute with palm down. Then they became silent and just stared at me. I did not respond. I got on my bike and peddled downhill for several miles before entering a small town. I saw a diner and went in so I would have people around me. I ate some food and drank some coffee while sitting in a booth near the window area. The group from the road did not come into town while I was there. The waitress informed me where the closest motel was. It was ten miles west along the road. When I got there, it was a large motel with a large number of people staying there for a dog show. The room was not cheap, but I did not care. I needed to make a phone call in the privacy of my room!

I had with me the phone number of a man I met a few years back. He had visited my motel in Stratton, Maine, while hiking the Appalachian Trail. We had two things in common: he is a trained martial artist, and he loves to hike mountain trails. When I had informed him about my plans to walk across America, he gave me his home phone number and told me to call him if I ran into any major trouble along the route. He had worked undercover in law enforcement for the state of North Carolina. I called his number, and he answered the phone. After greeting each other, I told him about the events of the last three days and gave him the detailed descriptions of what was said and what the young men looked like. He instructed me to stay near the phone and not to go outside. He needed an hour or so to do some research. So I waited.

When he called back, he told me he was retired now but the research he did enabled him to locate a certain website which is affiliated with a nationwide hate group. I will not go into detail about the group because I wish to live a normal life now and I do not want to stir things up. Basically, I had become a target for this group because the walk was generating more and more publicity the farther I went. Because my message of tolerance toward all people no matter their race, color or creed was being promoted to school age children and teenagers, they felt the need to stop me. Thousands of school students were hearing about "Journey for Peace," and many were following my progress. He told me my situation was very serious if I continued the walk. "You cannot be protected because I know some of these followers. First thing tomorrow morning catch a bus to the nearest big city. Switch buses there so no one locally (where I was then) will know your final destination. You will have to end the 'Journey for Peace' so this group will leave you alone. They are nationwide so you have no choice. Put a notice on your website announcing that you are done. I do not think this group will pursue you because their goal is to stop you from doing what you have been doing. Do not talk to any media and lie low in a safe area for a while. I suggest you return to Maine." I did exactly what he told me to do. He was right. They did not pursue me. They won! I know the name of the group, and I have seen accounts in the news about some of the violence they have put forth to others. My family was not bothered. I am not a martyr, and I will not put anyone in harm's way because of a cause no matter how important it is to me. I was devastated. Finding another path to continue the purpose I set as a goal was what I considered to do. I needed a path with less resistance. This book is just that!

"Journey for Peace" ended. I still have purpose in life, and my determination was not stopped.

King and Bartlett

For the next six months, I worked at a remote fishing and hunting camp called King and Bartlett. It is located deep in the Maine woods between Eustis, Maine, and Jackman, Maine. The hate group would not bother me there, and it was a great place to rethink my future. The manager, the owner, his son, the chef, the guides who came and went, and the guests who came to fish or hunt were all supportive, friendly, and fun to be with. The main lodge plus seventeen other buildings were constructed of logs and had very comfortable interiors. The earliest log cabins were constructed in the 1830s. The other cabins, workshops, community cabin, and storage building were built one by one over the years. Many of them were built by hand using hand saws, hand drills, and axes. They are all within sight of the crystal-clear waters of King and Bartlett Lake which has a bottom base of glacial rocks.

We worked long days, but we were very well-fed. We ate the same meals the guests were served. Three meals a day were prepared by Dean, a chef from New York City. Generally, there were ten to twenty guests at K & B each day. Most guests stayed for short period of time, and some took extended stays. I was able to get to know most of them. A few came in by a floatplane which would land on the lake, drop them off at a dock, then return to get them when their stay was up. Various people came from all over the United States because of the abundant wildlife, the landlocked salmon, and native trout. Picture this: you are surrounded by tens of thousands of acres in the Western Maine Mountains. You lodge in a cabin along the shoreline of a lake surrounded by forests. You have electricity generated by a diesel engine generator which came off a ship. It powers all eighteen buildings plus the large refrigeration system for the food. A truckload of good products come in once a week to supply the need. A chef from New York cooks, bakes, and makes deserts every day. There are two rivers and eleven ponds to fish on. King and Bartlett Lake is a hundred-and-sixty-feet deep fed by a natural spring at the bottom. I loved every day of being there!

It happened to be one of the regular guests (Marty) who gave me the idea of how I could continue to do walks yet not have any enemies. He suggested I do short walks and get various sponsors to help with expense. I became enthused again! I developed a plan and started sending out letters to various corporations and charities. While still at K&B, I received a letter from Charlie Frair, founder and executive producer of the charity, Partners in Ending Hunger. He believed a walk would be a great way to get their message out to people about ending hunger in Maine and New Jersey where their operations were located. The end result of Charlie Frair and myself communicating together was a long-distance walk in New Jersey and another one along the coast of Maine.

The New Jersey Walk

To set up a walk in New Jersey, Charlie had me contact Imthiaz Azeez, a member of the board of directors of the New Jersey Chapter of Partners in Ending Hunger. Before leaving King and Bartlett sporting camps, I bought a used van so I could have my own transportation again. From the gratuities I received while working at K & B, I now owned a vehicle which I planned to use on the walks. I was determined to keep purpose alive in my life! I could not let those people who caused "Journey for Peace" to end stop me from doing things of good meaning and purpose. Walking to benefit charities gave me a new purpose without having to worry about the hate groups. Being careful, though, was essential. Having the van to sleep in at night or to drive after walking, plus carrying a cell phone with me at all times, gave me a safer feeling.

The New Jersey Walk

I departed Maine in November after the sporting camp closed for the winter months. Mr. Azeez of the Partners in Ending Hunger Chapter of New Jersey, and I set up a walk from Wildwood, New Jersey, to Newton, New Jersey, to bring publicity to the charity. I followed the same route I had taken while on "Journey for Peace," except this time the walk was south to north and I had a young man, Skip, drive the van while I walked. He met me every five miles or so during the walk, and he left flyers about the charity at stores we passed. By having the van with me, I could walk without carrying a backpack. I didn't attract attention as I walked because I looked like any other person simply out walking. The attention we received came from newspaper articles, radio stations, and on television news reports. Mr. Azeez and his charity workers did a series of news releases while I walked. Skip and I had plenty of food and drink with us in coolers which made the miles go easier during the day.

Mr. Azeez walked the entire first day with me. All the publicity about the walk went toward the charity. On February 4, 1999, the walk began at the Greater Wildwood Chamber of Commerce Office on the Wildwood Boardwalk. The executive director of the Chamber, Andrew Cripps, along with Mr. Azeez and myself were interviewed by Channel 40 News of Atlantic City. This, along with a news release done by the Chamber of Commerce, helped gain publicity for the charity and informed people about the charity's functions. Andrew Cripps, Mr. Azeez, my sister Colleen, my nephew Connor (in a stroller), my surfing friend of many years Jeff Walden, and his wife Sue along with their daughter (in a stroller) all walked the first two miles along the Boardwalk. Mr. Azeez stayed along for the day. We walked to Stone Harbor, New Jersey, then out to Cape May Court House, New Jersey, which was about a fifteen-mile walk in total for the first day. Our legs were sore, but it was a good day. I learned a lot from Mr. Azeez about Partners in Ending Hunger. We had a ride back to wildwood set up so Mr. Azeez could return to his vehicle and I could spend the night at my parents' house. The next day, Skip joined me. We drove to Cape May Courthouse where Mr.

Azeez and I had left off the day before. Luckily, it was a mild winter, so battling cold temperatures or snow was not happening. During the two weeks of walking, the average temperature was around thirty degrees. The coldest day was the day we finished the walk in Newton, New Jersey. That day, the high was ten degrees with winds averaging twenty miles an hour. I was dressed warm that day!

Several times during the walk, I phoned Mr. Azeez to inform him of our progress. He was able to do news releases about the progress from his office. With the news releases and with Skip dropping off literature about the charity at stores, we garnished quite a bit of media attention which all went to helping Partners in Ending Hunger. The Atlantic City Press did several articles about the walk and mentioned the 800 number of the charity many times. The day before the walk started, we had a thirty-minute live radio interview on WZXL FM 100.7/WCMC AM 1239 which went very well.

The walk covered nearly two hundred miles. I covered all expenses since I could not find any corporate sponsors to help. Despite the media attention, it was still difficult to convince the corporate world of the value. But because of purpose and because of helping a good charity be known better, the walk was successful. I must admit, when it comes to marketing, I lack the skills to get financial help. In my next venture, I will have someone skilled with marketing to assist me. You will read later on in this book about my next venture. As an end result of doing the walk in New Jersey, it will show on my resume that I walked the length of New Jersey two times. This involved about four hundred miles in total because of a few zigs and zags. I saw the southern, western, and northwestern sides of the state better than anyone driving a vehicle ever could. These parts of New Jersey have forests, farms, horse ranches, small towns, Fort Dix, and the mountain areas in the northwest. It is the "garden state."

Coastal Walk of Maine

On March 15, 1999, the walk to benefit Partners in Ending Hunger in Maine began. Charlie Frair, executive director and founder of the charity, had Liz Warner become my contact during the walk. Charlie began the Hand to Hand Charity in Camden, Maine, during the year 1984 which became Partners in Ending Hunger. I am not sure of their current activities since it has been many years since the walk.

The first day of the coastal walk along Route 1 was typical Maine weather. Fox News was to meet me at the Welcome to Maine sign in Kittery, Maine, at 9:00 a.m. for an interview on Route 1. They were going to film my first step and let the public know about the walk. Unfortunately, it was snowing pretty steady, and the forecasts all showed a coastal storm with over a foot of snow possible. We waited until 9:30, then Skip and I decided we better start without the interview because the snow was coming down heavier. Visibility was becoming a problem. Skip drove ahead to find a parking lot where he could wait for me. I could only see the sidewalk I was on and the vehicles going by me at a crawling pace. The wind was so strong, I thought I was hearing freight trains going by. My Gore-Tex outer gear and the snow sneakers kept me comfortable. The Fox News van passed me twice, but they couldn't see me with all the snow and wind. I phoned Liz who then called the contact she had at Fox News. They decided it was just too severe to try filming an interview, so it was put off until later. Besides, they had a storm to cover which I am sure created a good amount of news to relay to the public.

Skip did a great job of finding spots to park safely every three miles. This was his first trip to Maine and his first full day in Maine. He joked about the brutal coastal storm giving him a "white" welcoming. I can remember how good a sight the van was every three miles: to get out of the wind every so often and give my face a break from the cold snow pelting my skin. Being from Southern New Jersey, Skip wasn't a seasoned driver in such snowfalls, yet he did excellent. He avoided the many snowplow trucks, drove smart, and found safe parking spots along Route 1. The road crews of Maine know how to plow! They are probably the best you will find anywhere in the country when it comes to moving snow and keeping roadways open. Our day ended in Ogunquit, Maine, after an exciting day and just over fourteen inches of blowing snow. Skip and I found a small motel and enjoyed a warm motel room with cable television.

The next morning, we awoke to find clear blue skies, no wind, and a beautiful white covering of snow everywhere. After a hearty breakfast at the diner near the motel, we shoveled the van out of the drift of snow around it. By noon, the roads were all cleared, so Skip went ahead, and I began walking again.

Biddeford, Maine, was a good stop along the walk. We visited a food pantry called Friends of Community Action while there. The people working the large pantry informed me that the Stephen and Tabitha King Foundation fund the pantry one hundred percent and also fund other food banks in the state of Maine. For those who do not know, Stephen King is one the most famous authors in the United States. He and his wife live in Maine. We toured the food pantry and were shown the operations within this important facility which helped the people of Biddeford, Maine. This might be a good time to write about the information supplied by Partners in Ending Hunger which we gave to every reporter, radio host, and television news crew who reported on the coastal walk. This is from the spring of 1999.

Hunger Facts

Twelve million (12%) American households experience hunger or food insecurity. Twenty-nine percent of the children in the United States suffer from or are at risk of hunger. Sixteen percent of all food pantry network clients are seniors sixty-five or older. Nearly 84,000 children in Maine suffer from or are at risk of hunger. Maine population is about 1,200,000 people.

These facts surprised most all the reporters. These statistics were not made up. They were compiled by the numerous agencies involved with relieving the hunger problem across the country and compiling each state's statistics. I learned from many of the food pantry workers that most senior citizens who came to them did not receive food stamps, welfare, or other government aide. They came because they needed food. The need today (2014–2015) is probably worse.

Portland, Maine

We visited a shelter in Portland where the homeless were able to eat, shower, and sleep for a few days. Think about that—a few days. The majority of the people there were young people of teenage years or people in their twenties. No cameras were allowed, and the privacy of those staying at the shelter was to be respected. I was escorted around the shelter by a staff manager who explained their operations and rules. Skip and I came out of the shelter feeling a sense of gratitude for the donors, the charities, and the staff who made such a haven possible for those in need. My eyes were opened to how many young people were homeless. This is only one shelter in one city. I kept thinking, *How many people across the country are in need of a place to sleep, a warm shower, and a meal?* The visit was an eye-opener for both Skip and myself. I recommend to people interested in helping those in need to visit a few shelters to see firsthand who the homeless are and to talk with them about their circumstances. Their stories are all not the same. I met one teenager who was not only homeless but had no family members left. He was virtually on his own at the age of seventeen.

Our next stop in Portland was at the Family Planning Center where preschoolers are cared for and given meals. I spoke to the staff there and about twenty of the children they were caring for. Because of the center, single moms are able to work at jobs and earn a living which keeps them off of welfare and gives them a chance to build a career. The time we spend at the center was enjoyable because children of that age have such imaginations! They tend to tell stories only they can come up with. Skip and I had a few good laughs listening to their stories.

I reported to Liz at Partners in Ending Hunger about our experiences so she could relay the information to her media sources. Most of our stops were planned by Liz because they were all part of the network set up to fight hunger. Every report we could get from the media helped to aid the charity and its causes. Before walking out of Portland, Maine, I visited a radio station which has a huge audience in Maine and parts of New Hampshire. They couldn't do a live interview, but they volunteered to broadcast information about the hunger issues in Maine and to give out the charity's eight hundred number. They told their listeners to look out for me along Route 1 and to honk their horns when they saw me. Sure enough, I got quite a few honks as I left Portland on Route 1.

Skip's hobbies are fishing and surfing. So when we visited Freeport, Maine, we went right to the L.L. Bean Store and right to their fishing department. The L.L. Bean Store is never closed. It is visited by people from all over the globe. It's historic, large, and most importantly has quality sporting gear and clothing. Skip enjoys salt-water fly fishing, so being at L.L. Bean was a treat for him. We spent several hours and bought a variety of things while there. It was a break from doing the walk, but it was a fun break. I just couldn't have let Skip not experience the L.L. Bean Store! We stayed at a small motel in Freeport that night then continued the walk in the morning.

To exemplify how extensive the coastline of Maine is, I will share a fact I learned while writing a monthly column for *The Maine Sportsman* which is a hunting fishing and outdoor publication put out each month. I covered the Sugarloaf Region during the 1992 and 1993 period by writing a thousand-word informational report of the area. The coastline of Maine has seven thousand miles of inlets, bays, islands, river outlets, and ocean frontage. This always amazed me. I can understand why Maine is so popular with people who like to sail, fish, lobster, scallops, and explore the coast. Along Route 1, we were seeing only a small percentage of the coast, but the towns we went through were full of history and beauty. The further east we went, the more we heard that distinctive Maine accent in people's voices. The Maine humor seemed more prevalent also.

As we continued along Route 1, we went through Brunswick, Bath, Woolwich, and then Wiscasset where the *Wiscasset Newspaper* did an extensive article about the coastal walk and about the charity. Aaron C. Miller interviewed us the day after I struggled through fifty-five-mile-per-hour winds with torrential downpours lasting over a twelve-hour period. My clothing was soaked, and my sneakers were dripping wet after walking eighteen miles during the on and off downpours and the constant wind. We visited a laundromat that night! In Wiscasset, Aaron invited us into his newspaper office where he did the interview and took a few pictures of us on their main street. Several days later, a person handed me a copy of the *Wiscasset Newspaper* from March 25, 1999, with the article and pictures in it. Aaron wrote a terrific article, and he covered the charity very well. Wiscasset and a lot of the coastal towns we went through are on my list of returning to someday. Maybe I'll get back there after this book gets to market. It will be fun to revisit those areas, especially after writing about them.

Down the road in Damariscotta, Maine, Skip and I took a day to relax and sit back for a day. Adam Hanson of the Lincoln County weekly caught up to use because of Liz's efforts. Joan Grant, photographer, took a photo, and Adam wrote the article. It came out on April 1, 1999. Both Aaron C. Miller and Adam Hanson are true reporters. My past experience with some of the newspaper writers is they tend to write from their own thinking or opinion instead of practicing true journalism. These writers just don't listen enough while doing interviews. Aaron, Adam, and a number of other reporters I had the privilege to meet cover the facts, listen, and then report in a just way.

I gave a speech once to a gathering of about thirty-five adults who were all involved in politics. The group included a mayor, a US senator, a county freeholder, and leaders of other government agencies. I spoke about "truth in journalism" for about forty-five minutes (without notes or a script). I gave examples of how different writers wrote articles concerning "Journey for Peace" and my other walks. They understood and agreed with me as I spoke about the lack of truth in journalism today. I complement the writers and reporters who do a professional job, but the lack of these good journalists is evident. I received a standing ovation when I finished my speech because they themselves experience poor journalism more than others. So throughout this book, I have and will continue to praise those writers and reporters who put out good articles without prejudice and in good taste.

We went through Newcastle, Nobelsboro, Waldoboro, and then Thomaston, Maine. Waldoboro is home to the Five Masted Schooner where we took pictures of various nautical artifacts and scenes. The coastal areas of Maine are full of nautical sights and maritime museums. A person could spend a lifetime exploring it all. When you are on foot, you see much more than a person does while driving along at thirty to forty miles per hour. I averaged three and half to four miles an hour at my fast pace while walking, but I slowed to about two miles per hour whenever there were special sights to look at. I am jumping ahead, but since I am writing about seaport towns, Searsport, Maine, is a must-see town for those interested in the history of nautical Maine. The Penobscot Marine Museum is there, and the town is full of history—American history. The Penobscot Indian Nation has deep roots and a long history in the areas, now the state of Maine. They were there before the European settlers arrived. The museum is a maritime museum which tells the stories of fishermen, lobstermen, scallopers, seamen, craftsmen, and everyone connected to the coast, bay, and sea. Searsport sits on the Penobscot Bay which empties into the Atlantic Ocean.

From Thomaston, Maine, I walked along the shoreline of the Penobscot Bay for several days. In Thomaston, we visited the food pantry at the Thomaston Baptist Church. It was a rainy day yet a very enjoyable day because of the five members of the food pantry who walked a half mile with me in town to become an active part of the hunger walk. Talk about Maine humor—they were the best! It rained on us, but our laughter made us shine. It seemed we all laughed during the entire half mile and our gathering outside of the church building. They told jokes and kidded each other with humor Mainers are known for. They took Skip and I inside the pantry and explained how they kept the needy in their community from doing without. As with many food pantries in Maine, they rely heavily on volunteers, help from donors, food stores, and charities such as Partners in Hunger to keep their doors open and the food moving. Because of seeing how the food pantries operate and how they supply people in need, I was learning valuable knowledge about how communities need food banks and people to volunteer. The Thomaston Baptist Church Food Pantry had a good system in place. I came away realizing it was because of the people who ran it with hearts full of compassion (and humor) that made it a true community project.

The major stop during the coastal walk was Camden, Maine. Camden isn't a big city. It seemed to be a large town with a business-oriented slant to it. I was told that the area had a healthy employment rate and a nice place to live since the coast was right there. This was where Partners in Ending Hunger had their headquarters and where Charlie Frair, the founder and executive, produced of the charity had his office. I met his staff members Tami-Lynn, Liz, Elaine, and Lisa while there. There were numerous reporters present along with the Camden Herald Newspaper and Fox 51 Television News. Charlie did the interviews since he was the expert on hunger in Maine. The walk was about helping to draw attention to the charity, and this stop sure did. The television report alone was viewed by most of Maine. After the media left, we all met together inside the charity building. Charlie asked me if I could try to meet with the governor and hand deliver a letter from the charity. He had been trying to meet with the governor for months but was unsuccessful. I agreed to try after completing the walk. I could stop at the state capital in Augusta, Maine, on our way home. But first, Skip and I had more miles to cover.

It took three more days to reach Ellsworth, Maine. This is the city I had planned to end the walk which began in Kittery, Maine. Bob LaForge of Hancock, Maine, met us a few miles outside of Ellsworth. He joined me to walk the last part of the coastal walk. Bob is a registered Maine guide who specializes in fly-fishing. I know Bob from working at Kind and Bartlett Sporting Camps.

We walked into Ellsworth and stopped at the steps of their city hall building. A reporter and her crew were there to document the finishing of the 225-mile coastal walk to benefit the ending of hunger in Maine. We were first interviewed by WLBZ Television News Center of Maine which broadcasts statewide. Bob did the interview with me. We watched it that night on Channel 2. *The Ellsworth American Newspaper*, which is Maine's largest weekly newspaper, had photographer and reporter Jessica Lee there to cover us. Liz Warner at Partners gave Jessica the information about the charity, and I told her about the walk itself. Her article came out on April 1, 1999.

The walk was a huge success for the charity. In just over two and a half weeks, we had over fifty media hits within the state of Maine and parts of southern New Hampshire. Four television networks covered the walk. Two radio stations let people know about the walk and over forty-five newspaper articles were written about our endeavors. Many of the reporters met me along Route 1 while I was walking. Some of them even walked along as they interviewed me. Money was raised because the media put out the 800 number of the charity. Awareness was generated about hunger in Maine and the United States. But the end result of attention is happening right now as you read this book! The statistics concerning hunger in Maine and elsewhere have changed, but the hunger in our country is still there. Remember, children and senior citizens are hardest hit by not having the luxury of food available to them on a regular basis.

Governor of Maine

Skip and I drove to the state capital building in Augusta, Maine, after leaving Ellsworth. I wanted to deliver Charlie Frair's letter as I had promised.

While Skip and I were walking across the parking lots in front of the capital building, he asked me if I thought I could actually meet with the governor. I told him it was at least a try. We found the location of the governor's office where about thirty well-dressed people were waiting within a large room hoping to meet with the governor. I walked into his outer office where his secretary sat behind a large desk. I asked her if I could deliver the letter I had. She asked me if I had an appointment. I chuckled then said, "No. I have been a bit busy. I figured I would just walk right in and see what could happen." She looked up at me with a serious look on her face, then she smiled and said, "I recognize you. You are the fellow who just walked part of our coast along Route 1. You are that fellow, aren't you?"

"Yes," I responded. "I saw you on the news just a day ago. Hold on. I think the governor might want to talk to you. Have a seat outside, and I will speak to him." I went out and sat with Skip. We both looked out of place among the others waiting. Everyone else had suits. We had jeans and flannel shirts on. Five minutes later, I heard someone call out my name. "Is Bill Flynn here?" I looked up to see Governor Angus S. King, Jr. standing in the room full of people. I stood up and identified myself. He greeted me and said he had heard about the walk. For the next ten minutes, we talked about a variety of things. He had read my book, *Pure Power*, so he was familiar with my writings. Alvin L. Barth, who was a state representative from the area I had lived in, gave the governor a copy of *Pure Power* when I started the walk—"Journey for Peace." I told the governor, "It is a small world. Mr. Barth would stay at my motel when he visited Eustis/ Stratton, and we talked many times." Governor King promised to look into the hunger problem right away. He did too! It was not long after that, he contacted Charlie Frair and Maine had a special committee formed to study and end hunger in the state. The impression I had of Governor Angus King is very favorable. He spoke with knowledge, yet he was "down-to-earth." He was elected two times as Maine's governor, and he was an Independent. I understand he also rides a Harley! I thank you again, Governor Angus S. King., Jr., for taking the time to speak with both Skip and me. Thank you also for your kind words concerning the message I gave to students and for your praise of this book's part I and part II.

One More Walk

On September 13, 1999, I took a break from my job doing construction work and started another long-distance walk along the East Coast toward Florida. I went alone but had my van with me and a bike to use. I would walk five miles then bike back to the van and move the van ahead. Three times a day, I did this which gave me fifteen miles of walking and fifteen miles of biking. The van was used to camp in every night and to store food, clothes, and other things for my use. My attempt on this walk was to generate sponsors by showing them my abilities of covering a lot of miles to help out charities. I did not seek any publicity. This I planned to do after covering a thousand miles or so. I had been in contact with close to a dozen charities who liked the publicity results of the Maine walk, but they all said

I would need to find sponsorship. Unfortunately, after covering 250 miles and the same mileage of biking, I was resigned to end the walk. Money was the problem, and I just could not use up all of my savings to continue. After two and a half years of walking, working to save up money to continue walking, and being turned down repeatedly by possible sponsors, I decided to stop and return to "normal" life. If I was not stopped short on "Journey for Peace," I know I would have made it across to California. It is the trying that counts! You will never know what you can do unless you try. By writing about my attempts and my efforts, the "Journey for Peace" will have a greater effect on people because many people did not know of the journey and its goals. Within these pages are the many people who became involved because of their interests of having a more peaceful society and a better civilization. Understanding personal peace and the problems of hunger within our communities is a basic understanding. Thank you for "taking the walk" by reading these pages!

CHAPTER 2

The Working Man

Over the years, I have thought about writing down my thoughts concerning working men and women. My first paying job was at the age of nine. Our dad was a hardworking person who instilled in us the value of work and the value of learning a trade. With his approval and my Aunt Floss's help, I worked at a clothing store on the Wildwood Boardwalk for three summers. The job was cutting letters which went onto T-shirts or sweatshirts to spell out people's names. My hours were three hours a day, five days a week. I received five dollars a week for pay. During my third year, I was given a job of stocking shelves, and the pay was increased to fifteen dollars a week. Any money we earned back then was turned over to Dad who put it into our savings accounts after letting us keep some change for spending money. My two older brothers and I found coins in the sand under the boardwalk which Dad allowed us to keep. Because the boards had a space between them, the coins people dropped fell threw them and into the soft sand under the boardwalk. We pushed sand onto them then shook the sand-free exposing pennies, nickels, dimes, or quarters on the screen. It was rare, but occasionally, a half-dollar or a dollar piece would show up. We averaged a dollar or so each morning and usually spent it on hot dogs, sodas, and pinball machines during the day. The best spots were under the storefronts where people paid for their food or drinks while still standing on the boardwalk. It was fun. It was like treasure hunting, and there were not many kids who knew what we were doing. We did not let our secret out. Can you imagine if we saved all those silver coins and wheat back pennies!

Mom and Dad grew up during the Great Depression Era. Our generation learned from our grandparents, parents, aunts, and uncles how difficult things were back then. A dollar went a long, long way back then; if you had a dollar. Most people did without. They struggled to survive, and many people went to bed hungry and without heat. Sharing with each other was common. Faith kept their sprits alive, and hope was a virtue they lived with. Nothing was wasted. Most of the things they needed were made by hand and by them. They cooked their own meals with whatever was available. If they had a fish to cook and eat, the fishes head was boiled in water to make fish soup with potatoes included. If there were any leftovers, that would be their next meal.

The working men and women of today who I want to reflect on are the people who work with their hands, risk being injured, use their muscles, sweat in the summer, get cold in the winter, put long hours in, learn their trades through experience, have callouses from doing hard jobs, clean up the messes left by people, use common sense to get their jobs done and all the other things involved with everyday work. The working person knows who they are. They are usually the least paid, yet the people above them cannot survive their positions without these people. I speak from experience. My experiences are working as an employee, being an employer for over twenty years, and being an owner of several businesses over the years. I am now an employee working for an employer. I know both sides of the coin. It is important for every employer to know and to have experience of being an employee so they can understand the life of a worker. Before someone can manage, they should know what it is like to be managed. A number of people may not agree with my thinking, but very few working people will disagree, I believe. There are owners who are also workers. An owner who works his or her trade is a working person. Here is an example of this: a farmer who owns his land, works his fields, fixes his buildings, and gets right in there with his employees—he or she is a working person.

A National Resource

Without the working man or woman, our country would literally stop functioning. These are the people who grow the food, catch the fish, build and maintain our buildings, roads, schools, and hospitals, cart away our trash, keep our utilities running, and clothe our families. The necessities of life are provided because of working men and women.

These honorable people are not afraid to "get their hands dirty." They sweat, toil, and survive the changing weather patterns. You know who you are. You are the most necessary and the most important people a strong nation has. You keep busy. You produce and provide. You service, transport, and aid the needy. Your time is valuable, and your muscles get a workout. Without you, many would starve, have little shelter, and barely survive because you provide the basics which humans need. You are the working man and woman, the backbone of our nation!

Bill Flynn
5/2002

This was written in 2002. It is now 2012. You can see my views have not changed over the years. Of all the workers out there, I have the highest regard and respect for the nurses who care for elderly and the cancer patients who are unable to care for themselves. What these nurses do on a daily basis is to be admired. Nurses, in general, put up with things most people cannot stomach. Their work is appreciated here in this book! They have purpose.

Within this chapter are included those who protect us every day or military, National Guard, police, fireman, first responders, prison guards, and our national security personal of various agencies all keep order and make our country and its people a safe place to live and to enjoy God's gifts to us.

Here is another short story concerning the topic of this chapter. This is something every working male can relate to because it is so true. I wrote this on February 5, 2001.

The Work Shirt

Ask any carpenter, mechanic, landscaper, painter, logger, handyman, or—for the matter—any male, young and old, who does physical work for a living, if they have one particular shirt that they favor. The answer will be yes! The shirts vary as much as the personalities vary, but their stories will be similar. "My wife keeps trying to throw it away."

"My mother wants to turn it into cleaning rags."

"No matter how many tears it gets, I just sew it up and it is fine."

"So what if it's ten years old. I like the feel of it."

"What stains? Those spots are marks of character."

"My girlfriend hides it, hoping that I won't look for it. But I find it every time."

"Just leave me alone and let me wear my shirt. It feels good."

Yes, girls, it is a male thing. You see, it takes a while to break a shirt in maybe years. When the right work shirt comes along, we have a real hard time parting with it. It is like a friend, a comfortable working partner. So please take care of my shirt.

Bill Flynn
2/2001

I hope you enjoy the humor of this story. When I wrote this back in 2001, I had the story printed onto T-shirts. The shirts were sold to fellow construction workers who got a kick out of it. They all agreed of how true it is about having one particular shirt they treasure. How many of you frequent a local diner or coffee shop in the morning? You may "connect" with this story. It was written for a particular waitress back in February 2002. Waitresses spend a lot of time on their feet and cover miles of walking back and forth from customer to kitchen all day long.

Rainbow Girl

Do you know the "rainbow girl?" She is a waitress who brings sunshine to everyone around her. Her charm, cheerfulness, and sweet nature lets you know she genuinely cares and likes those she waits on. Her smile is real. Her beauty is simple and appealing. She listens and really does hear. There is nothing phony about this gentle, free-spirited girl. Do you recognize her yet?

A rainbow is quiet, yet everyone is drawn to look at it. A rainbow portrays nature's artwork. A rainbow is a symbol of joy, happiness, and peace. Its brilliant colors are almost magical. The waitress I am speaking about is very much like a rainbow, only in a human way. If you know her, tell her so. Her cheeks may flush from embarrassment because she is a humble person, but she deserves the compliment. The "rainbow girl" pours your coffee, serves your meals, and brings your drinks. Most important, she makes your day! Do you know her yet? If not, you are missing out. She is real! I wrote this just for her.

You may know of a waitress just like the one written about. If you do, thank her for making your day a bit brighter.

Management

Is a manager a "working man?" No, not in the context of how I think unless the manager actually does physical labor and "jumps into the trenches" with those he or she is managing. If a person simply manages, then that person is a manager, not a worker. Yes, managing is work. But it is not physically as hard as the work the people do who are working under the manager. In most cases, managers are necessary and needed to keep things running smooth. Their position includes responsibility, organization, and overseeing. In some cases, their positions have been given to them because they are related to the owner or the financial backers of a company. These managers are usually not very good. The managers who excel are those who understand their workers, know their workers, and know what it is to do the work performed by those he or she is managing.

From 1972 to 1989, I owned and operated a small landscaping business. I spent every working day on the job with my helpers. I did whatever had to be done to complete a job, and I enjoyed the work we were doing. My help put in forty-hour weeks. I averaged seventy hours a week during the spring, summer, and fall. Ron Samartino worked for and with me nine of those years. Part III of this book is dedicated to his memory. Ron was one of my best friends and one of the hardest workers I have known. He made the hard work easier because of his humor and his positive outlook on things. When the "surf was up," we would hit the waves after doing eight hours of cutting lawns and gardening. Many times, we had our surfboards tied to the stake body truck so we could go right to the beach after finishing our last lawn. We didn't miss the waves when they were breaking good. Work hard and play hard—it's a good way to be. Ron played the drums and listened to rock music, heavy metal, or similar music. His favorite group while he was in elementary school and high school was the group named Rush. Ronnie knew every word to every song they put out. Because of our age difference, I would tell him about the music and the groups I listened to and saw in concert during the 1960s and early 1970s. Ron was born January 28, 1969. He and a few friends had their own band after they graduated from high school. It was called Exit 6. He is missed and not forgotten. He worked hard and played hard. He lived a healthy and active life until colon cancer struck him without any warning. "Follow the yellow brick road" was one of his favorite little sayings after seeing the movie *Wizard of Oz*. Excuse me for getting away from the subject of management. I think you can understand.

Here is something to think about. What would happen if every working person within the United States stayed home for a week? Would the country come to a standstill? I believe so. Now imagine if every worker continued to work but Congress and the Senate stayed home for a week. Would our country come to a standstill? No, because they do it often and even with longer periods of time. Yet they are still paid. What would happen if all the top executives, managers, and financial administrators stopped for a week, yet all the working people still went to their jobs? It would not stop our nation from functioning. Trash would still be picked up. Hospitals would still care for patients. Restaurants, stores, laundromats, wholesale outlets, gas stations, liquor marts, delis, and plenty of other places would still operate. The fishing boats, clamming boats, shrimp boats, scallop, and lobster boats would still continue their runs. Truckers would be hauling, loggers would be cutting, and the dairy farmers would be milking. Almost every small business in the country would still operate. The self-employed workers would still do their plumbing work, electric work, lawn maintenance, glass repair, construction, and so on. Here is my thinking and my comment which will probably cause many of the executives and the white-collar people to throw a tantrum. Sorry, but this is how it is. Here I go! Why do you think of yourselves as being more important and more valuable than the working person? Why are your egos so big? Can you survive on your own? Could you make ends meet if your pay and benefits were based upon a more just and fair society so the gap between you and those who are more important to keeping the country functioning is not a big gap at all? You can be self-righteous, and you can view working people as a class of people below you, but that does not gain respect. Government officials need a drastic cut in pay, perks, benefits, and pensions. Since they work for the people, they should be closer to the people! Executives, CEOs, managers, and so-called giants in the financial world need to get off their thrones and understand what working people do, how they survive, and how they live within their means. A person can be comfortable with having the necessities of life. A person can know peace living a simple life and knowing respect. Working people need to be respected a lot more by our society.

There I have opened up a hornet's nest. But I am not one to keep quiet when it comes to people who deserve more respect than they are given. Working people are the backbone of our country. We are humans, and there should be no kings or queens among us. The United States of America does not need a class system, and the leaders of our nation need to come closer to the average citizen. It is up to our leaders to make the changes, so this can occur. We are all equal under the law. We should be a bit more equal when it comes to keeping our country functioning. Those "at the top" think the workers cannot do without them. The opposite is true; those "at the top" cannot do without the workers. Remember, if the workers stop the country comes to a standstill.

On a lighter note, here is a story I wrote about two people I considered as my mentors when I was a teenager. I wrote this in 1994.

An untold, until now, story about Will and Bill Morey

I first met Will Morey Sr. during the fall of 1968. We met at 25th Street and the Boardwalk in North Wildwood. I was introduced by my aunt, Florence A. Hatt, who then operated the Pan American Gift Shop in Wildwood Crest.

I can still remember vividly my meeting with Will, even though it was twenty-five years ago. It was a big day for me. You see, I was fifteen years of age and very anxious to learn and work construction.

My first impression of Mr. Will Morey Sr. was how kind he was. I was nervous but he put me at ease. We talked for a while, then Will walked me to the beach side of the boardwalk. Looking down at the miniature golf course, which was then being dismantled, he told me of his plans to build a giant slide. "I'll give you a chance, Billy." He said, "If you work hard and pay attention, you'll stay on. I couldn't believe it. I was hired!"

The following weekend, I got to meet Bill Morey Sr. My first impression of Bill was, "My gosh, he's tough!" He put me right to work with a guy named Carl Manefretti. Carl was tough, but he had a good heart and a lot of patience. Carl called me "kid" because he said there were enough Bills around already. Bill Morey Sr. was tough, but he cared about me and taught me a lot about the construction trade. When the job was risky, he would have me work at his side or have Carl guide me until I learned what to do and how to do it safely.

I had two great bosses. Will taught me a lot about business and how to treat people fairly, and Bill taught me about construction and running a crew. I did not realize it then, but I had two of the best businessmen in the Wildwoods as teachers and bosses.

I visited Wildwood this July 1994, and I am not surprised at how well the Morey family is progressing. I worked weekends and after school with Bill while we constructed the original pier and giant slide. Will made me the first manager of Morey's Pier and guided me along during the summer of 1969.

We opened the slide on July 4 weekend of that summer, but I never took my nail apron off. Instead of nails, I was now putting money into my apron. Here is why: when we first opened, we didn't have any tickets, uniforms, or even organization. We all looked to Will, and he made the decisions. There were no ticket booths, and our office was the storage room under the slide. It was a quarter a ride, and we gave change out of our aprons. When a nail apron filled, we would tie it together and hand it to Will.

Will was everywhere that first summer. You would see him helping people at the top of the slide, stopping people at the bottom, collecting the quarters, and handing out mats. No job was too small for Will, and he had as much fun as us kids did with operating the slide. Working the slide was more than a job. It was the place to be! I and a dozen other teenagers worked for Morey's that summer, and we all had a great experience.

I learned a lot from Will Morey Sr. that summer. I watched and listened to how he dealt with the public. He reminded me of Walt Disney. He could have as much fun as us kids, yet he was one of the smartest adults around. Will cared about us, and we knew it. We are all adults now, and Will is much older. Some of the names I can remember who worked the giant slide that summer were Jim

McMichaels, Art Nazarro, John Gallagher, Mickey Massie, Cliff Massie, Joe Freeman, Ray Morey, Jr., Mark Longford, and others.

Will and Bill were surprised how well the slide did that summer. It was the cornerstone of what was to come. Each year, the pier grew, and the ocean receded. The pier is much wider and longer now, but my memories remain with the slide. I have known Will and Bill for twenty-five years, and I have only good things to say about these two exceptional people. Besides my father, John J. Flynn, of North Wildwood, Will Morey Sr. is the most honest man I've ever known. I try to follow in both of their footsteps.

A story I'd like to tell about Bill Morey Sr. is how he taught me foundation work. I was just out of high school, and Bill asked me if I would like to learn how to use a transit. Little did I know but Bill and I were going to lay out the entire groundwork for the Ocean Holiday Motel in Wildwood Crest.

The first day we went to an empty beachfront lot along Ocean Avenue in Wildwood Crest. Bill has a good vision for what "will be" when it comes to building. He showed me the blueprints and explained to me what we would be doing for the next week or so. The next two weeks were better than going to college to learn. Bill taught me every little trick in the book on surveying for the motel foundation. He was patient, thorough, and fun to work with. My biggest reward was the knowledge he gave me, and my biggest satisfaction came during the construction. Everything came together as the structure went up!

This may seem a simple story, but there was a lot involved. Bill could have chosen an experienced worker, but he chose to teach a young boy the trade. It took longer because of me and the time he spent explaining things. It's a simple story about a caring boss and friend.

I could tell dozens of stories about Will Morey Sr., but I'll refrain because of space here. Generally, though, Will took the time to know people who worked for him and looked out for their concerns. I am not a relative of Will's, but he made me feel I was part of the family. He was one of those rare adults in the 1970s who listened to us teenagers. His advice came with respect, and he didn't talk down to us.

I think his gift of listening was a big reason so many teenagers like working for Will.

Will is a rich person, but he has earned it, and he always put people before money. He enjoys his work, envisions the future, and cares about the community. Will Morey Sr. was one of those "good teachers" I was lucky to have in my life.

I have a lot of good memories of the Wildwoods. Morey's Pier and to help build the Ocean Holiday and the Port Royal were a big part of my youth. By this article, I wish to publicly thank Will and Jackie Morey and to remember the late Lew Morey Sr. who enriched my life with compassion, advice, and his saying to me, "If you ever need it, don't hesitate to ask me for help." Lew was genuine and helped more than once.

Work gives purpose to our everyday lives. Workers produce tangible things that are eaten, worn, lived in, and traveled on. Work has a substance to it. This is why most workers have a sense of pride with what they do. They produce! Here is just one simple example of this. The next time you are on a train, think about how much labor and skill is involved in building the entire train you are on. We should all notice more often and with more appreciation the things we use because someone invented, someone designed, someone forged, and someone built these things. For the young people reading this book and are not excited about working, get yourself motivated. Hanging out on the streets or sitting in front of a television day after day is not healthy or productive. Find work in fields you enjoy. If you enjoy fixing things, become a handyman or work at a repair shop. Auto mechanics seem to always be in demand, if you learn the trade well.

If you enjoy cooking, take a culinary course or find work at a restaurant. It is a great thing to be paid for doing what you enjoy. When I was a junior in high school, I wanted to become a forest ranger. I enjoy camping, hiking, and being in the outdoors. After researching about jobs available to me, I learned there were very few openings because the jobs were being filled by the men and women returning from serving our military in Vietnam. I totally agreed that those veterans should be the first in line to have the work, so I looked to other job possibilities. I enjoyed doing and learning construction, so I pursued that trade. When I discovered I enjoyed working for myself, I decided to start my own landscaping business and do construction during the winter months as an employee. I started out just cutting grass in 1972 then went on to trimming bushes and trees, planting flowers and shrubs, installing lawns, etc. To learn about the trade I studies from textbooks, Rutgers University students used in their courses concerning agriculture. Knowledge pays off with better pay and less mistakes. The youth of today have technology far superior to what we had in the nineteen sixties and seventies. Almost everything new during the nineteen seventies was because of the space program President John F. Kennedy promoted when he became president. To illustrate how far and how fast we progressed, here is a list of a few things for the young people of today to see and maybe to realize the changes my generation saw and experienced.

First, let's start with the construction trade. Power tools were a luxury in the late sixties. Carpenters still used hand tools. Every carpenter had a sharp set of handsaws, hand-operated drills with an assortment of wood bits, a few hammers of different sizes, and toolboxes filled with hand tools and parts. Our muscles did most of the work. In the landscaping trade, we used our muscles also. We swept by hand, tilled with a shovel, hoe, and steel rake, clipped by hand, and moved soil or stones with wheel barrels. Today, everything is motor driven. We never needed to go to a gym to build our muscles!

When computers came along for the public to use it brought a huge, new industry and created an entire new job market. New technology made every trade easier to do. Whenever I can recommend a career to a young person, my recommendation is to learn at least one trade besides knowing about the computer industry. Knowing a few trades is important because when the economy is down jobs become scarce. The person who can do carpentry, plumbing, or electrical work will always find work because they can jump from one trade to another. The need today seems to be in science and math. Health care and related industries will always be in demand because people are living longer. Personally, if I were in high school today, I would be looking into the fields of solar, wind, or alternative energy fields for a career. We will be using oil and gas as long as it lasts but the "thinking" of today is to seek clean energy. Good luck to the youth of today! There is a big future of discoveries ahead.

Brain and Muscle

It is amazing how some people do not understand the world of the working man or woman. Maybe it is because they simply don't care to know, or maybe it is about preserving their so-called image or status. To them, it is all about position, money, power, and influence. It is a class thing. Working people are not within their class. My favorite part of the New Testament in the Bible is when Jesus gave His sermon on the mount. Read Jesus's words of that day. He teaches us what is important and how God views our actions and lives. Jesus explained how people of virtue and faith will see their rewards. He also described how hard it will be for the rich to see heaven. Use your brain here. These are the words and teachings from the Son of God! The Sermon on the Mount is a powerful sermon.

Most of the Apostles of Christ were fishermen. They were "working men." It is good to know the first Christians were working people who used their muscles and their knowledge to catch fish which fed people. The examples within this chapter are about working people who use both their brain power and their muscle power to do the jobs they do. Unfortunately, their skills are not always praised, and their work is taken for granite. Within your everyday travels and daily routines, take notice a bit more of the people doing their jobs and what their jobs involve. For some of you, this could be a real "eye-opener." With your next visit to the bank, notice who deals the most with people, takes care of you on a regular basis, has the responsibility of making your deposit or withdraw correctly, and is on his or her feet all day. Yes, it is the teller. It is the bank teller who "connects" with you and does the work which keeps a bank moving. Then if you visit a store look at all the shelves and goods stacked and priced. Think about who put them there. Things just don't appear. When you see the trash men taking your trash, speak to them and thank them. They put up with smelly garbage, rain and snow, cold and heat, bags and maggots, traffic and much more. If you walk by a police officer, have eye contact and say hello. They are the ones who protect us twenty-four hours a day, every day. If you catch a bus to get to work or to return home from a day shopping, say hello to the driver, and thank him or her. Your safety is their responsibility, and they do it every day.

One of the arguments of the managers, supervisors, and executives is that people need them because things need to be organized. I agree with this. I do not agree with the gap between them and the people who produce the work. The financial gap is too big. The status gap is ridiculous, and the sense of power over others is disrespectful. Luckily, most working people have a strong sense of self-respect, and they know what they do is important to the community and the country. They know that "as a whole" their work is connected to the other workers. For example: when the concrete is delivered by the truck driver the masons can lay the sidewalks. Or when the framers finish building the structural part of the house, then the electricians, plumbers, Sheetrockers, trim carpenters, tile layers, etc., can do their work. Other trades have the same flow. When the shrimp boats come to port, they unload at the docks, beginning a process of work for others. The various jobs caused by the shrimps coming to market may end up at a table in a restaurant where people are enjoying a shrimp cocktail or scampi dinner. We could go back even further. Before the captain and his crew even catch the shrimp, the boat was constructed, nets were spun, machinery was built, and so on. The work of one begins a process. A piece of paper does not drive a nail, yet in most cases, the blueprint (paper) is needed before the nail is driven. Thus, you have the work of an architect.

When a recession hits our country or, even worse, a depression, it is workers who get hit the hardest, and they are the first to be laid off from their jobs. Self-employed workers see a dramatic decrease in work, yet their bills still come in as usual. Our government officials need to realize that a strong and healthy economy depends upon keeping the people working within the private sector and to have less people on the government payroll. Government is supported by the taxes of the people within the private sector. Without the taxes taken out of our checks each week, the funds slow down to support the government's expenses. Also the more people rely on the government, the weaker our nation becomes. People who work feel a sense of worth. They awake knowing they have something to do. They feel purposeful, and their energies are directed to accomplishing things. They also have less stress with knowing they have a paycheck. Do you know what "living week to week" means? There are a lot of people who are not in the workforce who do not know what this means. How many look toward Friday (payday for most)? Many workers live week to week because when they receive their paycheck, they can pay some bills, buy some food, gas up their vehicle, and maybe treat the kids. If there is money left, it goes toward other expenses during the week. You will hear people say, "Thank God it is Friday!" These are the ones who live week to week, and the numbers of these people are growing today (2013). Personally, I found it easier to exist financially back in the 1960s and '70s because a dollar went further and the government didn't tax everything we use or buy. Look at all the costs there are today. Are there any items not taxed today? A citizen should support their government, but us, American citizens, need to keep the government in check because we are a free nation and we need to remain so. Big government is too close to socialism or even totalitarianism. When we work, we receive our pay. It is hard earned, and it is ours. The government takes their share first, but the rest is ours to spend as we see fit. This is freedom? We need not lose any more of our freedoms because of a big government with too many controls put on us. The strongest virtue Americans have is their love of liberty. Workers know how important this virtue is because their work keeps liberty strong. They give to their country; they do not take from their country. If they are ever in need, then they can be helped. Our system is set up to sort those in need. We all find ourselves in need of help sometimes during our lives. Workers pay into these programs with every paycheck they receive. The system works except when it is abused. The abuse only hurts our nation! Too many people are relying on the government to support them. Many of these people can work but do not work because it is easier to receive a check, voucher, or assistance from the government. Government programs have caused many citizens to become less energetic or even lazy. This strains the people who are actually working. Who is to blame? I blame our congressmen, senators, and our president because they are afraid to make the hard decisions and bring the system into a responsible one economically. They are mostly after the votes to be elected back into office. Because of our current prolonged recession people have put off their retirements. Most people have lost their savings and are now living less comfortable despite working their entire lives. For those who are more fortunate, good for them! But for many, because of an accident, bad luck, illness, or investments gone, bad things are not comfortable. We can only hope these people maintain their self-worth and their faith in God.

I mention accidents because on October 14, 2002, at 11:45 a.m. My life changed drastically because of a fall while putting plywood on a new roof. We should have broken for lunch at 11:40 a.m. (humor)! The roof we were ply wooding had roof rafters spaced twenty-four inches on center. That is just enough space for a person to go through. The four-foot piece of plywood I was just about to nail slid off the edge of the rafter closer to me. My hand was on the plywood, and my upper body weight was on the board when it moved causing the plywood to fly up like a seesaw. I went head irst threw the roof with the plywood at my side. It happened so quick! When I realized I was free-falling through the air, it seemed like a second later I hit a pile of stacked two by fours two stories below the high cathedral ceiling. I consider myself very lucky. If I had fallen sideways on the roof (not through it), I would have fallen five stories onto a concrete walkway. By hitting the stack of lumber, my head did not get injured. My injuries were serious, but my spinal nerves were not severed. Doctors told me time would heal me but that life would change. After six hours in the emergency room and several x-rays and CAT scans with fluids put into me, I was given the report of my injuries. The fall caused two fractures on my spine, several fractures on my ribs, internal bleeding, damage to my back muscles, and damage to the calf muscle on my right leg. I live with a compressed vertebrate and a deep pain in my back which I have learned to ignore. During the recovery period, four different doctors told me not to chance further injury by surfing or continuing in the martial arts.

The compressed vertebrate was their reasoning for telling me I would have to give up my favorite two things. I mentally resisted at first. As time went on, I realized their advice was good. There are times when I twist a certain way and I get a sharp, hot pain, which brings me to my knees, and it is hard to move for a few minutes. If this were to happen while surfing, I would drown. My teaching of karate is over because I always taught by example. Students need to see the form and the correct movements to learn. I am happy I can still work and keep myself busy. I can do most things I was able to do before, and my knowledge within a few trades keeps me working. The injury to my calf muscle lingers because when I walk a mile or so, I get cramps. Oh well, that is life!

Workmen's Compensation saved me financially because of the medical bills and loss of work during my recovery. For those who have been injured and then return to work you know how hard it is to recover financially. Even though I returned to work in 2003, my income was a third of what I made before the fall. The financial loss to those who get injured seriously is a part of the risks workers have. I constantly think of those workers who have had accidents or illnesses due to work misfortunes and cannot return to work and I count my blessings.

Historically, has the gap between the working people and the executives ever been so great? This gap has been growing for decades. Working people cannot vote their own pay increases, yet the Senate and our Congress can and do. Let's say the "take home" pay of a store clerk is 350 dollars a week. How much do you think the clerk will have left after buying food, gas for his or her vehicle, paying the rent or mortgage, paying the utility bills, the phone and cable bills, insurance and maybe a doctor or dentist bill, purchasing some clothing and personal items. The list seems endless to people who make minimum amounts of money. There are always setbacks. One week, it could be the cost of needing a new tire or the car battery goes bad and you have to buy a new one. Or your eyes are getting worse, and you need to visit the eye doctor. The store clerk has to decide each week where the dollars will go and what things to do without. Because of living a life of necessities and of knowing how to do without luxuries, the store clerk can survive and even live a life feeling content. Sure, the struggles are hard, but working people know about struggles and push through each one. Whenever you hear a high-paid person complaining about their perks being cut or of not receiving a pay raise one year, think about the store clerk and the millions of workers just like him or her. Most of them own just one vehicle, and some of them exist without a vehicle. It is because they know how to survive and they how to do without when necessary. Even though they are hit the hardest during a recession, they survive and live in the real world. Working people know about survival! It is a part of life they live almost every day.

Our country is currently experiencing a major recession. We have been a strong productive and free nation because of how our Founding Fathers formed the system of government we have. One of the biggest problems our country has now is the size of the government. Our leaders need to cut back the size of our government and people's dependency upon it. Town, city, county, state, and federal government are all too large and need to be downsized. Private enterprises need to be allowed to grow. The government limits their growth by too much regulation and costs. Our judicial system needs to bring lawsuits under control. There are too many lawsuits, and most of them are simply about money, not justice. One of the biggest concerns small business owners have is of being sued. Lawyers feed on this trend and make large sums of money by encouraging people to sue. The lawyers themselves should be held accountable by judges when they bring frivolous lawsuits into court. Will I be sued because of this statement? Oh no!

Because this book is being directed toward students everywhere, I want to encourage young people to think deeply about the value toward human life work has. Think how important it is to have something to do every day and to be productive. Think of those you affect by inventing something new, building something people need or growing crops which feed people and animals. To really help people of the world, think of what field you want to work in. Humans need food, clothing, shelter, and health care to survive. The world needs less violence. People need protection from those wishing to cause harm. I strongly believe that purpose in life is more valuable than attaining wealth. How valuable is saving a life? How valuable is finding a cure for cancer? How valuable is adopting a child who has no parent? When you are young, you can choose a direction for your life. Think deep, take your time. Get good advice. Weigh your options. Pursue a course which you will enjoy doing. Keep in mind that God gives special "gifts" and natural talent in music or art. Put it to use and help people by doing it. You might have a natural talent for teaching. Follow your talent, and make it grow so you can affect people's lives in positive ways. Many farmers have a "knack" for growing crops and having good harvests. It is a gift from God, and they use it to feed the people. Those vegetables don't just appear on the grocery store shelves. They started with seeds and roots and grew. The farmers provide the product and other workers get it to you. This is the same with all those other food products you pass by as you walk up and down the store aisles. We seem to take things for granted too much. Our society is blessed with supermarkets full of food and supplies. It took work, a lot of work, to have all these stores filled and ready for the public to buy. Here is a sample agricultural question I'll throw in here! How are potatoes grown?

As I finish this chapter, our country is experiencing a dramatic change within the economic culture of America. The gap between the people of wealth and working people is growing tremendously. The middle-class workers are falling toward the bottom, yet the rich are getting richer. Our society is out of balance because of economic reasons. I blame this on too many strains put on the working class because they are paying the bills for those who are "feeding" off the government. Despite this, the United States of America is the best place to work, live, be educated, and to receive medical help. This is my opinion, and I share this opinion with most all Americans. This is not a boastful statement. It is reality for us. We have the freedom to move around from state to state in search of work. We can relocate to secure a job, or we can travel from job location to job location. In essence, we are free to pursue work and free to choose work. This is not true for many countries around the world. Our freedom is our wealth!

As I finish writing this chapter, 2013 is just about over. This will give readers a perspective on the time period of my writing even though many parts of this chapter are taken from thoughts and writings over many years. Work is not only about economics; my focus concentrates on making a living because of the struggles the working people endure. If you are a young person, plan your future career, but be ready for changes. No job is secure these days. Working at the same job for twenty-five to forty years is rare now. Our grandparents and many of our parents who worked during the forties, fifties, sixties, and seventies were employed by the same company for long periods. The global market changed that norm. New technology has changed the working climate. I wish the new generation a successful life. I hope most of them will enjoy the fields they choose to work in. Many people do not have the luxury of enjoying the work they do because they are working jobs out of necessity, not choice. While young, try your best to work where your interests lie. Set your goals to be within the fields of work where you will enjoy going to work each day and be enthused about advancing your possibilities. This is my advice after working for a living for many, many years. My advice is that you strive to not rely on government assistance unless it is necessary for food or lodging during a brief time. When people rely on the government, they tend to become lazy and nonproductive. I am not including unemployment benefits because workers have paid into these programs before receiving the benefits. I think everyone knows why I advise young people to be financially independent. If you are healthy, fit to work, and able to work, then you should work. Use your knowledge. Use your skills. Use your personality. If either your work is physical, mental, or artful, put your energies in a forward motion and be happy in life. Keep this in mind: if every worker in the United States stopped working for a week, our country would virtually come to a standstill. Think about my comment, then think about how the working man or woman deserves better respect than they are given today. Be a part of the "backbone of America," and your personal peace will be enhanced. For those bosses, CEOs, administrators, and managers, I recommend you to look in the mirror and ask yourself why you think you are so superior. Get off your high horses and realize how important every worker is. Without a base, a house would crumble. Workers are the base!

My Dad's Own Words

I am putting my dad's own written works in this chapter because he wrote about the Great Depression which hurt our nation tremendously. Dad wrote some family history, so we (my brothers and sister) would know about some of his history. Dad did not finish his writings, but the things he did write are interesting. My dad, John J. Flynn, Jr., was born in 1917. The Great Depression hit in 1929. That would make him twelve years old when our country failed financially. Here is a part of his writings. I have not edited it a bit.

"The depression hit in 1929, and all hell broke loss. Companies went broke, banks closed, people lost their jobs and all their money. Stop and think about all this if this happened to you. What would you do?

"I have seen, not hearsay, the constables coming up and putting people out on the street, selling their furniture, etc., to pay the back rent. I saw a man shoot at a constable through a door who came up to see him out. I also saw the people pounding on the door of the bank trying to get their money, but to no avail did they get it.

"Remember in those days, they had no unemployment, no welfare, no food stamps, no government programs until President Roosevelt got elected in 1932 and gradually introduced most of the programs we have today. That is why he was elected four times as president. Gee, I wish we had someone like him the last two administrations.

"Again, the Flynn family was blessed, God has been good to us, and you should all be proud of the name, Pop Pop Flynn worked all during the depression but only enough to live on from week to week (7:00 a.m. till 6:00 p.m. six days a week). Remember also, there was no vacation time paid or unpaid till the unions were and the sweat shops were eliminated.

"Well, as I said before, we were poor, very poor, but Mom Mom Flynn was a very good manager. The fifty cents daily I earned on

Saturdays (6:00 a.m. till 6:00 p.m. or till the load was sold) and during the summer of 1931 was greatly appreciated by Mom Flynn. That three dollars (a week) I earned huckstering (fresh fish out on the streets) was a big help to her. Remember that the average working man with a family was making about twelve dollars a week."

During the 1970s and early 1980s, Dad and I fished at nights during the spring, summer, and fall using his eighteen-foot Boston Whaler. We went out about once a week after a full day's work. It was relaxing and fun because we fished the Hereford Inlet between North Wildwood, New Jersey, and Stone Harbor, New Jersey, which has an active supply of saltwater fish species. We also fished the back bay areas when the tide was high. During those many nights of fishing, Dad told me story after story about how difficult the Great Depression was for everyone. Dad's memory was so clear! He educated me about how the unions got stared despite the resistance they got from the company owners and their "thugs." I remember how Dad spoke about the people being hungry. Many died because of hunger during that era. I encourage every student to research and study the Great Depression the United States had. There were no televisions then. People relied on newspapers and radio for news and entertainment. Refrigeration involved real ice. That is why they were called "iceboxes." Many, many things we take for granite today were not yet invented or designed. The Industrial Age in America came and went, but the products and discoveries of that era led to what we have today. Just think how important the workforce was during those years! Mom and Dad's generation knew about hard work and good work ethics. I pray our country will not continue to lose the value concerning those work ethics. Thank goodness our nation has the millions and millions of people who perform their duties on a daily basis. As you can tell, I have a deep respect for everyone who toils and protects us through their work. It is the American way! Be free, work hard, play hard, and protect each other.

CHAPTER 3

Adventures

To keep life interesting and to explore the world outside of our neigh-
borhoods, we all need some adventures. Young people, especially,
crave adventure and dream about doing things out of the ordinary
and of seeing places near and far. Curiosity and imagination draw
us toward adventures. A yearning to learn or a desire to see different things, people, animals, environments, or feel different climates
lead people to travel. After publishing *Pure Power* (part 1 and 2 of
this book), numerous readers encouraged me to write more in detail
about my exploits. Their advice is for me not to "gloss over" certain
things such as may adventures. Here in this chapter, I am following
their advice and recording past events people might see as adventures.

The first big adventure came when I was fourteen years of
age. My parents allowed me to travel from Southern New Jersey to
Cimarron, New Mexico, with a small group of fellow boy scouts of
various scout troops in South Jersey. The year was 1967. I still have
the topographic maps we each carried while hiking and camping
the northern section of Philmont Scout Ranch and Explorer Base in
Cimarron, New Mexico. It is right here on the table as I write. My
notes are on the maps from 1967. We each noted where we camped,
the trails we took, the mountains we climbed and where we went to
restock our food supplies. This map is jogging my memory! Many
things concerning the backcountry hike have escaped my memory
after forty-five years, but certain happenings are coming back to me
as I write while looking at the map and the various sketching put on
it when I was just fourteen years old. Each boy and each scout leader

carried their own map in case of becoming detached from the group. With the topographical maps and a compass, you could find you way to a predestined campsite. Our entire trail hike was planned by our leaders and the Philmont staff members who helped us. Before we began our journey on foot, each map was outlined to show us where we would be each day and where we would camp each night. We also practiced the "buddy system" so no one person would go off on their own without being noticed. Back in the nineteen-sixties, Philmont was the ultimate experience of the great outdoors for any scout. We went in August. My employer at the time was Arthur Greenspan. He allowed me time off from my summer job after my dad explained to him how important a trip to Philmont is for a teenage boy. I thanked Mr. Greenspan, and my parents many times for giving me the opportunity to experience such a great trip.

On the East Coast, we have a lot of humidity during the summer. You sometimes sweat while simply standing still. The one thing I will never forget about New Mexico is how hot and dry it was in August. The scouts from New Jersey were amazed how you could wet a bandana in the stream, put it around your neck, and in less than a minute, it would be dry. We also were amazed how fast our body sweat evaporated. This was something new to us all! Another thing my scout partner and I learned was to look at the ground more carefully before putting our "pup" tent up. We were in a hurry! We erected our tent and were just about to put our sleeping bags into it when out came a long, thick snake which we thought to be a rattlesnake! We yelled for adults who ran to us immediately. It turned out to be a bull snake which looks just like a rattler but is not poisonous. One of the adults used his walking staff to guide the snake away. The other adults took our tent down and moved it away. They pointed to the snake's hole in the ground. "You pitched your tent over a snake hole," they said with a smile. We pitched our tent far away from that spot! Another memory coming back was the night our group camped at a location where the Philmont staff kept an outpost supplied with food and various supplies for the groups to come to and refill their backpacks. It was mostly all basic dry foods. After a week on the trail, you could only dream about things like ice cream, fresh milk, fresh vegetables, or fresh fruit. We had powdered milk and tang to drink the entire trip. We could joke about have a "Philly Cheesesteak" or an Italian hoagie while sitting around the campfire at night. I am sure we joked about having ice with our drinks too. The water from some of the streams within the forested areas of our hike was pretty cool, though. With all the food supplies stored at the outpost, we were warned to be on the watch for brown bears. They were constant visitors to the area because of the food. The night we were there one visited us. The bear knocked over some stacked logs just outside of our campsite area. We were sitting around the fire when one of the scouts spotted the bear. The bear stayed away from us. It headed toward a building where food was stored. We were not alone. About five other scout groups were staying the night and had set up camp in various locations. There was a New Mexico Park Ranger at the site along with the Philmont staff. The bear ripped open a locked wooden door then pillaged through the supplies. Later, the ranger told us the bear had eaten a substance called Textrox which we used for cleaning our mess kits. He joked about how the bear would be in need of a lot of toilet paper! The bear had left the camp after a few shots were fired into the air to scare him away. We were hiking and camping in a wilderness area so dealing with wildlife was a common thing. Every night, our food supplies were hung from tree branches. We had rope and canvas bags. In areas where there are no trees, the bears were not common. Other animals were sometimes a problem, so you slept with "one eye open," so to speak. Compared to what is available today, heavy-duty canvas bags seem archaic. Lightweight materials were not developed yet. At least we did not have them. Our backpacks had wooden or metal frames. Canvas seemed to be the material of the day. Our tents and our backpacks were canvas. We carried small sewing kits and duct tape to repair things. We used wax from a candle to waterproof torn seams. You simply let the hot wax drop onto the tent seam or other things you wanted waterproof. We carried matches with wooden stems which we pre-dipped into liquid wax to keep them waterproof and ready to use. They are the ones you can strike anywhere, and you can still find them in stores today. I always carried flint and steel with me in case of emergencies.

Scouts learn how to use flint and steel and are trained to start small campfires with their use. The key to it is finding good tinder to ignite with the sparks given off by the flint. In extreme emergencies, human hair could be used if nothing else is around. The gunpowder in shotgun shells taken apart carefully works also. But learn from a survival person or a gunsmith before you mess around with ammo. I prefer to have a disposable lighter with me now. It is so much easier!

For the people reading this who went to Philmont as a scout or scout leader, you know how exciting the trip is. Our group's most exciting day was when we climbed to the summit of Baldy Mountain and had views which are spectacular. I still have a photo we took of our group on the summit. I think the elevation was about twelve thousand feet above sea level. It has been a long time since then, but the topo map I have shows 12,440 feet above sea level. Where I lived then, North Wildwood, New Jersey, is about ten feet above sea level. What a difference! I remember it as being a long climb up. We were above the tree line for quite a while as we climbed a rocky surface. Coming down is sometimes harder on your feet and calf muscles as we found out that day. I cannot remember how many miles we covered that day, but it was a big day for our group, and we felt proud of our accomplishment.

The adventure of traveling across this great country (USA) and of visiting places like Pikes Peak and the United States Airforce Academy gave me an experience you cannot put a price tag on, especially for a fourteen-year old boy from New Jersey. I had never seen mountains so high. I had never seen open spaces so vast! It opened my mind to do more traveling later. When I arrived home in late August 1967, I was only weeks away from my next adventure which I was excited about. I was going to high school! Elementary school was behind me, and now it was time for the "big time." That is how I felt back then.

Thumbing It to Surf

This adventure is just too dangerous for anyone to do today. I see myself as very fortunate to have been able to hitchhike across the country during a safe time when thousands of other people were doing it all across the United States. After graduating from Wildwood Catholic High School in June 1971 and then working the summer at Morey's Pier in North Wildwood, I decided to surf the waves of California. The cheapest way to get there would be to hitchhike my way across, so I did! It costs me twenty-five dollars to get from New Jersey to Huntington Beach, California, and it took me six days to get there. Kinda cheap and kinda fast—don't ya think? I would not even consider doing it now. Even if I was eighteen years old, it is not worth the risk. The world has changed quite a bit since 1971. Most of the people hitchhiking around the country back then were Vietnam Veterans returning home or young people out to experience the freedom inspired by the culture change of the nineteen-sixties. We were allowed to "thumb" along the entrance ramps of major highways. Almost everyone carried a sleeping bag and a small backpack. Long distance truckers picked up some of us to keep them company and to keep them awake while on their long hauls. Several truckers gave me rides, and one particular driver took me five hundred miles and fed me along the way. As long as I stayed awake and talked with him, my ride kept going west.

I was just a young kid yearning to surf the waves of the West Coast. For years, I viewed the pictures of surfers riding big waves within *Surfer* magazine. It was time to experience it myself! My hair was getting long, and I sported a dark tan from working outside all summer. I had the surfers look, yet some people referred to me as being a hippie. The older crowd thought that anyone with long hair was a "peace child." I was not. I was not into drugs, and I was serious about life. I did not live in a fantasy land created by LSD and acid. I worked hard and played hard! Actually, I am not much different today.

The first stop in California was on the beach at Huntington Beach. A young woman had picked me up on the east side of the Rocky Mountains and told me she would drop me off at a good surfing beach. She did! After thanking her, I walked onto the beach, set my basket weave backpack down, and went for a swim in the Pacific Ocean! What a thrill it was for this East Coast surfer! A local surfer told me where I could find a place to rent. He directed me to a hotel up the street. I went there and got a room for ten dollars a week. It was clean and had a bed and dresser. There was a bathroom down the hallway where you could shower and use the toilet. It was for everyone on the floor, yet it was clean and well cared for. I stayed there for three weeks.

My next mission was to get a surfboard. The hotel manager told me to go to a shop near the beach. When I went into the shop, I was stunned! There stood the famous surfer and surfboard maker Morey of Morey/Pope Surfboards. It was his shop (1971)! He noticed the look on my face, and he laughed. He said something like, "You must be from the East Coast. Did you just get here?" I told him about my journey and of where I lived. Then I asked him about buying a used board, and he helped me pick one out. I told him I would be surfing for about three weeks then return home for Thanksgiving. "Bring it back before you leave, and I will buy it back from you if it is still in good shape." It cost me eighty-five dollars, and when I bought it back, I received $70 for it after three weeks of surfing every day. You just cannot find deals like that today!

I surfed every day I was there. From seven o'clock in the morning until six o'clock every evening, I surfed, ate, and slept. What a life! The girls were everywhere along the beaches, California Girls. To be honest, the girls at the Wildwood beaches are just as fit and healthy looking as the ones I saw and met at Huntington Beach. Sorry about that, beach boys.

The waves along the West Coast are more powerful and break faster than the waves I surfed in Cape May and Wildwood, New Jersey. It took several days to get use to the power and the speed of those waves, but when I did, my surfing abilities improved greatly. The wave heights are measured from the back of waves, unlike how surfers measure waves from the front on the East Coast. We don't see a lot of big waves, so we cheat a bit.

The second week, I was at Huntington Beach the surf really picked up! The waves had great form and breaking at five to six feet. Getting "tubed" became easy and fun. Wipeouts were rough! The waves were so powerful that whenever you wiped out you were crushed. Your body is tested for its strength and its durability with every wipeout. We didn't use (or have) boards leashes in 1971. Use of leashes came along later. When you lost your board, it usually meant a long swim in and a long paddle back out beyond the breakers. I think I first used a board leash around 1975 or 1976. They are ok on average waves, but with huge waves, I do not want a leash. This is just my own opinion. Leashes on surfboards make things safer for the other surfers or swimmers. Back in the 1960s and the early seventies, a common practice while paddling back out was watching out for loose surfboards. If you could grab a loose board, you would hold it for the owner who was swimming in to get it. Without having leashes, we did a lot of bodysurfing to get our boards quicker. Surfers today don't have to bodysurf unless they choose to leave their boards on the beach. Some beaches have requirements where surfers have to have leashes. Wow! Regulations on how to surf! We were all so wild and so free back then.

Talking about rules, I just had a flashback. This happened along the coast around Maryland and Virginia. Four of my surfing buddies and I wanted to get to an island where we heard the surf was good and the beach was void of people. From where we were at, we could drive around to get on the island which involved about forty miles of driving and then about five miles of walking, or we could paddle across an inlet bordered by two rock jetties and frequented by fishing boats coming and going from the ocean to the harbors. The inlet is only about three hundred yards wide. We chose to paddle. We went across as a group then surfed half a day at the desolate spot. What a great day we had! We paddled back across the inlet as a group again and cheered with joy upon reaching the side where my van was parked. This was during the early nineteen seventies. There are signs there now telling surfers it is against the law to cross the inlet. Violators face stiff fines and penalties. Like I said, "We were wild and free back then." *Don't blame us for the signs*, I thought. They went up years later.

The adventure of hitchhiking across the United States to surf the waves in California is a high point in my life. I set a goal, and I got there anyway I could. To get home, I went to the airport and flew "red-eye." That was the term they used for anyone who waited for a vacant seat on flights late at night or during the early a.m. hours. They were very cheap, but you needed to be right there when a seat became available. I was home in time for Thanksgiving.

Tenting It

After returning from California, I needed a place to live. At the time, I didn't think living in a tent within a large wooded area was an adventure. It simply seemed to be a cool thing to do at the time, and I was young; eighteen years old. I worked construction during that winter then ran my grass cutting business spring, summer, and fall. I spent most of my time outside. Camping out for a year and a half was not a plan; it just fell into place. It was exciting and different. Mr. Stew Dempster had just bought over eighty acres of forested land with an open area bordering a busy state road. He received permits to develop a campground on the land. He asked me if I could cut the trees he marked where his gravel roads would be. He had just fin-ished building a new restroom facility equipped with showers, toilets, and sinks. He informed me the building would be functional and heated through the winter. I had a thought! I presented it to Stew. It went something like this! "Stew, how about I clear a spot back in the woods and I set up a campsite for myself. You let me stay here for free, and I will cut the trees when I am off work on the weekends. When you open your campground, you give me a site for one season in exchange of my work. I can use the bathhouse during the time I am out here this winter. How does that sound?" He thought about it for a few days then came to see me. We shook hands on the deal, and that weekend, I was clearing a site he had marked out. Stew had a masterplan of where all the roads would be and where all the future campsites would be. Stew wished me luck and told me he would be working most everyday out there building an office, game room, and his living quarters. This would be out near the road where a small field was.

My plan worked out great. After work every day, I road my 250cc Yamaha motorcycle from Wildwood to Green Creek, New

Jersey. It was only a six-mile run. I built a wooden platform then put an army surplus wall tent on it. I had about eight foot of length and five or six foot of width inside the tent. I carpeted the floor, put a cot inside, and used two coolers for my food storage. I built a campfire area with rocks and put benches around it. With all the trees I was cutting down on the weekends, I had a steady supply of firewood. I even stacked logs around the whole perimeter of my site. I stack them four feet high so my site could have a wind barrier during the cold winter nights, and with the log barrier, I had a pretty "neat" and cozy spot. This site was over a hundred yards from the heated bathhouse. That was the hard part. I awoke each morning at six o'clock when my windup alarm clock sounded. During the cold winter mornings, I just did not want to get out my nice, warm sleeping bag. But every morning, I did. Then I would run to that heated bathhouse using a flashlight to see my way along a path I had cut.

Besides having my 250cc Yamaha motorcycle I owned a Ford pickup truck which I used for my grass-cutting business. During the winter, I used the truck to go back and forth from Green Creek to Wildwood. You just don't ride a motorcycle during the ice and snow season! I always ate breakfast at a local restaurant in Wildwood where I mingled with the other "locals" at the Atlantic Diner. By eight o'clock each morning, I was on the job and earning money. Work, eat, and sleep mixed with pleasure time kept me in shape. I did not watch television for over a year and a half, but I generally took my dates to movies back then. When at my "home" in the woods, I stayed warm by sitting near a "toasty" campfire. I may have had to run a distance to use the bathroom, but it was modern, clean, and warm. I cooked my dinners on an open fire except if I brought back a pizza pie. The work I did for Stew Dempster covered my rent expenses. Life was good for this eighteen-year-old! I was never lonely. My friends thought it was cool to come out and sit around the fire. The girls usually brought me home-baked chocolate chip cookies or even a cake to eat. My friends were mostly former classmates, so we all knew each other for years. Sitting around the campfire, we talked, laughed, and joked around with each other a lot. We all had a great time! I kept at one rule, though. After nine o'clock at night, we had to be quiet. Sound travels at night, especially in the country. I didn't want the neighbors to complain because I had such a great place to be living. The closet neighbor was a farmer who came over one night when I first started camping. He told me he was curious about seeing a campfire in the woods. After explaining my deal with Mr. Dempster, he approved but warned me to be quiet at night. I remember him telling me he gets up at four o'clock in the morning to have breakfast and start his chores. I respected him, and my guests did too. Anyone visiting me parked out alone Route 47 and walked into my site. The sound of cars starting and doors shutting didn't bother anyone there.

We didn't have cell phones in the early seventies. My friends and I had to preplan things because of the lack of instant communication. If I planned to go to a movie or to a party somewhere, I let a few people know so they wouldn't come out to visit. Usually, they would all be at the party anyway. Going to a movie with a date was very common in the sixties and seventies. We usually went on Friday or Saturday night to Hunt's Theater in Wildwood. If there was a dance going on somewhere, we all met there instead of going to the movie. During the summer months, we didn't get together too much because we were all so busy working. When you live in a resort area, you work sixty to eighty hours a week during the season. I usually worked an average of seventy hours a week, yet there was always time for surfing or training in the martial arts. We sure did keep busy! We worked hard, and we played hard. Sleeping was never a problem. You closed your eyes and fell asleep instantly.

When Green Creek Campground officially opened, the first person to rent a seasonal site was Mike Boulageries. He rode a BMW motorcycle, and he also had a Winnabago camper. Mike became a close friend. He taught me how to ride a big bike when I bought a 750cc BMW motorcycle in the fall of 1972. It was almost brand new, and it cost me fifteen-hundred dollars. It had a windshield and flare with a roll bar for your feet. It was a great bike! It weighed over three hundred pounds and made my 250cc Yamaha seem like a toy. Mike and I rode most all of the roads in Southern New Jersey. We would simply get on our bikes and ride just for the fun of it. I stayed at

Green Creek Campground for almost two years. During the second season there, Mike helped me build a tree house to sleep in. He was a master carpenter, so he did the thinking, showed me what to do, and brought the material in which we needed. We ended up with an eight-by-eight platform in the trees. We built three-foot walls then used the army tent for the top part of my new living quarters. We expanded the tree house by building decks going here and there in the trees. I used a ladder to go up, and we set a fireman's pole into one of the decks to slide down on. Mike even ran electric up to the room so I could have lights and play music. The owner thought I was crazy for living in a treehouse until he saw the finished product and joked about upping the rent on the campsite. There were days when the government didn't regulate everything. Today, you would need a blueprint, permits, and be inspected. Mike and I would never be allowed to build such a novelty today. It was safe and fun to enjoy. The view was terrific. Sleeping with a bit of sway during windy nights was the only thing I had to get used to. The tree house stayed there for over five years after I left, and not one of the trees died because of the way we constructed the platforms. No one used the treehouse after I was gone, but it stayed up for people to see. The tent went with me. Stew told me people would see the treehouse and then image the fun we had while camping there. It sure was a fun time!

The Big Ride

The next adventure involved ten thousand miles, surfing in California and Florida and a 750cc BMW motorcycle.

After seeing the movie *Easy Rider* when it first came out, I wanted to take to the roads of America and see the country in a free and spontaneous way. So in the fall of 1972, I put a "sissy bar" on the motorcycle seat, tied a basket backpack on it, loaded my gear, and took off! From the many hours of work I had put in over the summer, my savings account was healthy, and my motorcycle was paid in full. I carried traveler's checks and a few maps with me along with my other gear. I am relating this adventure from memory. Things will come to me as I write about it. The route zigzagged because whenever I noticed something on the maps worth visiting I headed to see it or visit a particular area. My first detour was in Virginia to see the natural rock formation carved by water which created a bridge. I rode some forty extra miles just to see it.

Traveling by motorcycle included sleeping under bridges, in forested areas, rest areas, picnic spots, and anywhere I could sleep without having to worry about anyone calling the police on me. It was a safer and more peaceful society in the states than it is now. Now it would be unsafe to ride alone and to sleep at unprotected spots. Riding with a group is the way to travel today because you are safer in numbers. I was watchful when I rode across country, but I was not worried for my safety. There were many people doing the same thing I was, and it was a good experience meeting them along the roads.

I remember riding there and stopping at Gettysburg, Pennsylvania, and reading the monuments there. I stopped at Valley Forge also. There is so much history to learn about our nation, but when you actually stop and see a place than walk the land itself, you feel different about the place than how you do by seeing pictures or reading about it in a book. There is another place I visited which most of my fellow Americans will agree gives you a sense of feeling not usually felt. The place is the Alamo in San Antonio, Texas. Inside the building, you see the artifacts, the letter, the brave men wrote knowing they would soon be killed, the knives, swords, guns, and even some clothing they had are there on display for people to see and learn about. The feeling you get while viewing these artifacts and reading the journals actually written while defending the Alamo is a spiritual feeling. It is as if their spirits are still present within the chapel walls. Those who died defending the Alamo and Texas itself were courageous, brave, and very hard to beat. I encourage every student to learn about the Alamo and what it meant to Texas and the rest of our country. I consider the Alamo the most important place to see in Texas. The Alamo has been preserved because of people who are dedicated to preserving the memory of those people who defended freedom and independence.

These are just a few of the places I visited along the ten-thou-sand-mile ride. Luckily, my motorcycle averaged fifty miles to a gallon, and gas prices back then were cheap. We are now at about or over four dollars a gallon!

The Grand Canyon is a place you will never forget once you visit there. The immensity and the depth of the canyon is beyond description. I slept near the edge of the scenic outlook area the night I arrived there. I was hoping to see the sun rise in the morning because several people had told me the sun lights up the canyon walls and makes the color come alive at sun rise. They were right! The sight at sunrise is a display of natures' glory.

On my way up to the Grand Canyon, coming from Flagstaff, Arizona, a section of the forest caught my eye. It was a large growth area of Ponderosa Pines. Most of the trees were of mature growth. To see these trees for real was neat. We grew up watching Bonanza on television, and we always saw the opening to the show which portrayed Ponderosa trees. I stopped to look at the trees close up and the cones lying on the ground. Pine trees in New Jersey are smaller, a lot smaller. Southern New Jersey has a large variety of pine trees because our soil favors their growth, but I never saw a Ponderosa Pine until that day in Arizona. From studying about trees during my landscaping days, I remember there are sixty-nine varieties of pines. The number has probably changed since then because of the grafting technologies used in agriculture. The Ponderosa Pine compliments the beauty of nature.

Time for a little humor! I saw my first real live rattlesnake in Oklahoma. At the time, a guy from Maryland had joined me. He rode a huge Harley Davidson nicknamed Harley Hog. We were both heading west, and it was good to have some company. Somewhere along the road, I needed to make a pit stop, and the closest rest area was too far away. I signaled to him, and we pulled over to the shoulder of the road. We were in the middle of nowhere, it seemed. I grabbed my roll of toilet paper and ran up a small hill where some rock boulders were, lowered my pants, and began my business. Of all times for me to hear a rattler warning me, I was too close to him! He didn't appreciate me being in his yard and leaving a deposit near him. He was not a small rattler! My new riding friend figured it out quickly when he saw me running with my shorts down and toilet paper flying through the air. I wasn't really running. I was hurrying the best I could to get away. I can only imagine what the motorists driving by must have thought. I really didn't care. Wow! I got to see my first rattlesnake. How exciting!

Another bit of humor happened at Beverly Hills, California. For me, it was a mixture of humor, embarrassment, and getting a bit mad. When I saw a sign pointing the way to Beverly Hills, I decided to take a tour. In California, you could ride without a helmet to see more freely. Here I come, Beverly Hills! I cannot remember which road I was on, but it was a road with ups and downs; mostly ups. I rode slow as I gawked at large mansions, beautiful landscaping, and expensive vehicles. At the top of the hill, I decided to make a U-turn on a quiet neighborhood road. After driving clear across the United States on a BMW motorcycle, you would think I knew how to keep my bike upright. No! I fell over doing less than five miles per hour. The foot roll bar saved my leg from being crushed. The bike lay on its side—all three hundred pounds of it. There were a few people from the neighborhood looking at me as I struggled to ride my bike. I removed my basket pack to lessen the weight. No one came to help me. Why not? I was nineteen years old with long hair riding a motorcycle through their Beverly Hills neighborhood. I must have been a sight! Finally, with all my strength, I pushed it upright then pushed it to level ground where I could tie the basket backpack onto the sissy bar. I can remember I waved to those watching me and yelled, "Thank you for all your help." I had to laugh, though. I dropped my bike in Beverly Hills! I had gone through rainstorms, windstorms, across the desert, over the rocky mountains and even rode hands free along the long stretches of western highways. But here I was, gawking at rich things and I fell.

I have told this next story a few times over the years. When arriving in Los Angeles, California, it was about seven o'clock in the morning. The day before, I had found a place to camp somewhere along the coastal highway coming down from San Francisco. I pulled into a diner and parked my bike near the entrance where I could keep an eye on my backpack strapped to the sissy bar. The only person inside the diner was the waitress. I took a seat at the counter, and she came over to me. She asked me if I was sure I wanted to stay. I was confused. Why would I not want to stay? I was hungry. She informed me that her diner was the breakfast spot for the local chapter of the Hells Angels. I just wanted some breakfast. A few minutes after ordering my breakfast, I heard the roar of dozens of motorcycles. About forty members of the Los Angeles Hells Angels came into the diner. All of a sudden, the place was busy, and I was not sure if I was welcome. Every seat at the counter was taken and some of the booths too. The man who sat next to me on my right side asked me if that was my BMW outside. I said yes. He asked me how long I had been in Los Angeles, and I told him I had just arrived. I explained that I had ridden from New Jersey and that I was touring the country. His facial expressions never changed. He seemed to be upset that I was there. I asked him, "Am I in trouble?" Then all at once, the bikers around me laughed really hard. The man slapped me on the back and laughed too. He was playing with me! He told me I was okay. He basically said something like, "If you had colors on, we would have stomped on you, but I can tell you are just some young kid out for a ride. You don't belong to a gang, do you?" I told him I ride alone and I did not belong to any gang. He continued asking me questions as we ate breakfast. I began to like the guy. I could tell he really wanted to know about my ride across the country. I told him about riding the roads in Southern New Jersey, and I named the motorcycle gangs from the area. He said he was familiar about the gangs because some of his club members had come from the East Coast. When I mentioned I was planning to surf for a few weeks, he yelled, "What! You mean you surf and you ride a motorcycle?" I didn't understand why the bikers were laughing at me again until the man to my left told me that surfers and bikers do not usually get along. I asked him, "Why not?"

"They just don't," was his response. I spent over an hour with them. When I was ready to leave, the man to my right told me he was the president of the chapter and the man to my left was the lawyer for the group. The lawyer handed me his card and told me to keep it with me for the rest of my trip. I still remember his words, "If anyone messes with you, you can call me. We'll see you get some help. But don't lose my card. I signed it so certain people will know you are okay with us." I carried that card with me for the entire trip. I knew he meant what he said. When I left the diner, I felt good. I had actually met, sat with, and talked with some of the Hells Angels. Up till then, the only thing I knew about the club was from movie with Marlin Brando in it or from stories about them in the newspapers. That morning in Los Angeles was real! They were real people, and they let me learn about their club in a brief way. I only wish now that I would have saved the lawyers card because somewhere through time, I lost it, like so many other things we don't think about saving.

I surfed for two weeks at Huntington Beach before heading south to Mission Beach for a few days of bodysurfing and sightseeing. My ride back across the states was along Interstate 10 until I got to Florida. Riding across Texas gave me the knowledge of just how big of a state it is. It took me three to five days to cross the states and to make my side trips. If there was something I wanted to see or a place to visit, I would just get off the interstate and go. I was riding just like Easy Rider. It was great!

Speaking of being free, I just remembered the group of Hippies I met along the Sur while riding the Coastal Highway in California. I had pulled over onto the shoulder of the road because the steep drop from the road to the ocean below amazed me. I sat on a small guardrail. I could see for miles, and I watched sailboats and ships traveling along. It was a clear, sunny day with only a slight breeze. On the land side of the road, there was a slope with a dirt road coming down it. That was where I saw a group of about fifteen genuine "flower child" hippies. The women wore very colorful dresses of lightweight material which went to their ankles. Their breasts were easily seen as they moved their bodies and swayed their long hair. They all had fresh picked flowers in their hands and beads hung from their necks. The men mostly had old, cutoff jeans and wore sandals. They all had long hair some had beards. My own hair was long but not nearly as long as theirs was. My hair covered my shoulders. Their hair covered their backs. Remember, this was 1972. They were singing and dancing as they came over the tops of the slope and down the dirt road. I went over to meet them when they all sat down in a circle on a grassy area.

There was not a shortage of grass (marijuana). The smell of incense and "pot" filled the air around them. They had wine which they had made themselves and fruits from their orchards. I was invited to come and stay at their commune where they had orchards, gardens, goats, chickens, and other farm animals. About fifty people lived as one family sharing the buildings they constructed. A few of the girls I was sitting with were my age. When I say I was really tempted, I really was! But after thinking about how good my life was already, I decided to stay with what I had. Looking back at that moment of decision, I can only imagine what my life would have been like if I went and stayed at their commune. I was riding free but not as carefree as they were. I enjoyed the natural highs I get from surfing and riding my motorcycle. The short time with them was fun and spirited. I am glad I had the experience of meeting and spending a few hours with them.

The adventure of traveling across this great county (USA) is available to us all because we are a free people. We can travel by bus, train, automobile, motorcycles, campers, and even on foot if you dare. Hitchhiking is a thing of the past, but there is always the idea of polling your friends and traveling with a group of friends in a camper. There is so much to see and do right here in the United States! I will be back out very soon.

Hawaii or Bust

A year after taking my motorcycle tour, a surfing buddy of mine joined me on the adventure of a lifetime! We talked about going to Hawaii and surfing big waves, but we had to come up with a plan on how to travel cheap. In August 1973, our opportunity came. A high school classmate asked me if I could accompany her to Hollywood, California. Her mother would not let her drive her car across the country by herself. She wanted to move out there, and she knew how much I liked surfing California waves. The deal was, if I helped drive her to California, she would pay for the gas. After a talk with her mother, Gary was included in the trip, and we were set to leave in October after my work was completed. It was perfect! My lawn business was done by then, and enough cash for the trip could be set aside for airfare, food, and lodging. I planned to buy a surfboard in Hawaii also. The only luggage Gary and I needed would be some clothes and a toilet kit which could fit into a backpack along with a sleeping bag. I always traveled with a sleeping bag.

It took us seven days to drive from Wildwood Crest, New Jersey, to Hollywood, California. We stayed only one night in California. Gary and I were on a plane to Hawaii after saying farewell to my former classmate and wishing her luck. We got a cheap rate by flying "standby."

Gary liked photography, so I had brought an 8-mm camera with us. I still have the films he took of us crossing the United States, landing at Honolulu, and the five weeks of surfing the North Shore of Hawaii. I have the film on VCR with music put to it since the camera didn't have sound. Remember, this was 1973. It is in color, though. We arrived in Honolulu late in the day. We hadn't had a clue where we would sleep that night. Our only concern was to get to the north shore where all the waves were. We walked around the city for a few hours seeing the sights and hearing the sounds of a busy city. We caught a bus to the north shore late that night, and we slept on the beach just near Sunset Beach. The following day, a surfer told us about a place where we could rent "floor space" in a beachfront house full of other surfers. We went there and spoke with a guy of our own ages who was managing the single-story house. He described the house as a surfer's commune. There was no furniture. You literally rented enough room on the floor to fit your sleeping bag and store one piece of luggage. There were two bathrooms, one for the girls and one for the guys. Showers were to be taken outside, and surfboards were to be stored in the yard near the beach. I stayed for five weeks, and my rent total was fifty dollars. Can you believe it? We stayed right on the beach within sight of Rocky Point and Sunset Beach for ten dollars a week! We even got to meet Tim Lynch who was the number 5 surfer in the United States of America at the time. He stayed with us for a few nights and got us into a few parties where you needed to be invited. Gary filmed Lopez, Purpoise, Habbman, and Crawford surfing Pipeline, Sunset Beach, Rocky Point, and the beach right in front of our house called Kami Land. I hope my spelling is correct. I am taking these names from a letter I had sent home to my parents over forty years ago. My dad saved that letter all those years.

I surfed only two giant waves at Sunset Beach when it was breaking at thirty feet. I learned fast to go back to the smaller breaking waves at Kami Land where it was breaking ten to fifteen feet during the last two weeks of my stay in Hawaii. The surfers you see riding the big waves deserve a lot of respect. There is a degree of skill and knowledge they possess which sets them apart from the average surfer. I was an average surfer, but I just had to try surfing huge waves at least one time in my life, and I did two, and that was it. Gary filmed me because he knew I was only going to try it that one time in my life.

At Kami Land, I met and surfed with Danny Ho of Hawaii. We surfed numerous days together while I was in Hawaii. He had a yellowish surfboard just like the one I surfed. In the films, it is hard to tell us apart. We both wore cutoff jeans and had long sandy-blonde hair and dark skin. His skill was above average. He surfed as if he could feel the waves next move. He made me feel comfortable out on the water because he treated me as a fellow surfer and not as an intruder. We were referred to as "Mainlanders" by most of the locals, yet Danny was a friendly Hawaiian and enjoyed surfing. I did have an "in," though. Tom Everly of Hawaii (at the time) made me a board using a design I drew out on paper with exact measurements and descriptions. Tom is a world-famous surfboard designer and maker. He made my board in his garage and charged me eighty-five dollars for it, but he kept my design. I agreed. I surfed with that "gun" from 1973–2002. I sold it on eBay two years after breaking my back. Someone out there has a one-of-a-kind surfboard with Tom Everly's name and my first name written on the stringer. It sold for about four hundred dollars. An eBay dealer sold it for me in 2004, and I included a copy of my book, *Surfers' Love Story*, with it. It will be cool if whoever bought the board reads this book and realizes Danny Ho enjoyed a few good rides on the board also.

Gary stayed in Hawaii after I left. I have never seen him or heard from him again. He might have met up with one of those beautiful island girls. Who knows? The experience and the fun of being a beach bum for five weeks in Hawaii during the early seventies is something money can't buy. Because we had to live cheaply and enjoy basic things made the experience even better. I even did the forty-five-foot jump into ten feet of water at Wiemea Falls. I have it on film because my friends back home would not have believed me otherwise. We were wild and loved our freedom. We took risks, and we got our natural highs. I still love my freedom! There! I have recorded a few adventures in life!

Chapter 4

Purpose

The purpose of this book is to encompass various themes, to take my own personal experiences and thoughts to explain the themes, and to encourage others to give meaning to the short time we have here on earth. I especially want to encourage young people to question things to see answers. Entertaining the readers is another element within this book. Inspiring thought by sharing some of my own thoughts is also a purpose. Most of all, I wish to leave something of value long after I am gone. This book gives purpose to my life because of what I share by writing. It is life going forward.

Every human being has a purpose. We are here to give God praise and honor. We can live to be a hundred years old, or we can live only seconds, but because of life, we are all God's children. The baby who dies at birth or the human fetus who is aborted has a soul because with life comes a soul. These human beings have a special place with God in heaven. This is my belief. Babies depend on their mothers, fathers, and mothers to make choices for them. Unfortunately, the unborn fetus which is alive within the womb of the mother does not have a choice as it is aborted and killed. Millions and millions of healthy fetuses which are unborn young humans are not given the chance to live and grow as we are. I am not the judge of these actions. God is! The newly born humans depend on other people because they are fragile and innocent. Yet most grow up to be children, teenagers, young adults, adults, and senior citizens. Each has a purpose no matter how short or how long they live as a physical being. Who really knows what their spiritual purpose is after their physical death. During their lives on earth, some will become parents and maybe even grandparents. Others will not have children yet will give their time and efforts helping the youth.

The essence of purpose is love. The essence of life is love. We are here because of God's love. If you were given a choice of two people, you would have to spend time with and one of the persons was a person who knows love while the other is a person who knows hate; who would you choose to be with? Most will choose love. We all have people who dislike us, and we all dislike some people we meet. I believe this is normal. But when we have hate in our hearts, this goes too far and invites evil into our lives. Hate diminishes happiness. Hate destroys your inner peace. Put purpose to work if you feel hate toward others. Make it a goal to erase your hate by practicing understanding, forgiveness, and try to change your thoughts. Bring humor into your daily life more often. Good humor melts away hate. It is really hard to hate anyone who is humorous and has a good laugh about things. We know there is a growing hate throughout the world today. We have terrorism happening almost everywhere on earth. We can deal with terrorism without hate by using force against force because of security, not hate. When children are taught to hate certain people because of religious differences those children grow up to become adults who will hate and even kill others because of the things they are taught. Instead of teaching children how sacred life is and how blessed it is to help those in need they teach martyrdom; a false martyrdom. Where does all the fighting benefit civilization? If the energies spent on fighting and killing were put to advancing agriculture and health, we would not have a hungry person on earth!

Have you ever asked yourself what purpose you have in life? I'm sure most of you have, and I am sure most of you know your purpose. I began asking myself that question when I was a teen back in the nineteen sixties. The youth were asking many questions during the sixties. It was a time of change, a youth revolution against the "establishment," and a time of encouraging peace. The slogan of the time was "Peace, Not War."

Following the Vietnam War (not conflict), look at how many years our nation enjoyed peace without having our young people going off to fight in foreign lands. We didn't go to war with the Soviet Union (USSR), yet the wall came down in Germany. Economics, trade between countries, sporting events shared internationally, student exchange between nations, the Internet and objective education between different cultures brings peace not war. Too much government control of a society does not help peace because it limits freedom. Freedom aids peace. This has been proven by our short history as a nation. When people enjoy freedom, they govern themselves better. The youth of today enjoy the use of the Internet and can use it freely in most countries. It is a positive thing for people to be able to communicate with others across the globe. Communication and free dialogue prevent wars. It helps people see their similarities. It communicates fashion, music, art, cooking traits, sports, and other life events. The Internet is like a classroom. A person in South Africa can see and talk with a person in Alaska in real time. It is an amazing thing, yet the future of the web is so great we can only imagine its future. The only limit to the Internet is too much government intervention. We need to keep this great source of information and entertainment as free as possible. It does not need to be taxed or overregulated.

The sad reality is that we will always have wars and terrorism is here to stay. We can prevent wars, and we can fight against terrorism by promoting education, commerce, and open dialogue. Unfortunately, the terror groups have hate in their hearts and do not respect life. Those groups and individuals have to be dealt with directly, and our nation is doing just that. We must be careful, though. We should not police the world. We do not need to be involved in wars around the globe, and we need to protect our own borders better than we are doing now.

One avenue of preventing wars is to promote agriculture. When a nation's population suffers from hunger, they are more vulnerable to those who want to be in power. A society where the people are working, have enough food, clothing, and shelter, enjoy good health care and medical aid, and can afford good security is a society which does not want violence. Dictators control their nations. The key word here is *control*. The United States of America enjoys freedom because of the foundation set forth by its founding fathers after setting themselves free from the British control of the colonies. As a nation, the United States has been heading toward bigger government and more control of its people. This is not good. I do believe our people will vote against a lot of the measures which limit their freedoms. Even the poor in our country can survive because of our charities, church groups, and government assistance supplied by the taxpayers. Here is a statement heard over and over. It comes from the older generation who grew up during the Great Depression Era. "We were poor, but we didn't really know it because we had our necessities. We were poor, yet we were happy." Because they knew how bad it was during the Great Depression, their lives following that time of hardships were happy times even though they were economically poor. They did without luxuries, vacations, and things not needed to live. The food on the table, clothes on the body, and a roof over your head were their concerns.

Struggles

My dad often told us, "There is a reason for everything that happens." We might not know the reasons at the time of things happening, but I do believe Dad is right. The reason we have purpose is to give meaning to our lives and therefore adding a certain degree of dignity to our humanity. Why do some people go through life without having to struggle while others struggle most of their lives? I believe it is fate. I also believe the people who struggle more than others do have stronger characters because of the energies and the extra efforts they use to get through their struggles. Take, for example, this simple comparison: you have two groups of four people in each group. They are all standing atop a high mountain peak looking out at a spectacular view of forests, rivers, and lakes below them. One group is more joyful, more spirited, and more bonding than the other group standing near them. Why? It is because the quiet group was airlifted to the summit by a helicopter and the excited group hiked for hours to reach the top. The group who was flown up did not have to struggle to reach the summit. The four people who hiked up endured sore feet and strained muscles, a blister or two sweating, bug bites, and a test of their lungs' health. They earned the sights from the peak, and they knew it. They rejoiced with each other because they felt the accomplishment their group made. Their food tasted better, their water felt more refreshing, and the cool air cooled their heated bodies. The other group stood and enjoyed the sight, but they did not enjoy an accomplishment because there was not struggle involved. They enjoyed their visit atop the mountain, but they did not experience the "whole" mountain like the other four did. Now take this example and compare it to your life. Which group do you belong to? Which group do you wish to belong to? I know your answers will go either way. You know from reading this book which group I would want to be with. To struggle is not always a bad thing, the degree of our struggles which make them favorable or unfavorable. No matter how severe our struggles may be, there is a reward for enduring them. The reward will not always be in our lifetime. Some rewards will come later. God rewards those who suffer due to circumstances they have not caused.

Purpose from Loss

When a young person dies suddenly and tragically, the whole community is affected. I have not forgotten how our entire high school body felt and mourned the sudden death of William McKee. We all knew him as Billy McKee. He lived in Sea Isle, New Jersey, and attended high school at Wildwood Catholic High School in North Wildwood, New Jersey. He was a star basketball player, a friend to us all, and one of the most popular students in school because of his positive nature and good humor. Billy's car crashed while driving in a wooded area during their senior after-prom picnic. His death shocked us all. I, along with my fellow schoolmates, have never forgotten Billy McKee. I am writing about him within this chapter because of the positive effect he had on me and others.

During the wake for Billy, my good friend Jimmy Young and I decided to give Billy's death some meaning and some purpose. Billy had come to our aid many times while Jimmy and I were freshmen and he was a junior. If Billy saw the seniors towel whipping us or punching our arms while in the locker room after practices, he stopped the seniors, and they listened to him. Billy was a tough guy with a big heart.

Jimmy Young and I put our hands on top of Billy's closed casket. Together we verbalized a promise to Billy that we would never drink and drive once we got our drivers' licenses. Jimmy and I shook on it then joined the hundreds of other people outside of the funeral home. To this day, I have never once drunk and drove because of the promise we made to Billy McKee. Billy was a member of the class of 1969 at Wildwood Catholic High School. My brother Danny also is a member of the class of 1969, W.C.H.S.

Future Purpose

None of us know what our future holds, but it is good at least to have a plan. Looking forward to something and making plans keep our thoughts active and hope alive. How many times have you heard people say, "I hope too," when talking about the future? I have set a goal for myself which will take a lot of planning and a sense of hope. First, I must finish writing and editing this book then get it published. I also have a completed manuscript which is a sequel to my book, *Surfers' Love Story*, which is already on the market along with my other book, *Secret Tales of the American Wealthy*. When I have all four books on the market, my goal is to travel around the United States in a camper while stopping at flea markets or wherever I can set up a table to sell the books. My plans are to stay out there and do the signings for at least two years while a person back home runs a website selling the books and following my progress in real time so people anywhere can see where I am and what I am up to. I will live out of the camper and stay in warm weather zones as I travel. I might be on the road right now as you are reading this. Who knows? I might be selling you a book at some market and asking you to make a comment on the website about your hometown. My idea of keeping an open journal while selling books will be for people to write their thoughts in it. With enough thoughts recorded, I could compile a book titled, *Thoughts of America*. It should be a good journey, and hopefully, I can financially make it work. I hope to see you out there!

I Was Given More Time

Life has its surprises. I am adding this personal revelation to the book to show how much I value the years of putting my thoughts on paper. It has everything to do with purpose. I am currently proofreading and editing this manuscript for the third or fourth time. I have lost count. It is Christmas Day 2014. A week from now, I am having all my handwritten pages typed up and put on a disk. Then I can send the manuscript off to the publisher to have it "finally" put into print and onto the market. There are years of writing, thinking, and experiences within the covers of this book, but I feel it is all worth it. Here is what happened.

On February 26, 2014, I suffered a slight stroke. I was home at the time. It was at night, and I was alone. It came on suddenly. Luckily, I was near my bed. I fell onto the bed as my face, and the left side of my body went numb. I could not get to my phone. I simply laid there thinking this is my time to go. My thoughts were clear, but my body did not want to move. I do not fear death. I was not scared, either. I simply prayed to God saying I accepted His wish if these were my last few minutes alive. Believe it or not, but my only worry was if this book would not get out to give purpose to my life.

As you can tell, God has allowed me to still be here. I woke up the next morning and thought, *I am still here!* A lot of the numbness was gone. For several months, I still had very little feeling in part of my left hand and the left side of my head. I still have a posted note near my kitchen table, where I write, stating,   "To the family: if something happens to me, please have my manuscripts put into book form."

I was employed at the time, and I live alone, so I kept my slight stroke to myself. My feelings were returning, and I figured I could get better. I have. If I made it public, I may have lost the job I would be returning to, and that would hurt me financially since I have been living week to week for years now. I know most people will think I am crazy, but over the years, I have used meditation to heal myself or get through tough times. The reason I am cured for now is not of my doing. It is because God has granted me some more time for a reason. This is what I believe. Many people will think differently. That is okay.

My writing hand was not affected. What a blessing! As of today, the only effects are that my left two fingers on my left hand are not always reliable. It is a minor thing. I feel healthy. I feel good about life. When God calls me, I accept His wishes. God is our judge, not any human. Personally, I hope to be around for another thirty years.

After Many Delays

Patience has saved my mental equanimity. I say this because of the many delays I have experienced trying to get this book out. I thought I would have it out back in 2015. It is now 2017! A combination of setbacks has delayed me yet has never changed my purpose. Finances and difficulties with production of my work may have slowed me down but has not stopped me. This book is too important to let go. I truly believe the lessons and messages recorded here will help people, especially students of all ages.

For those who have waited for *Life Going Forward* to be published, I am sorry for the delays. I have added this explanation in February 2017 so you readers can understand and see this book depends more on substance than when it was published. I have just added it to this chapter and put it in as the final typing of my manuscript being done.

CHAPTER 5
Listening

Listening to others is a virtue. It is important because when we listen to others, we understand more fully how people feel, think, and live. By listening, we show people we care about what they say. By listening, we show a good quality of character. When we hear the words, we can understand where people are "coming from" better. The words, plus the manner in which a person expresses the words, make us more aware of what the person is trying to communicate to us.

A child who is ignored becomes unhappy. If this is done on a regular basis, the child may feel unimportant which can lead to having low self-esteem and other unhealthy psychological problems. Children want to be heard. It is a need they have. They also need to be taught a balance between being paid attention to and of being overbearing. Our grandparents and parents told us children it was not polite to interrupt adults when they were speaking. The key word here is *polite*. Do we hear this word used much today? We were told to listen when spoken to. This instruction was part of being polite. I use the word *courteous*, but the meaning is similar.

Teenagers will talk more freely among themselves than they will around adults. So when your teenage son or daughter speaks to you, listen! Teenagers who communicate with their parents are usually those whom their mom or dad have kept the communication lines open by listening to them over the years. It goes both ways, though. The teens need to listen also. Debate—don't argue. Take "five" if you have to. Don't talk over each other. This is not easy! My own solution to someone who does not want to listen, not want to hear the words

I speak, is I walk away. I let the person think about whatever is going on or what was being discussed without me there. When they are ready to discuss and listen without emotions being out of control, then I will join them again. When I was a teenager, my temper got in the way. I was not in control of my emotions. By learning and practicing the martial arts, my temper has rarely surfaced since those years. I learned control. I learned how to neutralize my ego. I learned self-discipline and of how to walk away from negative situations. The years of learning, studying, and teaching of the martial art of karate has made me a better person. I am a better person because I "listened" to my senseis. Sensei Joe Hess taught me how not to fight by having self-control. I have not caused a fight since entering Joe Hess dojo when I was sixteen years old. He taught us how to be ready if we were attacked by someone or by a group. He taught us the importance of defending others if they were in need. The most important thing he taught us was respect. He took the time to listen and talk with us teens. He was a policeman at the time, so we would see him regularly in town. It was common for him to pull up to a group of us teens and talk with us from his patrol car. He joked with us and talked about things we were interested in, like sports, girls, and the dance in town. We respected him, and we all listened to him. He is probably one of the best police officers Wildwood, New Jersey, ever had.

Are there times you just don't' want to listen? Sure, there are. One of those times for me is when a person is talking foolishly. Another is when a person is speaking hatefully. I will listen to people who have different views than my own because sometimes I learn from them. Even if I do not want to hear hateful, bigoted, or racist talk, I will listen so I will know where these people are coming from and why they feel like they do. By knowing about a subject, you're enlightened by knowledge even if your view differs. I cannot turn myself off to the realities of the world, so I listen and learn. And I speak my own thoughts even if some people don't like them. Free speech makes our country strong because the people are allowed to voice their beliefs. This is why we citizens of the United States of America stand strong on protecting our constitutional right of free speech.

Within the workplace, listening is very important. The restaurant manager listens to his or her customers to know how they feel about the food, the menu, the staff, and the price. Most all corporations have customer service departments and encourage customers to give their feedback on products and service. On a large scale, if a corporation or financial institution does not listen to the people who are the base of their success, then they will suffer and maybe lose some of those people to competitors. When politicians don't hear the voter's concerns, they will probably be out of office next time people vote. Of course, many politicians stay in office because they have too much control. This is why we need term limits on government-elected offices. Listening is not one of their more important issues. Control and influence are. The president of the United States has a two-term limit. Why shouldn't every other elected official have term limits? With term limits, people just might be listened to because the politicians won't be able to amass so much power in office. Maybe we can return to representatives instead of career politicians. Can you hear me?

People who cannot physically hear rely upon their other senses more than others. They observe better than the people who can hear. They "listen" with their eyes, their smell, their touch, and vibrations. Anyone of us could lose our hearing at any time. If that time ever does come, we will need to sharpen all our other senses to compensate for the loss of hearing thru our ears. It is the same with the loss of any other sense we have. One piece of advice I give students is to learn sign language. If learned at an early age, it is not too hard to learn, and they can always use it to communicate with those in their school who rely on sign. It could also turn into an occupational asset after their schooling is complete. It is an asset to know how to communicate in several languages; sign is one of those.

By putting my mailing address on the information page of *Pure Power* readers were able to write to me. Because of their suggestions and advice, I have written a bit differently and included more information. I listen to positive criticism and positive advice. I am an ordinary person writing an extraordinary book! I want the book *Life Going Forward* to be the celebrity, not me.

As for listening, if you know a student, please tell them about this book and how some very talented people in positions of schooling and in government have recommended they read this book from cover to cover. Maybe the student will listen. After this book is out, I will be speaking at schools again. It seems that bullying has increased. As with speaking about nonviolence in schools, I can speak about bullying. Students do listen to me. I know from experience. I do enjoy listening and speaking with the students of all ages. I do not have all the answers, yet I have a ton of experience "under my belt": fourth-degree black belt, Ren Shi (expert teacher) USA-GOJU KARATE (May 1, 2002). I was awarded this promotion by Edward Verycken who is tenth-degree black belt of USA-GOJU KARATE. You will see his name several times within this book. My diploma reads: American GOJU Karate Association.

Chapter 6

Egoism

Most all of us have a degree of egoism. If you do not, you must be a saint living among us. Egocentric people are few in number compared to the rest of society. Is ego a bad thing? Like many things, it is not, as long as it is kept in balance. If one's ego slants toward conceit (an exaggerated opinion of oneself), the ego has entered into the realm of vanity which is not a good thing. When there is a balance between thinking of oneself and thinking of others, the ego is in balance; self-analysis can keep us in check. But we must be honest with ourselves when we do a self-analysis. To keep out egos from sliding toward conceit, we can ask ourselves a few questions. Have I been bragging boastfully about myself? Are my thoughts and conversations more about *me* than about other people and things? Am I getting too upset when I am corrected by others when their corrections are right?

A conceited person lacks self-esteem so they prop themselves up by bragging and trying to gain other's approval. On the other hand, a person who is self-confident does not have to brag about their accomplishments, their talents, or their skills. Conceit is negative. Self-confidence is positive. There is a big difference between these two attributes. Sometimes, people may accuse a person of confidence with having a bloated ego. They are usually wrong. Confidence is about knowing. A person of confidence has "been there," "done that," and they simply "know by experience." People with confidence stand tall, show little doubt, and they are usually the quiet ones at a party or gathering unless participating in conversation. They are not the "loud ones" who strive for attention. The next time you hear a conceited person talking and bragging, listen to him or her very carefully, and observe his or her actions. Watch their eyes. The eyes can tell you about a person's sincerity. Listen to hear just how much of what he or she is saying is really true. How much credit are they taking for what other people have done? Is he or she trying to gain approval from those around him or her? Do you believe this person when you hear them speaking? Are you impressed, or are you turned off by his or her inflated ego? By listening more carefully and by observing more closely does this help you understand a person better?

The Martial Arts and Ego

Because of learning, training in, and then teaching the art of karate, I was able to neutralize my ego. The credit goes to the teachers (senseis) I encountered over the years and the many books I studied which were written by the masters of old. My two primary senseis were Joe Hess and Edward Verycken. They are both tenth-degree black belts now. Sensei Verycken leads USA-GOJU, and Sensei Hess founded the Hess style. What accomplishments these two have had!

Personally, I stayed within the art and did not get involved in the sport. The sport is where you complete at tournaments against other people. When you compete, you are awarded prizes, trophies, and sometimes money if you place in the top positions. The art mostly involves one particular dojo (school) of which you are a member. The art concentrates on kata more than on sparring. Conditioning of the physical body is emphasized greatly. It is the learning and performing of kata which develops focus, control, balance, strength, and endurance. The more advanced katas you learn and perform regularly, the better your chi (strength from within) becomes. As I explain the art, keep in mind that I am only experienced within the United States. I am not writing or speaking about how the art is in other countries. I could not because I am not familiar with other cultures. The art I stayed with all my adult life is USA-GOJU.

Over the years, I observed that participants within the sport have a stronger sense of ego because they compete against others. A true martial artist competes against oneself. He or she is constantly trying to improve in kata (a dance form) and in technique. If one is excellent in kata, then everything else falls into place. To learn your katas, you first train in basic moves for long periods of time. No matter how many years of experience one has, you will always continue training with basic moves and techniques to keep them sharp. As you progress, you learn advanced moves and techniques. If you are ever confronted and attacked, your basic moves and techniques will protect you and maybe even save your life. I know they will because of my own experiences over the years.

If you are a student of a martial art, I encourage you to continue. It is one's own choice whether to complete in tournaments or not. To find a true marital arts teacher these days is not easy within the United States because there are very few who teach the traditional art. Commercialization of art has caused teachers to pursue the money, fame, and profits more than ever.

The school I founded in Maine is not-for-profit. It is called Neko-Ashi Dojo-Maine. We had our first class in January 1990. Because of my back injury, the doctors told me to stop surfing and teaching karate. My spine was injured too much to take any quick twisting or abuse. I hope it is not egotistical to say I retired as Renshi (expert teacher) fourth-degree black belt USA-GOJU Karate in 2004. The school is still there because of Ron Perkins who is one of the original students of Neko-Ashi Dojo-Maine and is now Renshi-fourth-degree black belt USA-GOJU Karate awarded to him by Master Edward Verycken. Ron volunteers his time, and the students love him. He is one of my students who is now giving back to others what he learned. I was able to teach because of Edward Verycken who taught me and promoted me.

Effect of Ego

Do our egos or other people's egos affect our daily lives? I believe it does but not on a large scale. It depends on one's particular situation. Maybe you work in a place with a number of people sitting at their desks or inside their cubicles and you have to deal with a few inflated egos.

Then I guess it does affect your daily life. Maybe you are a bartender or a waitress working in a bar. Telltales and bragging are not strangers to the bar scene. It could be annoying, or it could be entertaining. It depends upon the client's stories and/or the degree of their boosting. Most people who drink alcohol will loosen up and talk more than usual as they become intoxicated. Egos emerge as the drinks keep coming. In the construction trade, there is always one or two on the job who boost regularly about knowing how to do things within the trade. They try to boost their image and their income by doing this while the foreman or bosses are around. The tradesman who knows his trade does not have to boost. His results and his production speak for him. The confident ones do their jobs and usually talk about sports, politics, or hobbies. Most crews get along pretty well despite a few bloated egos.

Where would you say the biggest egos exist? Would it be in our government officials who are at the top levels? Would it be on Wall Street where the major financial groups gather? Is it in your local police department? Would you list the "Hollywood Crowd" or the top rappers from across the country? Is it within the national news and commentary media, be it radio, television, or print? Is it at your local gym? Just for fun, make up your own list and compare your list to some of your friend's lists. Do it while you are hanging out together. It could stir up the conversation concerning egos and probably enlighten you on how your friends or associates think about the subject. We all have a degree of egoism. Most people keep or try to keep it to a minimum. Over the years, I have enjoyed many conversations around the campfire. Some are humorous, some are philosophical, and most are about currents events happening in the world. I cannot remember having any conversation concerning egoism, but it would fit in with some of our philosophy discussions. If I was to start a discussion today, it would be about the connection of egoism and the pursuit of fame which the current generation adores. Everyone wants their "fifteen minutes of fame," and some will do almost anything to get it. It is not only the young generation who participates in "putting themselves out there" for everyone to see on Facebook, YouTube, and other outlets sharing their personal thoughts, photos, and other things with the world. I have done similar by writing this book, but my purpose is much different. I do not seek any fame. If it comes about because of my writing success, then I will be happy because it will lead to more people (especially students) reading my books. Fame does not excite me, and I believe people are making too much out of it. My own idea of fame is of people who have done terrific things for humanity. Think of some of these people then put their achievements next to those society glorifies today. Marketing creates fame today. It is a façade at times. It concerns money, popularity, sales, hype, and vanity. This is the fame most of society today want to be a part of. This desire has much to do with egoism. It is not a healthy desire because it does not lead to good things in the long run. I realize I am in the minority with my thinking, and I will be called "old fashion." I have to be honest, though. Whoever invented duct tape, now there is a famous person (humor, my friend)! If it is fame you desire, pursue it by doing something of value toward humanity or the environment. This is my advice.

Later in this book, you will see I did a chapter on celebrities. I will be honest. I wrote about the celebrities I have met to give a bit of variety to this book. On the other hand, those times did give me some insight because by meeting these people on a personal level, all the hype and "stardom" didn't interfere with the time spent with them. I hope everyone can spend some time with a few celebrities during time when the cameras are not around and when they are "being themselves." It is quite an education because you learn and witness their human side, not their "public image" side. I learned early in life that the "famous stars" or celebrities are not always fun to be with. Egoism surely is prevalent characteristic of many celebrities. Luckily, I met and spent a short time with some really great and fun people who are also celebrities, a few being really big stars or famous people. We are all humans. I simply cannot idolize anyone. I do enjoy being around someone who is very talented or has done some very extraordinary things. It is good to have a bit of variety in one's life.

One of my readers suggested I write about egos. I hope I have at least opened the door of thought upon this topic. Keeping one's ego in balance is not always easy, but it is one of those positive things we can work on.

CHAPTER 7
The USA

As a citizen of the United States of America, born and raised within this freedom-loving country, I feel blessed. This chapter is more for those who have not been to the United States of America and are reading this book. For those who are in the United States, maybe my thoughts and words will encourage a deeper study of the country's history and geography.

As I am writing this chapter, the 2012 presidential elections have just ended. President Obama has been reelected and will serve his second term of office. Every presidential election causes more people to vote because it is the highest elected office in the nation. We have a balance of powers which is shared by three branches of government: the executive branch, the judicial branch (appointed), and the legislative branch which is Congress. We, the people, elect the president and the members of Congress who represent us. Our vote is power! Ever since we gained our independence from British Rule, this country has been strong because of the values set forth by the Founding Fathers. Liberty, freedom, rights of citizens, and our trust in God were and still are the cornerstone of our nation. We have a written Constitution and a Bill of Rights which has been proven invaluable to our survival as a free, sovereign nation. Christian and Judeo beliefs are intertwined within the founding of the United States. The teachings of Aristotle, Moses, and Jesus are reflected in the original documents and statements recorded of what our founders said and wrote. Look at the Bill of Rights and look at our Constitution, along with the Declaration of Independence, and you will see the reflections. The best source of information about the United States is at the Library of Congress in Washington DC where almost every published book, article, document, etc., are stored. I would say that if you want to learn about the United States and its history, the Library of Congress is where to do your research.

Our justice system was formed by people who believed in fairness, equality, truth, and law. Religious freedom was extremely important to the colonialists because many of them fled their homelands and came to the American shores to escape religious persecution. Religious freedom was and still is important to us.

Historically, we have not always been fair, but corrections came as the nation grew. Take for example the issue of slavery. The words and belief that "all men are created equal" were ignored for a long period of time. Slavery existed in our northern states and in our southern states. The slave owners used these human beings to do their work without pay. Human beings owned other humans. They bought and sold these people as if they were property. The slaves were considered property. It took a person of principle to see that the rights of all men and women were protected. It took President Abraham Lincoln to hold our nation accountable to its beliefs. He knew the slaves who were brought from Africa or who were born into slavery involved a great miscarriage of justice to an entire group of people. President Lincoln stood firm on his beliefs, and he knew how important it was to keep our country from dividing into a north and a south. We had Civil War. The Civil War hurt us tremendously because of Americans fighting and killing Americans. I doubt it will ever happen again. I recommend you read Lincoln's Emancipation Proclamation. The Thirteenth Amendment is a result of the Civil War and a result of President Lincoln's leadership. There are hundreds of goods books written about the Civil War. The Library of Congress has the information you will need to seek out the right books.

We need to learn from history, especially when it comes to wars. The slaves were freed and given citizenship. Eventually, they were given the right to vote, but the right to vote came with struggles. Our current president, President Obama, is the first US president of color. We have come far since the days of slavery! Someday in the future, we will see a woman become president. I was really surprised the first time I learned that a woman didn't have a right to vote in our country for so many years after the government was formed. I was surprised because as I was growing up, my mom always voted, and it was ordinary to see women at the voting stations. It was just one of those normal things we saw women do. It took the women themselves to fight for and gain the right to vote. The Women's Suffrage Movements happened long before I was born. They protested and marched until the men got the message!

It is good out nation corrects its wrongs as it grows. The fundamental belief that all men are created equal always included women, but it took a long time for the men to admit it. We are all equal in God's eyes. Our country has strict laws written now which protect people from discrimination based on gender, race, religion, disabilities, and the color of your skin.

One of the tragedies caused by our nation's fast growth due to people coming from Europe to settle in the New Land is how the Native American people were treated and pushed off lands their ancestors lived on for centuries. The European culture and the Native American culture clashed. One lived off the land and waterways while the other put property ownerships, as a priority and limited the land's use to whoever owned it by written title. Entire tribes were moved off lands they had called home and then forced to live on reservations set up by the government. Even though they were here first, they were not citizens and were not given the rights citizens enjoyed. The influx of so many people coming from across the Atlantic Ocean and the Pacific Ocean pushed the Indian Nation from their homelands without much regard for their natural rights as a "people."

I encourage every student attending a college or a university to take a course in American history to learn and to know about the country they live in. Despite wrongs and tragic events, our country continues to grow and to do good things. We started as colonies and then grew as a nation after the Revolutionary War which freed us from British control. The nation grew in size by buying lands. The Louisiana Purchase was the largest purchase of land the United States made and opened up the country to have states from the Atlantic Ocean to the Pacific Ocean with the Gulf of Mexico shoreline to the south. European countries had claimed land across the "new continent," as it was called originally. By buying or trading for these lands, the US government increased the size of the nation to what we have now. Another major land purchase was when we purchased Alaska from Russia. Alaska is vast and contains a rich supply of oil, minerals, forests products, and water and has a healthy supply of fish and other sea products. At the time, it was a new frontier, and little was known about its resources. It was a great buy!

The United States of America is the most charitable country in the world. Because of our help during WWII, Hitler was stopped and defeated. Because of our tremendous medical research, lives are saved, prolonged, and enriched throughout the world. Because of our space program, technology has changed the world in almost every field. Our production of food is the best in the world. Agriculture in the United States of America is one of our biggest strengths. We grow and harvest the most varieties of food on earth. We grow, lumber, and produce wood, wood pulp, and forest by-products not only for ourselves but also for many countries who buy from us. Because of the geographical size of the United States, we enjoy vast areas of unpopulated lands and numerous national parks, national forests, and wetland areas. We enjoy a peaceful border with Canada. I would guess the border runs over three thousand miles or more. Canada is a lot like the United States of America and has rich resources. Our relations with Canada are strong and will remain strong because of our similarities. I have visited Canada about thirty to forty times since 1972, and I have always enjoyed my visits.

The United States of America is a young country compared to other countries. Our history isn't an old history like France, Italy, Spain, Greece, or England has. History should deal with facts. Most historians do just that. They show you the documentation, the photos (if available), the deeds, the writings, etc., to prove the facts. Almost every town, city, and country has a museum where you can visit to see the local history. The largest and the most complete place to witness our nation's history is the Smithsonian Institute located in

Washington DC, our national capital. During my childhood years, our family visited the Smithsonian Institute numerous times. My parents wanted us to learn about our country and its history. The displays you see, the inventions and the inventors you learn about, the aviation and space exploration history, the numerous buildings you go through, and the shear immensity of the institute are worth a visit at least one time in your life. It will take a few days to see, and it is worth every minute you spend there. Every school student in America should see the institute. It opens one's eyes to science, aviation, agriculture, textiles, medicine, the human body, history, transportation, and much, much more. It is a school trip unmatched by any other school trip involving education. It and the other places in and around Washington DC can take time, but the visit is worth the effort.

The Land

The United States is so huge and so geographically diverse that the people who live here rarely get to see the whole country. For you who live in the United States of America, ask yourself these questions, and you will realize how much you have yet to see. This does not count flying over the land and seeing it form the air. How many states have I been to? How many mountain ranges have I driven over? How many of the Great Lakes have I visited? Have I sailed along the coast of Maine's seven thousand miles of coastline? Look it up. You will discover Maine has an immense coast when all the islands, bays, tributaries, coves, inlets, and beach areas are measured. Have you seen the active volcano in Hawaii? I could continue, but I am sure you understand what I am saying about the size and diversity. I also understand that many people are content to stay home and enjoy the world they have within their own communities.

Unfortunately, it is costly today to travel. Gasoline prices are high. At four dollars a gallon, it isn't easy to travel. It is costly just going to work and back! For those who are confined to their living quarters due to medical reasons, the computer and a large field of cable networks on television enable them to see and experience the world. Before we had the Internet and cable networks, we all read and looked at the pictures in National Geographic Magazines. It was not until 1975 that our town of Wildwood, New Jersey, began the process of having cable television instead of us using antennas attached to our rooftop chimneys. We had three television channels before the cable came in. They were broadcasted from Philadelphia, Pennsylvania. Today, you can sit in your living room and view the world! We also watched our television with black and white screens. Later on, we were able to see shows in color when the colored TVs became affordable. There were no satellites in space until after our Space Program got started. We can all thank President John F. Kennedy and the leaders back then for pushing the space program forward. The world watched the day on American astronaut stepped onto the moon! What an amazing achievement it was. Everyone in the United States was glued to their television sets that historic day (it was night in Wildwood, New Jersey), as the news network showed the film footage supplied by NASA. During that era, the United States and Russia were competing for space exploration and research. Now we are partners and work together. The Space Station is an example of how we and other nations can work together to achieve progress.

With the technology we have today, we can view in the real time. With webcams set up all over the United States, you can see the waves breaking along the beach in Ocean City, New Jersey, even if you are sitting at home in Kansas City, Kansas. You don't have to be in Pennsylvania to see (in real time) their forest, rivers, or farmlands. You can be in New Hampshire and watch people walking around in a Texas City. We have come a very long way in a very short time compared to past centuries. And it seems there is no limit to progress improving every day.

The variety of landscapes across the United States rivals most every country. We have deserts, mountain ranges, shorelines, forests, farmlands, lakes, rivers, waterfalls, two oceans, the Great Lakes, the Bering Sea, islands, glaziers, tundra, swamplands, canyons, the Gulf of Mexico, peninsulas, numerous caves of varying sizes and depths, active and inactive volcanos, wilderness areas, national parks with natural wonders, and so much more. Have I left anything out? Oh yes, the cities and the excitement within them!

Future of America

The future of the United States of America concerning energy is very promising. Natural gas production is growing, and our natural gas reserve is considered the largest known at this time. Clean energy is in our future because wind, solar, thermal, and other sources are progressing. The one source of energy we have plenty of is coal which is powering many of our energy plants. Coal research is the key to us becoming energy independent. Nuclear power will be with us for centuries. The financial costs of each source of energy will determine which sources get used the most. The consumers usually determine which supply is used the most because if it is affordable it will sell. Americans are concerned about the environment, yet the market dictates heavily on what is used or not used.

Energy plants have been progressing steadily. We have energy plants burning wood chips, garbage, waste products, and other materials which use to go into the landfills and produce nothing. Cities and counties across America are building and operating such plants because they are now profitable. Recycling products is profitable and healthy toward the environment. We are recycling more today than in any time of our nation's history.

We have an abundance of meat products and dairy products because of the ranches, hog farms, chicken farms, dairy farms, and processing plants. Americans enter grocery stores across the land and see the shelves full every day with these products because of the people who tend to the livestock. Americans take for granite the food they see in the stores and expect it to be there every day without stopping to think how it gets there or where it comes from. I am generalizing, but most Americans are like this. The United States of America is the land of plenty. We should be thankful to God that we are and we should see that those with very little are taken care of. But those with very little who are not willing to work or contribute their energies should not reap the benefits others deserve. People who take and do not give hurt society. There will always be a percentage of people who do not even try to support themselves despite being able to. These are the "takers." Luckily, America has more "givers" than "takers."

Water and Veggies

In another book I authored, *Secret Tales of the American Wealthy*, I wrote about the importance of water and its connection to the wealthy people of America. Water is a necessary product. The wealthy know water's value, and they know ownership of water rights, water sources, and desalination plants are the key to having wealth in the future. The United States has a mixture of private and public ownership of water and water facilities. Keep an eye on the water industry! A country with clean water is a healthy country, both economically and health wise. Steam energy has been around for a long time, and its future is solid. It is just one more use of water besides keeping the population healthy. Think about how much water is consumed every day in America. When water becomes scarce due to droughts or pollution, people realize how much water is taken for granite.

Sometimes, we need to look back in time to see what could benefit us now. Years ago, most everyone had a vegetable garden in their yard and cultivated fresh crops to use for their family and neighbors. Can you imagine the amount of food we can grow if every homeowner took the time to plant a garden and harvest their own vegetables or fruit each growing season? If you have never had a vegetable garden or a few fruit trees in your yard, I recommend you try it. It is a peaceful hobby, and you get to enjoy eating your own grown food fresh from your garden. The state of New Jersey is called the garden state because the people in the central and southern parts of the state used to have vegetable gardens in their yards and because of the many small farms there. The farmlands of New Jersey still produce record numbers of crops because the soil and conditions are nearly perfect for a variety of vegetables. The "Jersey tomato" is the best tasting tomato you will find anywhere. Here is a short story and humorous story I wrote in 2002.

Jersey Grown

George, a potato farmer from Maine, and Ralph, a tomato farmer of Southern New Jersey, enjoyed a relaxing day together last summer. Here is one of the conversations these two elderly farmers had.

Ralph: George, see those tomatoes over there? There is a perfect example of natural beauty. Have you ever seen such radiant color? Have your eyes witnessed more beautifully shape contours?

George: They sure do stand out, Ralph. Yep, they've got my juices flowing. You must have something special down here. What is it—the water, the salt air, something in the ecology?

Ralph: I can tell you this, my friend. New Jersey has got the best stock you'll find anywhere. Look at those stems. They are incredible—a picture of good health and vitality. Maybe I've spent too much time on the farm. George, but that skin just seems to invite me. I'm going over there. I want to smell those sweet ripe and juicy tomatoes!

George: I'm right behind ya. Let's go.

Ralph and George got up out of their chairs and walked over to four bikini-clad girls sunbathing on a large beach blanket.

Ralph: Excuse me, girls, are you from around here?

The girls sat up, and one answered, "We all grew up here, but we attend college now, out of state. Why do you ask?"

Ralph turned to George, saying, "See, I knew it! They're Jersey grown."

We, the People

Because of our geographical size, we are not a densely populated country. We have places where you could go to within our country and not see a human being for weeks, months, or even years. Alaska is one of those places. The land mass in Alaska is extensive, and many parts of the state are remote. Montana is another state with wide open land. Montana is called "the big sky country" for a reason. There are only a handful of big cities in the state, but there are many ranches and small towns to see. I remember riding across the state of Texas on my motorcycle and feeling lucky I had plenty of fuel in my tank. The spaces between towns, cities, and gas stations cause you to be prepared! It is a beautiful state. It also has variety. Texas has a coastal region along the Gulf of Mexico, a forested region along the eastern side of the state, a wealth of history, open ranges and ranches with thousands of acres for each one. Check out the states for yourself, and you will see each state has its own characteristics and appeals.

The people who live, work, and play in all the states come from a variety of backgrounds. I would guess we have the most ethnic and cultural varieties than any other country in the world! This says a lot for our nation! The language most used is English, but you could hear almost every language in the world spoken somewhere in the United States. The main reason for writing this chapter is to paint a picture of the United States by using words, sentences, and paragraphs so people elsewhere can have a particular view of our nation written by one ordinary American—myself. The media does not show the basic virtues of a nation. They like to sensationalize things in order to get ratings or to sell their products. The people of America have ancestors from every corner of the world. Because of marriages over the years between different ethnic groups and races, we have a very unique America culture. Many religions are practiced within the United States of America, and many philosophies are taught and practiced. Because of our belief of having religious freedom, we will find churches, temples, masques, and other buildings of worship spread throughout the land. The Christian faith has the largest number of followers in the United States with Catholics being the majority in number. The Catholic Church started when Jesus told Peter the apostle that he would be the "rock" upon which the church would be built. Christmas is the biggest holiday season in America. Christmas represents the birth of Jesus Christ. People shop for Christmas gifts months before the day of December 25, a national holiday. It is also a time when many employees receive their bonuses which adds to the festivities of New Year, January 1. New Year's Eve is probably the biggest party night of the year. I think the closest celebration to New Year's Eve is our Fourth of July celebration of Independence Day. July 4 has a lot more barbecues! Oh, what a great smell!

I have touched upon a few things concerning the United States of America, but there is so much more. The music, entertainment, fashion, cultural art, sports, literature, Broadway in New York City,

Disney World in Florida, Niagara Falls in New York State, Las Vegas in Nevada, and so on. I encourage the people of other countries to become familiar with America and the people living here. You will be surprised how freely you can travel around within our borders. There is much to see and much to do. It depends on what your interests are. It depends upon the seasons. We have skiing in the winter or the Florida sunshine. You choose, like we do. Do I hit the mountains for skiing and snowboarding, or do I hit the beaches in Florida and get a tan? Do I hit the surf in Southern California, or do I go snowmobile the trails in Maine? Sounds good, but personally, because of finances, I'll stay home this year. I am sure I am not alone.

Since I am writing to benefit students across the world, I need to mention how extensive our educational institutions are. Within every state, there are colleges, universities, and institutions of education for specific careers. Some of our states' geographical sizes may be larger than the country you live in. For example, Israel is about the size of the state of New Jersey which is not a big state. For the benefit of those not familiar with our states, I wish to list them in alphabetical order: Alabama, Alaska, Arizona, Arkansas, California, Colorado, Connecticut, Delaware, Florida, Georgia, Hawaii, Idaho, Illinois, Indiana, Iowa, Kansas, Kentucky, Louisiana, Maine, Maryland, Massachusetts, Michigan, Minnesota, Mississippi, Missouri, Montana, Nebraska, Nevada, New Hampshire, New Jersey, New Mexico, New York, North Carolina, North Dakota, Ohio, Oklahoma, Oregon, Pennsylvania, Rhode Island, South Carolina, South Dakota, Tennessee, Texas, Utah, Vermont, Virginia, Washington, West Virginia, Wisconsin, and Wyoming.

There they are: all fifty of the states which make up the United States of America. Now just imagine how many educational facilities and campuses there are in this one nation. The educational resources are phenomenal! What other nation of the world has such a vast resource of education? Education of every field you can think of is available in the United States. Medical education is offered in every state! Keep in mind that some of our states are larger than many nations of the world. It boggles the mind when I think of how large our country is and how much it offers to us. And yet we are such a young nation compared to others. One of the beautiful things I have seen as I traveled across these many states is that each state has its own characteristics and their own ways. Every state has their own set of laws. Every state has a governor and a state senate besides having representatives in the Congress and Senate which represent their state on the federal level. There sure are a lot of politicians in our country! And they sure do get paid well! One of our major problems right now is that our representatives have become career politicians and do not understand the plights of the average citizen even though they say they do. Many, if not most, of them have not had to work, and I wrote about it in the chapter on the working men and women. The disconnect they have is because they believe they are more important and above the average people. This hurts our nation. We need a smaller government, and we need representatives, not politicians. This is not only my opinion but the opinion of the majority of US citizens. Because we value freedom, I believe the votes will bring back basic representation again. Businesses are being overregulated which causes underemployment. Small businesses need to be freed up from being over regulated and taxed so our country can prosper once again. During the Industrial Era after World War II, our country prospered because people had jobs. Now the government is the problem. It may change. If it does not, our economy will suffer. I have to laugh when I hear certain politicians say, "I feel your pain." Are they living week to week? Are they walking to work? Are they counting their change to go grocery shopping? I think not. The majority of Americans are starting to ask these questions because their tax dollars pay the salaries of the politicians. This is how it is right now, but it will change. When the sleeping giant (the citizens) is awoken, it reacts strongly. It always has. When liberty is at stake, the "sleeping giant" comes alive! This is not only my view, as I have said.

The United States is a beautiful country. For those who get a chance to come and visit, they are not disappointed. There is so much to see and do!

CHAPTER 8

Storytelling

Have you ever sat around a campfire while camping and listened to everyone telling stories? If you've been in the Girl Scouts, Boy Scouts, or Explorers, you sure have. Maybe you've been with a group of friends or family members staying together in a lodge somewhere in a remote area. Did you and your group tell stories? There is something about certain places and the environment around you which causes stories to be told. Scary stories, humorous stories, stories of "remember when," alien stories, and mysterious talks are usually the popular ones. Here is a short story I wrote for Kori and Keely Weinberger when they were young children. Lynn and "Willie" Weinberger are their parents. Willie was a close friend and high school classmate of mine. He passed away a few years after my walks were done. He is missed and always remembered. Here is your story Kori and Keely!

The Storyteller (Fiction)

"Please tell another story," the little girl pleaded. "But I have just told you two long tales, my child. Are you not tired?"

"Not at all sir! You tell such great stories. My friends and I would love to hear another."

"Well, I guess I can tell one more," the storyteller answered with a twinkle in his eyes.

Six young children sat before him as he explored the collection of tales stored within his memory. Their eyes fixed upon the old man as they waited with quiet anticipation. When he spoke again, the children leaned forward, intent on hearing every word and see-ing every gesture of the storyteller. Reality disappeared as the story-teller grasped their imagination and took the children on a journey where walls do not exist. His voice controlled the mood he needed to project, and his expressions mirrored the atmosphere throughout the tale. When his voice lowered (sometimes a mear whisper), the children learned forward. When his voice thundered and his arms flew wild, the children retreated and huddled together. He cast the spell! They felt the wind, rain, sunshine, the cold, or the heat. They saw the people, trees, animals, the mountains, and the valleys. They heard the sounds, tasted the food, and smelled the scents. They were there, wherever the storyteller took them!

When he ended his story, he lowered his head and closed his eyes briefly. He then heard a familiar voice saying, "Please tell us another story, please." Along with the storyteller, I wrote another story. This one involved a troll. Keely's favorite characters were trolls, so I came up with this one for her. If you have a young child, you might want to read this to him or her. I intend to include several children's stories in this chapter of "Storytelling."

Keely and the Troll

You cannot convince a nine-year-old Keely that trolls only exist in fables. She is fascinated about these beings which are spoken of and written about in Scandinavia Folklore. The lore came to America along with European immigrants of old. Ask Keely and she will tell you the trolls too came across the seas, probably hidden within the cargo areas of many ships. Laugh if you wish. Keely knows the truth.

Trolls usually live in caves and hide under bridges. So when Keely and her family visited Vermont this summer, she hoped to see a troll. Her uncle Buddy gave her a tip as she left for Vermont. "If you see any old covered bridges near high mountains, check carefully under them. Trolls can camouflage themselves better than any other being on earth. They favor the old wooden bridges."

One misty morning while touring Vermont, her dad stopped their van near a long covered bridge. "Daddy, I saw something run under the bridge!" Keely yelled as they pulled in.

"It was probably a deer," her sister remarked.

"No. It was a troll! I know it was!" Keely emphatically stated.

"I'll go with you, Keely, and we'll see what it is," her mom said calmly. So Keely and her mom investigated. "Nothing under here," she said as they stood under the wooden structure.

"Can I stay here a little longer, Mom?"

"Well, okay, but not too long. I'll be up with the others. Don't wander, Keely."

Keely remembered her uncle's words, "Trolls can camouflage themselves better than any other being on earth." Then she yelled, "I know you are here, Mr. Troll! I saw you run under here." Just then a trickle of dirt floated down from the bridge above. "You are on that big beam. I can see you!" She really couldn't see anything, but she sure did fool the troll.

Thinking he was spotted, he showed his face to Keely saying, "How could you see me? No one has ever caught me up until now."

Keely jumped with joy. "You are there! You are!"

"You mean you tricked me?" the troll asked as he climbed down to her.

Excited and a bit scared, Keely waited until the troll was on the ground and right in front of her. "You are smaller than me," she remarked.

"Yes, I'm a dwarf troll. You caught me! I'm so ashamed."

"Don't be ashamed. I tricked you, just like you trick people."

"You are a smart little girl. I can't stay. But because you caught me, here is magical ring. It is over a century old. If you are ever in danger, just rub the ring's stone, and the nearest troll will come to your aid."

With that said, Keely was given the ring and told to close her eyes. When she opened her eyes again, the troll was gone, and the magical ring was on her finger (Bill Flynn, 11/99).

The following story is true. I wrote this just before Christmas in 1999. Sandy and I were true friends. We are soul mates, but destiny determined for us to be apart. We went our separate ways in the early nineteen nineties. Here is our story.

A Shining Star

Love is the strongest force on earth. True love is eternal and remains with our souls despite our bodies returning to dust. When the love between two people reaches a level which surpasses the physical and mental parts involving love, then the two persons become spiritually bonded and eternal "soul mates." Here is a story of two such people.

Every time Bill sees a sky full of bright stars, he is reminded of his youthful soul mate, Sandy. One night, many years ago, Bill nicknamed his friend "Sparky" as they sat on the beach together under a canopy of twinkling stars. While forming a circle by joining his thumbs and index fingers, he tried to explain to Sandy how important she was to him. "Imagine this circle as my own little world—a speck of sand compared to the universe. The circle is made up by the people most dear to me. Some are immediate family, and others are my closet friends. You are a part of this circle, and you are my shining star, illuminating my world. I'll nickname you Sparky because you shine as beautiful as any star above us."

Their times together would envy any young lovers. Sandy and Bill experienced many romantic, sentimental, and humorous nights together under starlit skies. Whether it was walking long deserted beaches, sitting alongside peaceful lakes, or standing together atop the jetties, their love proved as true as nature itself. The magic their bonding produced is known only to Bill, Sandy, and the heavens above.

Call it fate, destiny, or God's Will, but their lives took different courses. Their memories have no shadows, and their bond is enternal. Apart physically, Bill and Sparky have only to look up at the stars and think back upon their magnificent times to feel the warmth love gives.

Here is another children's story. It is fiction, of course. I cannot remember how I came up with this one. I guess my imagination was running wild.

A Furrube's Story

You won't find me in the dictionary, and most adults deny that I exist. Why? Because I only show myself to children who know how to imagine.

I am a Furrube. I resemble my cousin, the porcupine, except my fur is very soft and long. Only my small face and feet are without fur. I can stand just like a woodchuck, and I run on all fours. My two front feet are actually very tiny hands similar to a human newborn baby's. My best friends are rabbits, and we have a great time playing hide-and-seek in the grass or along the edge of the woods. If you listen, I make sounds just like a hamster, but I'm much louder, and I laugh more than hamsters do. My home is a comfortable nest of leaves and pine needles tucked secretly within a bush. I sleep during the day, and I play most of the night. Oh, what a life!

No one will find me, though. I am the master of hiding. You can spot me in a field, but I won't let you come close unless you know the Furrube password. Do you know how many times I have been within reach of you and your friends and you have not seen me? Then and only then will I give you the password so you can see me up close. Oh, yes, I have a special talent. I know sign language. So if you too know sign, then we can communicate. I talked with a boy and a girl once who knew how to use sign. But the adults didn't believe the two children and grown-ups said the Furrubes did not exist. But then those same adults stopped believing in Santa Claus many years ago. He even waved at me as his sled flew over my field. Imagine! Santa is the only adult to have ever seen me, and he even knows the Furrube password.

Do you want to see me? Well, just let your imagination guide your eyes and listen for me near a grassy field just before it gets dark. If you learn sign language, I might talk to you. I'll be with the rabbits, playing.

Okay! Here are two Irish tales I wrote. Believe them or not, that is up to you. I put a bit of a slant on how the Irish got to America.

It's the Truth...It Is!

Have you heard the legend of Danny McCree? "No," you say? Then I'll tell it to you as it was said to me. Danny was the first Irishman to set foot in America. "Crazy," you say? Then explain why the crew who sailed with Columbus spoke of him. Or explain the shamrock designs found among ancient native writings discovered in the New Hampshire Mountains. And how did Danny McCree's unique knotting style appear centuries ago within Native American villages along the northern Atlantic coast?

He hadn't planned on a long voyage when the left the Erin shores to fish. Some say it was a leprechaun's trick, and others say it was a storm at sea which caused Danny's craft to eventually end up across the ocean. Say what you will, but a handwritten letter, tucked into a bottle, was found ten years after he had disappeared. Written in Gaelic it read: "I am Danny McCree. I lost my way and crashed my boat on a rocky shore. The sun rises from the sea and settles onto the land here. It you find this bottle tell my family I am alive but not sure where I am. There's plenty of trees and animals. I met some people. They look at me strange, just like at home! The lasses don't wear clothes, and they all have long hair. They're a sight to behold. I tell you.

"I'm gonna explore this land of many trees and scarcely any people. I'll use my skills to survive, and I'll watch for a craft, but I'm not too hopeful, the way the people have looked at me and felt my clothes. I must be the only white man ever here. I'll leave my mark as I explore. Look for the shamrock, and you'll know I was there!

"If you're not convince enough yet, then I recommend you either find a leprechaun and ask him or read this again after a few more shots.

"Tis the truth, it is!"

Those Tricky Leprechauns

How did Leprechauns get to America? Why are European treasure now being found within caverns in Virginia, Pennsylvania, New York, and as far as south as Georgia?

The secrets of the Leprechauns are gradually being discovered because their magic is wearing thin these days. One of their most guarded secrets is the secret of the "Gold Tunnel." No engineering project can compete with the tunnel which connects Ireland and North America!

Because Leprechauns are small, the circumference of their tunnels average only one foot. These tricky and secretive "little people" began the tunnel after hearing about the discovery of a new land across the ocean. During the tenth century AD, the kind of our treasures! Let us begin a passage where no human could ever discover us. We will build tunnel under the ocean floor, and we will call it the Gold Tunnel. Every Leprechaun was contacted and called to a historic meeting within the Great Room near the sea. The Great Room is a huge cavern hidden with the cliffs of Ireland along the ocean's edge. During the meeting, they chose their top engineers, their best tunnelers, and their hardiest workers. Three of the cleverest magicians were picked to help troubleshoot throughout the project's construction. Since Leprechauns are experts at finding things, finding the best route for the Gold Tunnel came easy. Magic came in handy too. Their biggest concern was keeping their activities secret and making sure the Viking pirates were unaware of their project. Keeping the entrance secret to all humans involved a lot of tricking and magic. Although it took several centuries to complete, the Gold Tunnel was done without detection and became one of the Leprechaun's greatest feats.

The tunnel has hundreds of small resting areas along its route under the ocean. Each resting area has supplies, magical dust, four small beds, and a chest to hold treasure. In the "New World," which is now known as America, a network of tunnels reaches north, south, and west. While the secret about the Gold Tunnel has been broken, the tunnel itself has yet to be found! It is said that the rainbows over the ocean sometimes point to the Gold Tunnel. Who knows?

Some of the stories I've written were printed on the backs of T-shirts and sold in stores. I may try this again sometime. Here are a few of the stories we sold on the shirts.

Surfer Girls

Move over, boys; we, girls, are showing our stuff! No longer do we sit on the beach watching while you have all the fun. We are cool. We are smooth. And we carve over signature on the walls of the biggest waves. Our style is our own. Whether riding the lip, crouching inside the tube, or simply cutting back and challenging the white water, we, girls, bring new life and new air to the art of surfing.

The waves called, and we responded. We are here to stay and here to have fun. We know the music! Our bodies flow, our hair flies, and our muscles respond as we roller coaster left to right. We are in the water, on our boards (short and long), riding the waves and loving it!

This next one was sold at our local American Legion Headquarters. The sale of two dozen shirts put a few dollars into their general funds. I had three dozen shirts printed, and they sold within three weeks. The fastest selling story was the one you just read, Surfer Girls. Two dozen T-tops went off the shelves at a surf shop in one week! Here is the next one.

Structure of the United States of America

Here is an analogy of how the United States of America was constructed to last and survive for a long, long time.

Our nation's original leaders were architects of exquisite standards. These men had vision, intellect, commonsense, fortitude, and unity. They built a foundation upon the words, "One Nation under God." The material they used comes from the principles and teachings of Aristotle, Moses, and Jesus. Liberty, justice, equality, and civility were molded together, forming a solid base. Walls were built, not to keep people out but to protect those who entered desiring to be a part of the new nation. The windows of opportunities and doors open to success lured people from everywhere. The engineering proved stable. The nation's citizens are the house, and they carry on the dream of the architects.

The United States of America will remain strong, free, and just as long as the foundation is intact. Many have died, shed blood, or sacrificed much to keep this structure standing. Be careful of the future, and remember the powerful statement embedded into the cornerstone, "In God We Trust."

Two other short stories were done. You have already read them. They were "The Work Shirt" and "I Am the Boardwalk." The story "I Am the Boardwalk" sold easily because of its popularity. I put laminated copies on pieces of wood to represent the planks which make up the Boardwalk and sold several hundred of them. I stopped with the shirts and boards in order to concentrate on writing books. Who knows what lies in the future? Another world-famous boardwalk is the one in Atlantic City, New Jersey. I wrote this story in March 2002.

I Am the Atlantic City Boardwalk

Chances are, you have walked along my grand deck. I am the "walk" of the celebrities, the presidents, the rich and famous. I have heard every language, seen every culture, and witnessed every fashion trend the world has offered. Yet I have never moved beyond the beachfront of Atlantic City.

Over a century ago, humans built me. I am here because of you. Storms have battered me, fires have raged, decay is constant, but you have always repaired and improved me. I really should be one of your national monuments. Don't you agree? I have more visitors than Mount Rushmore, and I'm as old as the Washington Monument. And don't forget, I have seen more national beauties than any other landmark in the United States of America!

Where else is there a simple wooden structure with such grandeur and rich history? Look at me now. I am bordered by sand and the beautiful Atlantic Ocean on one side and the massive new casino hotels on the other. I am brighter than ever. I do miss the diving horse, though. Things do change, and events come and go. I will be here as long as you humans enjoy your recreation, peaceful strolls, and the romance of the Boardwalk—the Boardwalk of the Stars!

If you've ever been to a beach along the ocean, you probably have seen children building castles near the water's edge. Here is a short story I wrote in February 2001.

The Sandcastle

While enjoying a beautiful day on the beach, five-year-old Jason and his twin Katie busied themselves building a castle. Their parents supervised as Katie and Jason shared their plastic shovels, buckets, and youthful imagination. Their small hands mixed sand and ocean water as their father had taught them and they used shells that they had gathered for decorating the castle. Blocks of sand used for the walls were designed by using their tiny shovels.

Near noon, Jason and Katie stood admiring their castle which was now as tall as themselves. "Mommy, what do you think of our beautiful castle?" Katie smiled proudly.

"It is terrific! You two have done so well," Mom praised.

"We need a moat and a small bridge, just like I saw in our books," Jason said to his sister.

"Yes," Katie responded.

So they dug a trench around their castle, and their father found some driftwood for their bridge. Running back and forth to the ocean, they filled the moat with ten buckets of saltwater. "Any king and queen would love your castle," their father told them as they all admired the finished sandcastle. Jason and Katie beamed with pleasure as other beachgoers came to see the castle.

Later in the day, the tide changed, and the ocean slowly crept toward the sandcastle. Mom and Dad sat with their children and explained how the ocean would dissolve the castle and return the sand to its natural state. "Your castle will remain with you. You will always be able to visit your castle even though the ocean will melt it away. Don't be sad when the water comes to claim your castle. You'll see what I mean later," their mom explained. The ocean rose, and the twins watched helplessly as the castle disappeared, dissolved by the tide. They were sad.

While tucking the children into bed that night, Dad told Katie and Jason to close their eyes and picture their castle sitting on the beach. Seconds later, Jason and Katie opened their eyes, smiling and happy. "Mom was right! Our castle is still there!" The twins said as one.

This next story involves my thinking of how teachers need to "connect" with their students better. Knowledgeable teachers speak more with their students in the classrooms because they know about the topics they teach. When teachers get to know their students beyond just grading them, then the students tend to respect the teachers better. I wrote this in December 1999.

A Tough Lesson

John Anderson has taught English literature to thousands of students over the years, but he never experienced a class such as the one he has now at Woodville High.

He knew something was different the very first day, but because he was new to Woodville, he figured the students needed time to adjust to him. Every class, each day, he assigned literature to read and reports to be written. The students of the first period followed their assignments, received high grades, and were respectful. But every morning, Mr. Anderson noticed that his thirty-two students gave him the same curious look until he read them their assignments. Night after night, he pondered why they gave him this look. He dared not to ask them because he was the teacher and the teacher should always be in control! "What is their curiosity?" he pondered. "Why do thirty-two adolescents of different genders, religions, back-grounds, and home environments all have the same expression every time I begin a class?" Well, after a full month of this, John Anderson the teacher just had to inquire.

At the start of the next class with his first period students, he stood looking at their curious looking faces and asked, "What? Why have you given me this look every day since school started? What are you curious about?" The students stay quiet and nonresponsive. "Please tell me," he pleaded.

A student stood and spoke for the class saying, "We mean no disrespect, Mr. Anderson, but we have been wondering when you are going to teach us. Most anyone can give assignments and grade our reports. We need a teacher, sir. Will you teach us, Mr. Anderson?"

In the chapter on adventures, you read about my trip across country on a motorcycle. During a motorcycle rally in our town back in the year 2002, I wrote this short piece as the sound of motorcycle engines filled our island. I handed out a few dozen copies to some of the bikers who came the following year. They liked it!

Free to Ride

What is better than getting on your motorcycle and "hitting the roads" for a week or two? Forget about having a particular destination; just get out there and ride! If you've done it, then you know the high. If you've dreamed about doing it, then just do it. It is one of the best natural highs any adventurous person can have.

Ask any biker who has ridden coast-to-coast, north to south, south to north, or crisscrossed the states how their trip was and you'll hear what we call "Stories of the Road." Their trip may have only lasted for a few weeks, but the memories last a lifetime.

Spontaneity and love of freedom flows through the bikers' veins. A good bike, a little gear, and a stash of cash is all a biker needs to enjoy life and experience the people, places, and things that make the United States of America such a great nation to explore. You can go now. You are free to ride.

Here is another story for children. It seems to be their favorite one. I wrote it in April 2001.

The Clumsy Dragon

He is known as Clagon. For more than a century, he terrorized the people of Europe. Whenever Clagon appeared, people hid to avoid the mean dragon. His huge dens were located high in the mountains. He had a den in Greece, Italy, and Norway. While flying from den to den, he ravaged villages, capturing and then eating sheep, goats, horses, and even people. Everyone and everything feared Clagon. This large dragon would swoop down from the sky and grab his victims with his huge talons as fire shot from his nose destroying whole villages. No hamlet was safe. No village was secure. The only hope of survival was to hide underground or within small caves and hope Clagon would not see you.

Then something strange happened. Clagon became clumsy. People began to witness the fierce dragon dropping his prey and bumping into small hills. His flames began missing his targets. It is said that on one occasion. Clagon spewed out his flame and missed an entire village. His firebomb hit a large tree and ricocheted back onto him, catching his wing on fire. Clagon quickly dove into a large lake to save himself from his own fire.

He wasn't seen for decades, and the people rejoiced. Where did he go? Was he dead, or was he hiding in one of his smelly dens? How was he surviving without eating his prey? The answer finally came from the words of a wizard who saw Clagon and spoke to him. The wizard said, "Clagon is too embarrassed to be seen again. He is hiding in a large cavern, high within the mountains of a foreign land. He flies only at night, so as not to be seen and he feeds on the creatures within the sea. Clagon dives into the sea and uses his wings to propel himself through the water. Ever since burning himself, he is afraid of fire. Clagon still lives! But until his clumsiness ends, you are still safe. Keep an eye on the sky, though. For someday, I know Clagon will heal, and then he will remain fiercer than before!"

I have never been to a bull fight to see the matador and a bull go at it, so this short story is purely made by my imagination. I wrote this on May 9, 2012.

The Matador

He is tall and lean. He sports a curled, black mustache. His eyes have an intense look in them. The colors of his attire are black, red, and white. He is a courageous and daring man. He is Spain's champion!

A bull comes into the open-air arena. He weighs nearly a ton. His horns are thick, pointy, and long. He hears the cheers of the spectators as he spots the matador. He senses this man is his opponent, so he locks his eyes on the man riding a horse. The muscular bull stands his ground then stomps his hoof defiantly. He charges as the man, and horse comes toward him. They meet! He feels a sharp pain in his shoulder as he throws his head sideways. The bull turns, only to see the man riding back toward him. He swings his horns and catches the horse's flank. Another sharp pain! This time, his upper neck feels aflame. The people in the stadium cheer. The bull is in a huff! He feels wetness on his hide. He spies the man, now standing in the center of the arena. The matador holds a red cape in front of his body. The bull's nostrils flare. His hoof beats the ground. He lowers his head and aims his sharp horns at the man behind the red cape. He charges! The cape is hit, but the man steps aside just in time to escape the bull's horns. A third sword is stuck into the bull. Now losing energy, the bull attempts another charge. This time, he hears a roar come from the crowd as he falters and dies from the fatal blow of a fourth sword. The man survived. He acknowledges the people cheering him. He takes several bows then retrieves his swords from the still giant. The matador has won! He can return home without injuries this time. But first, it is time to celebrate at the festival and drink some fine Spanish wine.

As you can see, the stories in this chapter are mostly fiction. I listen to the ideas and advice people give me. Numerous readers suggested I put my short stories into the books I write. Although this book is nonfiction, I decided this chapter would be a good place to include some of the short stories I've written over the years. While most are fiction, real events, feelings, and real people caused a lot of them to be written. For example, this next story is based on what a chief of Penobscot Indian Nation in Maine said to a small group of us one night. He spoke for a good length of time about life, beliefs, and the life after death. I took mental notes of the things he said, and this is the result. I wrote this in February 2001, but his talk with us was long before that. He spoke with us (a small group of friends) sometime in the nineteen-nineties.

God Is Energy

"Sitting around a campfire deep within the Maine woods, the old Native American Indian shared his thoughts to a group of young children. Neither he nor they knew that this was his last day of his life. For many seasons, I have contemplated who the Great Sprit is and why things point to His greatness. However, when others or I refer to God as Creator, Supreme Being, Father, Great Sprit, Jehovah, Lord, Yahweh, or the Great One, we are all speaking of and praying to the same God. When I die, I will learn the truth, I hope. When I say the truth, I mean about all things.

I envision the Great Sprit as the Master of energy. I will venture to say that God is energy! The elders spoke of this around campfires many moons ago. I was a child then, just like yourselves. I have been taught that God is everywhere, knows all things, and is eternal. So my children think about the things I say. Creation involved energy. Nature is constant evolution of energy. Life depends upon energy. Even when our bodies die, as mine will soon, energy returns our body to earth. My body will return to the great cycle of nature while the fate of my spirit lies in God's hands.

Energy is constant. Whether I speak about our own planet or I speak about the universe around us, keep it in mind that energy is everywhere. Nature lives and continues because of energy. A tree dies yet takes on other forms. Its seeds produce new trees. Its wood turns to soil or is burned to warm us. Energy continues! The sun, which we enjoy, is a huge source of energy. I believe God designed this. There are many other suns out there, and I have often wondered whether there are other places like ours with people similar to us. It is possible, children.

Energy keeps my heart beating and by brain functioning. Energy keeps the river flowing and the fish swimming. Energy allows the birds to sing and the animals to grow. Energy is ever changing, yet the cycle of life remains constant and the principles of energy keep to God's plan. The more I learn, the better I appreciate the gifts the Great Spirit created for us all. Fire is energy. Earthquakes are energy. Tornadoes are energy. Blizzards, storms, lightening, and floods are all forms of energy. Are they bad? I think not. They are necessary. They are as necessary as a quiet and peaceful sunny day.

So why do I say that God is energy? It is simply a thought of mine. I believe that energy has come from God. He didn't create it. It is a part of His very Spirit. Energy is all around us and within us. As I have said earlier, I will know the truth after I die and my spirit travels to heaven but only if the Great Spirt allows me.

Thank you, my children, for being so kind and attentive to an old man rambling on. I will see you all tomorrow. For now, I will retire to my bed under that majestic spruce tree."

On New Year's Day of 2002, I wrote this one. I wasn't contemplating making any New Year resolutions.

Now Is the Time

If you could change anything in your past, what would it be? If you say nothing, then I say, "Get real!" There are countless things we would all have changed it given a chance. Who wouldn't prefer clear skin over acne? Who ever wanted to be taller or shorter, heavier or lighter? Are there words you would rather not have said? Wouldn't it be great to correct a time of carelessness that caused an injury or even a death? Sure, it would! How about those times of selfishness? Did you really want to leave your son or daughter and have them grow up without you there every day? Would you change having the first cigarette, first drink, or trying those drugs if you knew where it would lead you?

Yes, there are many things we all would change if we could. But we cannot go back. We live in the present, and we make mistakes every day. We are human! Right now, we can change our future by asking ourselves, "What could I change right now!" *Now is the time.*

I won't explain this next story. You will see why. I wrote it in July 1999.

A Maine Story

While visiting Maine, an elderly man walks along a small dirt road through the forest. A little girl, carrying a bouquet of wildflowers, comes toward him on the road. "Hello, my child, where are you going?"

"To join my twin brother at the pond, he is waiting for me there. Where are you going?"

"Oh, I'm just getting some exercise and enjoying the peace of these woods." The six-year-old gives the man some of her flowers saying, "My mama says that when you give something to a stranger, God smiles." Looking surprised, he thanked her, and they parted. Not far down the road, he saw a group of children playing in a field near a log cabin. He sits on a rock and remembers his own children laughing and playing simple games. He decides to visit them again after decades of lost contact.

Coming back along the dirt road, he sees the little barefooted girl again, "Where is your brother?"

"Timmy is still at the pond, it's our favorite place," she said, smiling.

"I have to get back to my other brothers and sisters now."

Continuing on, the man sees little footprints going off the road onto a footpath. He follows the path to a secluded pond. A weathered picnic table sits within a cleared shoreline and grassy area. Across the pond, he sees a deer browsing, and he hears a loon calling to its mate. The pond surface reflects the blue sky and puffy white clouds as the man admires this heavenly spot. A wooden sign, nailed to a tree, is marked *angel pond*. Wondering where the little boy could be, he looks around. Near a tree, he finds a small engraved cross with a bouquet of wildflowers placed around it. It reads, "Timmy (age five), our little angel." The old man kneels and places his flowers atop the others. Tears moisten the ground as he says, "Here, Timmy, here is something from a stranger."

Ten years ago (2002), I wrote this story imagining I was eleven years old again and camping with fellow boy scouts. I am glad I wrote it because of the young children who read it. It is mythical and has a wizard; it is popular with seven- to twelve-year-old children.

Magical Campfire

Children! Let me tell you about a special campfire only a few will ever see!

Many years ago, I learned about the rare and magical campfire. Four other scouts and I were sitting around a campfire we built. It was nighttime, and our camping area lay deep in a forest just below a steep, rocky mountain. Little did we know that the firewood we gathered held magical powers which would be released when burned and could only be witnessed by children; therefore, receiving the magic released.

What an experience! We five, eleven-year-olds sat entranced as the logs burned. Our eyes stared at the shooting flames, the swirling smoke, and a weird blue glow below the red flames. Magical powers flowed onto us through the fire's heat and into us as we smelled the smoke. Not one of us were ever the same! It was a good magic, a special magic. You see, anyone who receives this magic will never be afraid of the dark ever! Also the magic unlocks many of the secrets the forest holds. Sorry, I can't tell you the secrets. But if you ever see a magical campfire, then you will know the secrets too.

I can tell you this: there is a wizard of the forests. He is the cause of our firewood having magic. You see, if the wizard of the forests touches a tree, then the tree receives some of his magic. He does it on purpose so that someday a childlike yourself might be sitting near one of these campfires just like us five scouts were many years ago. Even though the adults cannot see the magic, make sure an adult is with you so your campfire stays safe. The magic won't work without an adult nearby. This is one of the wizard's rule.

You have read the chapter on simplicity. I put this short story to print in May 2002. Since the late nineteen-eighties, I have simplified my life by doing the things I write about. At the age of thirty-two, when stress caused me to have a heart attack, my thinking changed. The doctor who treated me told me I needed to say "no" more. Before having the stress syndrome heart attack, I said yes to everyone even if my days were already full. This short story may change your life! Take is seriously.

Keep It Simple

When I rolled out of bed this morning, I made a promise to myself to simplify my day.

The first thing I must learn is how to say "no." The second thing I must learn is how to say "Oh well" more often. Why have I let so many trivial things bother me? Why have I allowed insensitive and ignorant people to ruin my day? These things are history! From now on, my days will be less stressful and more productive. My priorities will gain more attention, and the things I don't need are going on sale. I realize, after years of gathering "stuff," why some people say, "Less is best."

I will no longer try to please everyone. I will focus on what and who is important today. To simplify my life, I will pay attention to my senses. I will listen better, see what is around me clearer, and notice the things I touch, taste my food; not just eat it and appreciate the good scents around me. I'll keep it simple with bad scents. I'll hold my nose.

Each day will get simpler. I will be happier, healthier, and more relaxed. Simplicity is really an easy philosophy to follow. All I have to remember are three words. *Keep it simple.*

A pleasant experience for many of us is to socialize in the morning at a coffee shop or diner. The following short story is so true! I wrote this for a restaurant owner.

The Coffee Shop Talk

In every small town, within every busy city, neighborhood, or somewhere along a country road, there is a daily tradition taking place. It is people gathering and solving the problems of the world over a cup of coffee. Who in America has not participated? Whether your seat is at booth, a stool at the counter, or around a table, the conversations are common to several themes. The talk about weather is as common as bees around honey or snakes in high grass. Discussions about sports, politics, and current news reports compete with the local gossip. Have you ever sat back and listened? It is quite interesting and a real education on human nature. Do people really go for the coffee? I think not. There is always more talk than there is coffee poured. Everyone has a story. Someone will relate an experience about, let's say changing diapers. Ten minutes later, the topic is foreign policy or corporate takeovers. It happens every time! "How did we get from diapers to world affairs?" Someone will ask, and everyone will have a good laugh. Within those ten minutes, there are usually ten other topics touched upon also. This is coffee shop talk.

Then there are the people. There's the working man and woman who don't stay long, the retired person whom usually stays an hour or more, the conversationalist who involves everyone in the dialogue, the silent, more reserved person who favors the newspaper or uses the newspaper to shield their timidness, the lonely individual seeking some sort of community, or the traveler who brings fresh ideas and conversation to the regulars there.

I would guess that the only place to gathering which tops the variety of characters and topics covered is a neighborhood bar. Coffee shop talk is as American as peanut butter and jelly sandwiches. Or something like that. We'll discuss it over coffee (Bill Flynn).

Writing is a positive form of expressing one's thoughts and feelings. Distractions are not helpful when writing. I choose to have a quiet place to write. I do without watching (or having) a television for years so I can put my extra time into writing. A dream of mine is to have a small cabin within a forested region which I can retreat to for periods of time to write. When I want to have a peaceful environment to write in, the cabin would be there. The rest of my time will be traveling and working. I will see this dream become reality! That is if God allows me. Writing and finishing this book is a purpose of life for me now. Only time will tell if it happens. If you are reading this, it happened!

It is now December 2014. I have finished this manuscript and am proofing and editing it for the third time. My goal is to have it out by July 2015. It will take time because this manuscript is all handwritten. It will have to be typed, checked for mistakes, and then sent to the publisher which all takes time (and money). I am writing this short footnote because after going over my various short stories I had a thought: "I sure did write quite a bit!" I am referring to the whole manuscript. I consider writing as an art, and I enjoy putting my thoughts on paper. Once a book is on the market, the reward comes through the comments of its readers. My sincere hope is the book becomes the celebrity and I can stand in the background.

CHAPTER 9
Celebrities

Celebrities are defined as famous people. Whether their fame comes from their talent, their looks, their deeds, an unusual event, or from aggressive marketing, celebrities enjoy a position of stature and fame. My preference is knowing or meeting a person because of their talent or artistic skills. I am not impressed by celebrities who are shaped and created through marketing. In the United States of America, we have more celebrities than ever before. Much of this is because the public thrives on stardom, royalty figures, financial success, vanity, or craziness. There is a falsehood about it. Just think of a few genuine celebrities of the past then put their deeds, skills, artistic abilities, and proven fame over many decades against that of celebrities of today, and you may realize what I am trying to say. Think of some of the comedians of the past for an example. They performed live and made people laugh about the most common things. They made themselves laugh, and you laughed with them. In sports, you saw legends making history with their athletic abilities. Think of Wilt Chamberlain who made history on the basketball court. He was so good they had to change a few rules of the game to make things fair. Arnold Palmer is known even by those who do not follow the game of golf because he dominated the sport and was genuine. He still is. John Wayne was the true American for several generations. His nature was and still is admired by millions of fans. What you saw is what you got by the man young boys looked up to. Mohammad Ali is certainly the greatest boxer in American history even though there are many great boxers of the past. The generation growing up during Ali's career saw a spectacular athlete, humorist, Olympic star, and a person people admired. Mohammad Ali told us he was the "greatest," and he proved it. Some celebrities become more popular after their deaths, and some celebrities die young. A few of these individuals are legends and are (or will be) written into the history books. Michael Jackson is such a legend. His artistic skills are legendary. John Lennon is a legend. The Beatles are legendary. Their fame, their songs and music, their controversies, and the number of fans they had and still have worldwide are historic. They wrote, sang, performed, recorded, and compiled music as a group then went separate ways. Yet they are all considered The Beatles. The proven celebrities will be in the history books and museums. The "marketed" stars are in the tabloids now but will barely be remembered over time. Marilyn Monroe is recorded in history. Her fame and sweet charm acting and photos reached the world during a time when technology was just beginning to increase. Charlie Chapland is legendary. He did not need a stunt man to do his feats of courage and skill. The Three Stooges and the Marx Brothers did their own stunts also. They made us laugh then, and their films still have people laughing.

In every field of entertainment, fashion, sports, the art world, science, and medicine, there are legends. Not all are or were celebrities. Within the political world, you have celebrities. Some will be recorded in history because of their achievements or certain happenings. Some are more popular because of how they "connect" with the public. Former President Bill Clinton is recognized wherever he goes throughout the world. He has stayed active after leaving office. He gives speeches, supports charities, and visits countries everywhere. He is active in very big projects, and he has a major influence on people. I give Bill Clinton as an example of a genuine celebrity within the political field because he seems to be the most active one out here. It seems to be his nature to "keep at it" and never retire.

The cliché "fifteen minutes of fame" is well-known. The American public has put fame as their top desire. The tabloids make billions of dollars because of this. Many people seek fame and a large percentage of the youth today want fame in some sort of fashion. It is not always a pleasant experience once they receive their moment of fame because many times it is achieved by deeds, action, or words spoken which are not favorable to most. The desire to be in the spotlight certainly drives people to do some crazy things. And unfortunately, the desire pushes some to do harm against others.

Seeking fame because of the riches it can bring is one factor why people want to be in the spotlight. It may be enjoyable at first, but the "costs" of being a celebrity is sometimes negative. Personal privacy is given up because of the public's desire to read about and to view pictures of the celebrities. It can overwhelm a person. The bigger the star, the less they can do publicly. Their security is also affected because of their "celebritism." Despite the negatives, most celebrities enjoy the attention, the riches, and the lifestyle. The desire to be recognized is a normal human want. It is not a bad thing to want some attention from others. Many times, it is a boost to receive recognition from others. Like most desires, it is the degree or overbalance of the desire that draws it toward obsession.

I am writing this chapter because I know there is an interest in the subject. I wish for my book and writings to be in the limelight. I prefer a quiet life without any glitter or fame. In order to bring attention to this book, I realize I will have to be "out there" for a few years. The more books I sell, the more students will have a chance to compare their thoughts with mine. This is a good thing. I encourage those students to write their own thoughts down as they think upon certain topics.

Here is a question which can start a conversation while sitting around with friends or neighbors. Who is your favorite celebrity, and why is this person your favorite? So far, I have named a few celebrities. Because of space, many are left out, but you should get my point. I am sure that any of today's celebrities whom I have not mentioned would want me to include them. Today's stars and celebrities seem to have huge egos and they seem to "expect" people to "fall all over them." Sorry. I am not one of those people who need to see or meet celebrities, but some of us will probably bump into a few during our lives. I intend to write about the few I have met, conversed with, or heard about through firsthand knowledge. My comments are my opinions, not always in sync with other's opinions. I generally try to write in a positive way, but in order to explain a few factual events of my meetings, I have to cover some negatives too. Within the following pages, some of my dad's stories are included.

Babe Ruth is a legendary baseball player. He is considered one of the best players of the game. Just the mention of his name, all sports fans picture him. One day, many decades ago, my grandfather took Dad to a baseball game where Babe Ruth was playing. The "Babe" signed and gave baseballs to the youngsters awaiting to see him near his team's dugout. Dad met the "Babe" and received one of those signed baseballs. It was one of Dad's most cherished memories. As a young child, I remember seeing the baseball atop our mantle in the living room of our house in Washington, New Jersey. Here is the story which goes along with that ball.

Fifty years ago, our family moved from Washington, New Jersey (Warren County), to North Wildwood, New Jersey (Cape May County). It is about three and a half to four hours of driving. My parents used their station wagon to move all our things. They must have made a dozen trips! On the very last trip from Washington, Mom drove the station wagon. Dad was in North Wildwood with my brother Dennis and my sister Colleen. Dennis was five years old, and Colleen was two years of age. Myself and two older brothers were with Mom. I was eight, Danny was ten, and Jack was eleven. Halfway to Wildwood, Mom stopped along the road so we could all eat lunch. She had made sandwiches and packed drinks. We stopped where a picnic table sat in a grassy area bordered by trees and underbrush. After lunch, my brothers and I grabbed our baseball gloves and a baseball to have a catch. There was just enough space on the grass to throw and catch our ball. We were three youngsters having a catch. We lost our baseball when it went into the woods. There were a lot of sticker bushes (thorny) in the underbrush. One of us went to the station wagon and got another ball to play with. We lost that one too! Mom called us, and we resumed our trip to Wildwood.

While unpacking the station wagon, Dad found the shoebox which held Babe Ruth's baseball. It was empty! He called to us and asked us if we had seen the ball. It turned out to be the baseball one of us had gotten after losing one to the woods. Dad took Jack with him, and he drove all the way back to the picnic spot to search the woods. It was night when he got there. Dad and Jack searched the woods using flashlights. Who knows how far that ball was into the woods. The sticker bushes didn't help any. They came home without Babe's baseball. At any rate, we had played with, thrown, and caught a baseball held by Babe Ruth. One of us also missed catching the very same ball. I asked Dad many years later while we were fishing during a warm and calm evening aboard the family's eighteen-foot Boston Waler if he had gotten mad at us for losing his prized baseball. The same baseball our grandfather protected for Dad while he served in the Army during World War II. Dad answered me by saying he should have realized that young boys will play with a ball if they see it. He told me he was upset at first, but then later, he thought about Babe Ruth. Babe Ruth handed out balls to the kids so they could play with them. He was generous to the kids. Dad then said, "The Babe would have wanted you boys to use that ball. How could I get mad about my sons having fun by throwing and catching a baseball without knowing it was the ball Pop and I protected all those years. To you guys, it was a baseball. You three boys were doing just what Babe wanted you to do, having fun playing a great sport."

Sally Starr

Our parents took us to Cape May, New Jersey, one summer day to see the television personality, Sally Starr. This was around 1958. I was only five years old then, but I can still remember her all decked out in her cowgirl attire and sparkling hat. Her show on television featured cartoon characters such as Popeye and Olive Oil. It was broadcasted out of Philadelphia, Pennsylvania. Every young child in the tristate area (PA, NJ, DE) watched her show because of the cartoons and we all knew her because she brought the cartoons to us. I think her show was on Saturday mornings. It has been a long, long time since then. In Cape May, she was up on the balcony waving to us kids. We were near where all the party fishing boats were docked. As I write this, I am aware that Sally Starr is still alive and well. She is a true celebrity. Her show and her example as a loving person gave joy to millions of children. Before seeing her and hearing her voice, we only knew her from television. She seemed more colorful, more energetic, and more charming in person. She was definitely more colorful! We only had black-and-white TV back then. That day in Cape May was an exciting for me and my brothers.

Jan Michael Vincent

It was just after my graduation from high school when I met Jan Michael Vincent. The year was 1971, and it was a hot summer day. I was resting on the beach after surfing the waves for a few hours at Diamond Beach near Wildwood Crest, New Jersey. North Wildwood, Wildwood, and Wildwood Crest are all part of the island known as the Wildwoods. While I was sitting there, a young man approached me and asked if he could use my surfboard while I rested. He explained to me he was from California and he would be in town for a month or so. He had the look of a surfer, so I told him to "go for it." He surfed really well! He ripped up waves for nearly an hour, then I went out for about an hour. When I returned to the beach, he was still there sitting on a towel. He said he had just arrived in Wildwood, and he asked me to fill him in about the island. We talked for a while, then I told him I had to be at work in a few hours. He said he was staying at the Thunderbird Inn on 24th Street. I offered him a ride back to there, and he accepted. We walked up the street and then two blocks down to where David von Savage let me store my surfboard in his father's garage. As I was putting my board into the garage, Mr. Von Savage (David's dad) came out and said hello. Then to my surprise, he said, "Jan, nice to see you again."

They shook hands as I asked, "Mr. Von Savage, how do you know Jan?"

Mister Von Savage was the mayor of Wildwood Crest. He had met Jan the night before at dinner. Jan explained it to me because he knew I was not aware of him being a movie star and Hollywood actor. I simply saw him as a fellow surfer. Mayor Von Savage laughed about it saying, "Billy, you brought a Hollywood star to my house, and you didn't even know it." Mr. Von Savage went back into his house, still laughing as he waved good-bye. I had always liked David's dad. He had a great sense of humor.

I gave Jan a lift back to the Thunderbird Inn on my 250cc Yamaha motorcycle. He invited me to come over the next afternoon for a pizza lunch. I agreed. Then I went home, grabbed a shower, and went to work. I was working as the manager of the fiberglass slide on Morey's Pier. What a great job! We were working and having fun doing it. The slide was the favorite spot on the boardwalk for teenagers to hang out and mingle. I was paid $3.50 an hour for working around my fellow teens! What a life. Actually, that was good wages back then. Most teens who worked the boardwalk businesses only received about $2 an hour.

It was sometime around nine o'clock that night when Jan and a beautiful actress came up to the slide. Hundreds of people gathered around him and his date. It is funny: I did not recognize Jan until he told me about his acting and some of the roles he had played, yet here was a crowd of people gathered around because they recognized him and his date right away. Even so, I still saw him as a surfer because he impressed me with his skill. With everyone around and dozens of cameras flashing, I told Jan to take a few rides on the Giant Slide. He and his date climbed the steps up to the top along with the regular crowd of riders. They took several rides, and they had a ball! The slide was one of those simple yet thrilling rides everyone had fun on. We generally had ten to twelve people coming down the slide every fifteen seconds. Clearing the bottom landing was our biggest concern. That was where we had many close calls because of people leaving the landing and people coming down to the landing at top speeds. Jan and his date were among them. We hurried them off just like the others. It was pure fun. There were always people laughing and showing joy as they exited the landing area. Jan thanked me and my fellow workers just before being swarmed by people asking for autographs and pictures. Jan yelled back to me, "Pizza tomorrow for two!" I gave him the thumbs-up.

The next day, I took my lunch break from work to have pizza with Jan. The Thunderbird Inn was only a block away from the slide. He invited me into his motel room. Two pizza pies had just been delivered along with some Coca Cola drinks. An older man was sitting at the round table located near the door to the large room. Jan's unit was on the first floor. You could walk right out and be on the public sidewalk within seconds. The man was Jan's agent or manager. I vaguely remember his title, but he was pleasant and invited me to "dig in." Our conversation dealt mostly with surfing, girls, and motorcycles. I heard very little about the Hollywood scene except that the movie they were to shoot was titled, *Coming Home*. Jan seemed more interested in normal conversation like I did, which made me feel comfortable. Just as we finished, the pizza someone came into the room. I heard the screen door shut, then a man came past me as Jan and the agent made room for him to sit with us. He looked over at me. I looked at him. I knew instantly who he was. It was Robert Mitchum. He didn't say a word to me. I said, "Hello." He asked Jan who I was and what I was doing there. Jan explained everything to him, and it seemed to be okay. I did not like the disrespect he had just shown me. I let it go since I was a guest of Jan's and not of Robert Mitchum's. Up until that moment, I had liked Robert Mitchum because of the many movies I had seen him act in. But after only meeting for a few moments, I did not like the man. It was a negative situation following a fun time eating pizza and conversing with Jan.

The next thing that happened was a shocker of a lifetime. Mr. Mitchum had a large cigar box on the table. He opened it. I saw a small pipe, a stack of joints (marijuana rolled in paper), and a quantity of something else inside a plastic bag. I asked, "Mr. Mitchum, what is that?" The first words he spoke directly to me were, "My boy, this is a pipe. This is hashish. We are going to smoke it." I felt extremely nervous about being in a room with such an amount of hash. All I could think of was how much jail time a person could receive if caught with it. My face must have shown my worry. In a gruff voice, he asked. "Do you have a problem with it?" He lit the pipe, and the smoke gradually filled the room as he smoked the hashish. I stood and thanked Jan and told him I was leaving. "Check me out later, and let me know how the waves are," he said as exited the door. I was only a few yards out the door when I got hit hard by a rolled-up newspaper. It bounced off my back as Robert Mitchum yelled, "Don't come back, punk!" I did not respond. In fact, I did not even look back to give him any satisfaction.

The only ones I told about that episode were my surfing buddies who I knew kept things between us. It was years before I told anyone else. I was shocked that day. My eyes were opened to the reality of what celebrities can be like in real life. It is humorous and sad at the same time. Robert Mitchum, the huge star of Hollywood films, cursed me out and hit me with a rolled-up newspaper. I hope he enjoyed his hashish! He was a great actor, but in my book of life, he does not gain my respect. Sorry for being negative, but it was real and a big lesson for me. As I have said many times, I prefer the natural highs of surfing and riding free on my 750cc BMW motorcycle.

Evel Knievel

Bob Knievel is a celebrity I can really enjoy writing about. Within the little time I spent with him along with some of my hunting partners, I can honestly say he impressed me tremendously. He was genuine. He was a good man. He impressed millions of people with his dangerous stunts on motorcycles, and he was the first to attempt the things he did. Bob "Evel" Knievel showed the world what a daredevil is. Wide World of Sports covered his major jumps. The Ideal Toy Company marketed the many products depicting Evel Knievel. When he was at his peak, everyone in the United States and Canada knew who he was. He knew how to market himself. He could ride a motorcycle like no one else. Many tried to copy him, but they could not come up to his level of skill and daringness. He took risks and paid the price whenever he crashed. Yet when you met him in person, it was hard to tell he had broken so many bones in his body. When he shook my hand, I felt his strength. His grip was powerful. This was probably due to all the riding and holding on to the handlebars of his bikes for so many years. Evel was a tough person with a big heart. His hometown of Butte, Montana, benefited because of his charity. I found Bob to be one of most down-to-earth persons I have ever met. Bob Evel Knievel was not fake. He was the real thing! He enjoyed being around the average Joe. Evel could tell stories about real-life experience and hold your attention for hours. He did with us! We sat in a diner in Butte, Montana, listening and conversing with him for three to four hours one night. No one grew tired or became bored. It was just the opposite. Before beginning his stories with us and some other hunters, he joked by asking, "Anyone have a tape recorder? If you do, keep it off." He allowed us to snap a few photos of us with him. In fact, he allowed me to take pictures up at his ranch where he lived. I took two rolls of film while at the ranch but lost the film cartridges while camping out and hunting elk within the backcountry south of Butte near the town of Melrose. Lew White (my hunting companion) and I searched his vehicle, our large tent, our foot lockers, and all our coat pockets. We never did find the film. Oh well! I did have one roll from the night Evel treated us to fried chicken, ribs, and drinks. He seemed to favor a shot and a beer. We ate a great meal and listened to an American legend tell stories. It was a fun and memorable night.

While visiting Evel Knievel's ranch, we got to see Evel's motorcycles all lined up, side by side, in a three-sided garage. It has been long ago (1974), but I can still envision the bikes. I asked if I could try one out, but he said no in a polite manner. He told me when we came back out next fall maybe we could do a few small jumps together just for fun. I was thrilled, to say the least! Evel asked Lew if he could join us hunting next fall. Lew and I had told Evel about how we were to camp out within the backcountry while hunting elk and mule deer. Evel liked the idea of roughing it, so we all agreed to communicate and plan for a hunt the next year. We met his young son Robbie while at the ranch. I understand he followed in his father's "tire tracks" and became famous in Australia for his jumping feats. The last letter I have received from Evel was sent to me on January 8, 1979. Maybe this was the trip that got Robbie started in Australia, or maybe not.

1\8\79
Dear Bill,

Just a short note to thank you for your letter of December 10, 1978. Enjoyed hearing from you.

I will be going to Australia for a tour which will include forty appearances near the end of

January. So will be out of the country for a while. The family are all doing well.

Thanks again, Bill. Hope to see you again, but in the meantime, best regard for a Happy New Year.

Sincerely,
Evel Knievel

The day after seeing Evel Knievel's ranch and meeting his son, we left Butte and headed to Melrose, Montana. Lew White, Mike Voll, and I hunted for three weeks just outside of Melrose. Melrose, Montana, had a population of 105 people at the time. We ate at the Quack-Quack Café whenever we were in the town. Montana is a great place to visit and to live in. There is a lot of open country, small towns, and I found the people to be very honest and fun to be with. Meeting and spending time with Evel Knievel made our visit even better. He did not forget us. I received two letters from him that winter. It just goes to show how a person of such huge popularity and fame can take time to communicate with us average people if they want to. From what I gathered, Evel did most all his communications personally. I only saw one secretary at his office in Butte. He was not the kind of person who needed anyone to manage his affairs or to speak for him. He was a true American and a true superstar.

The Country Belles

They were known as the "All Girl Vocal and Instrumental Band." They were out of Gibsonia, Pennsylvania. Wow, could they ever perform country music! We saw them perform live during a special gathering during the deer hunting season in Pennsylvania back in the nineteen-seventies. We were in western Pennsylvania. We had nearly twenty guys in our group from Cape May County, New Jersey, and Philadelphia, Pennsylvania. The place where we went to see the Country Belles perform had tables set up to seat three hundred people. Every chair in the place was taken, and there were only a few women in the crowd since deer hunting involves mostly males. The food was served without menus. It was venison stew, salad, and buttered rolls. It was all you could eat. Our group sat within talking distance of the Belles. Throughout the night, during their breaks, we conversed with them. Their performance literally "took the house down." They played and sang so well that men were stomping and dancing to their music even though there were no women to dance with. I was one of those guys dancing up a storm.

I have often wondered if the girls ever became larger celebrities or recorded any hit songs. They sure did have the talent, and they sure did keep three hundred hunters enthused that night. Maybe one of the Belles will read this and be happy they are remembered all these years.

Bill Irwin and Orient

Bill Irwin is the first blind person to hike the entire Appalachian Trail. Along with his seeing eye dog, Orient, he hiked 2,168.9 miles through fourteen states to achieve this. His book title, *Blind Courage*, tells all about his and Orient's experiences. *Blind Courage* by Bill Irwin and David McCasland is an exceptional tale. I assume every Appalachian Trail hiker has read this book. If not, they sure should because of what Bill and Orient accomplished. Just try to walk through the woods or up a mountain with your eyes closed. You won't make it too far!

I was very lucky to have met Bill and his dog, Orient, while they were on their long hike. Phil Pepin of Stratton, Maine, called me to ask if Bill could stay a night or two at my motel in Stratton. I owned and operated the Stratton Motel at the time, and many of the A.T. hikers would come off the trail and stay with us. On page 172 of *Blind Courage*, Bill mentions staying at the Stratton Inn on November 1, 1990. I gave Bill and Orient the front unit which was a two-bedroom condo. I only spent an hour talking with Bill because I knew he needed to rest and to enjoy his privacy. Meeting Bill was terrific and inspirational. I am sure that those who met Bill Irwin along the A.T. felt the same way. Linda Bachelder of Stratton was at the motel when Bill and Orient departed. Linda worked as an employee there for many years. She told me when Bill stepped outside it was not long before members of the media were around. They had been searching to find Bill the day and the night before, but Phil Pepin managed to keep his whereabouts secret. I fielded the phone calls for Bill the night he arrived. I only let certain calls go thru as directed. The media people were calling every motel and hotel around the area. My answer to them was, "You will probably see him around town tomorrow." Bill had told me he was exhausted and needed just one night to rest and think. Every major newspaper along the East Coast had carried his story and were following his progress. *USA Today* and other national newspapers reported on Bill Irwin and Orient. The news media can really be bothersome at times. But with what Bill and Orient were accomplishing was historic and they deserved acclaim. They were celebrities of the best kind. They were inspiring people to get motivated and showing people you can do exceptional things despite have a disability. The following year and every year after, I heard Bill's name mention often by the A.T. hikers. I met on the trail or at the motel. I have a ton of respect for Bill Irwin the man and Bill Irwin the hiker. My source for his total miles walked is from his book, *Blind Courage*. I encourage you to read the book.

Ted Williams

Ted Williams is one of the greatest American Baseball players in the history of the sport. This short story has never been made public because it comes from my dad who knew and associated with Ted Williams during the nineteen-fifties and early sixties. What I write here comes from what Dad told me over the years. I was too young to remember Ted Williams even though I may have met him. John J. Flynn, Jr. (my day) was a sporting goods salesman for Edward K. Tryon Company located in Philadelphia, Pennsylvania. Dad's nickname was "Boston." Dad lived in Boston for a few years on Mercer Street before the Flynn's moved to Philadelphia, Pennsylvania, in 1928. He was a young boy while living in Boston. I am quoting now from Dad's own writings: "Jack Sharkey and Jim Maloney—2 prominent fighters of the day sponsored the trip to the Circus. The trip to Fenway Park was Father Burk's gift to us as altar boys. My first year there I had the honor of Babe Ruth coming into the stands amongst us and took the vendors ice creams and gave each one of us an ice cream cone and a pat on the cheek. At the circus was Tom Mix, Bill Cody and Buffalo Bill."

Dad wrote these accounts when he was in his late seventies. Father Burk really gave those boys a great day at Fenway Park! Dad told me the guys in Philly gave him his nickname of "Boston." Everyone seemed to have a nickname back then. It stuck with Dad, and I am sure Ted Williams (#9, Boston Red Sox) called Dad by his nickname also. Dad told me he and Ted Williams had a few things in common which they enjoyed talking about together. They both served in the military during WWII. Ted Williams enjoyed fly-fishing, and Dad was an avid fresh water and saltwater fisherman. Ted Williams was a great sports star, and Dad sold sporting goods for a living. The one thing that brought them together was because Ted Williams had his own line of fly rods and fishing tackle which he demonstrated to the sales force of Edward K. Tryon Company. Ted Williams sat at a table with Dad at that luncheon. Dad said they talked about baseball, fishing, and the war, along with other things. Because John J. Flynn, Jr. was a top salesman of Tryon's, Ted Williams relied upon Dad to help get his product selling. I do not know how things went, but I do know from Mom telling me that Ted Williams visited our home in Washington, New Jersey, to talk with Dad. Her account is humorous. She didn't realize how famous Ted Williams was. All she knew was he was tall, good-looking, and he played baseball for a living. Mom said he gave us baseball bats which we played with until they broke.

Our Celebrity
John Flynn—My Grandfather

We all called him Pop-Pop. I am including my grandfather in this chapter because of his contact with President Franklin D.

Roosevelt's son, Jim Roosevelt. John Flynn Sr. knew people in high positions within the Democratic Party during an important time of American history or of his "connections" during the nineteen-thirties and beyond Dad informed me of how his dad worked so hard to make our country a better place to live in and to feel free in. I was surprised and thrilled when Dad showed me the picture and note sent to Pop-Pop from Jim Roosevelt following the Democratic National Convention held in Philadelphia, Pennsylvania, in June 1936. It is a copy of the photo taken while President Franklin D. Roosevelt was signing one of the biggest pieces of financial security our nation ever saw—The Social Security Act—on August 15, 1935. And the copy of the photo has Jim Roosevelt's note to my grandfather on the back! What a piece of history.

I am sure most of you have encountered a celebrity or two in your life. Maybe you met a celebrity when you were in a restaurant, movie theater, or at a concert. If you grew up during the nineteen-sixties, you probably saw quite a few at concerts. I know we did! Our group of schoolmates went to every concert we could go to. My list is long, but I will spare you the length. We saw Elton John perform in Wildwood Convention Center in the early seventies during a big rainstorm. Only about three hundred made it there, but Elton played and talked to us throughout the storm. Water was coming through the ceiling onto his piano, but he continued after a few staff members moved his piano to a dry area on the stage. He joked about his music being "watered down." Elton didn't want to leave while the storm continued outside, so we got a bonus of him playing and singing for an extra hour or so. That night was memorable! My fellow classmates and I saw at least forty big name performers or groups from 1970 to 1975. When I was fifteen years old, I saw Santana perform at an open-air concert at the University of Miami. My brother John was a freshman there (spring of 1969), and my dad allowed me to visit John during our Easter break from school. I took a train from Philadelphia to Miami to visit him. I was able to watch Santana from the front edge of their stage. It was great! My favorite concert was Neil Young playing at a small theater. About twenty of us drove from Wildwood, New Jersey to Philadelphia, Pennsylvania, to see him perform. Because of the size of the theater, there were only a few hundred of us young people there. He took the time to talk directly to us in between his songs and ballads. He explained to us how he wrote some of his songs and of how ideas occurred to him. Neil Young was and still is a personal type of person who really is into his music.

The funniest event was Cheech and Chong. They gave a show in Wildwood at the Convention Center. It was about 1972 or so. The hall was packed, and they were late. An hour late, they ran onto the stage and yelled at us all for not giving them a ride. They were staying at Diamond Beach which is a few miles south of the Convention Center. If you have ever witnessed Cheech and Chong together, you can imagine how funny they were. They ended up walking the whole distance. They said that even the police rode by them without giving them a ride. There were two uniformed cops standing near the stage. Cheech and Chong really let them have it in a hilarious way. They used lines like, "We are glad you had to wait. Couldn't you see we were getting high? Any other time you would arrest us. But no, you just drove by because you were in a rush to see the concert. Well, we are the show, and our thumbs were out." They didn't use those exact words, but it is close to some of the things they were saying. They belittled all of us for not giving them a lift. They had us laughing for hours, and the police promised them a ride home. In fact, just about everyone there offered them a lift home as their show came to an end. The three-hour performance by Cheech and Chong that summer night was the funniest show I have ever seen performed live.

Fascination

It is a natural human reaction to want to see or meet people of extraordinary talent, skills, or fame. This is why we go to movies, concerts, and shows. We want to be entertained. We want to hear and see comedy. We want to root for a team or an athlete we favor. The problem we have today is celebrities are marketed to such a degree that is creates a falsehood. The celebrity is put into a position which makes his or her life a chore instead of a joy. Once the marketing begins, the simple things of life are harder to enjoy. Marketing has actually created celebrities who have done nothing involving talent or skill. Their fame is centered on vanity, craziness, or partying with the so-called in crowd. It seems these created celebrities don't last long and fade away in time. Americans seem to be infatuated a bit too much with celebrities, stars, and foreign royalty. This, of course, is just my own opinion. It is caused by the media, advertising, and the tabloids by constant attention toward this part of society. I may be called old-fashioned by expressing my opinion and believing that we need to "cool it" some on our ideas of fame and idolization. Today's celebrities are chased and hounded by photographers because the photos can sometimes bring big money. Personal privacy is ignored because of financial gain and the statures of being the person who "got the shot." Even celebrities need some personal privacy. They rarely have it today. It is the price anyone who seeks stardom should be ready to pay.

We have some very serious problems across our planet. Let the celebrities entertain us, but let us pay more attention to the environment, humans in need of the basic things of life (food, clothing, shelter), and the need to prevent wars everywhere. Education, communication, and new technology are important in preventing war. My message to the young people reading this chapter is, "It is good to be entertained and to have fun. Keep a balance between having fun and having purpose. Put less concern on fame. Put more concern on your own life. Keep it, life going forward!"

CHAPTER 10

Good-Natured

It is a pleasure being around people who are good-natured. Think of a person you know who always seems to be in a good mood and has a pleasing effect on people. It is a state of mind. It is a positive spirit. It is a virtue, not a majority of people have. It is the seeing good in people. It is because they do not let negative things, thoughts, feelings, and people control them. It seems that good natural people are also healthy people. But then there are many cancer patients who have a good nature despite the pains they experience and the physical drain to their bodies caused by the cancer, the medications, and the treatments they go through. The next time you blame a minor injury or a temporary cold for making you grouchy, think of the young children dealing with cancer or other serious medical problems who give the nurses and doctors a smile each day and put an effort toward not complaining. Or think about an elderly relative you have who knows their time on earth is nearing an end yet cares more about others than themselves.

Having a good nature within the workplace keeps others from complaining or becoming gloomy. The salesperson who makes people feel comfortable and projects a friendly attitude makes people want to come back. Whether the person works in a store, a fast-food establishment, or a real-estate office, people tend to return to places they feel good about. The product, its price, and quality are very important, but it is not everything. With the amount of competition there is, a business needs an edge on other businesses. Making the customer feel happy is a good edge to have.

During many years as a volunteer Boy Scout leader, I just couldn't wait till we went camping again. The scout troop I was with had a team of adults who enjoyed laughing, telling jokes, and projecting positive attitudes. It was contagious! The boys would sit around the campfire for hours having as much fun as the adults. Boy Scout Troop #185 of North Wildwood, New Jersey, averaged a membership of fifty boys and eighteen to twenty volunteer leaders during the nineteen-seventies and eighties. We camped during the fall and winter months because our town is a resort area, and everyone worked long hours during the spring and summer. The boys learned outdoor skills and endured the harshness of winter but loved every minute of it. We cooked all our meals over the campfire or hot coals from the fire. The boys learned how to buy their own food, package it for the campouts, prepare their meals, and use the campfire or solar oven for cooking. Mealtime is a busy time on a campout but a good time. We ate pretty good! Because of the adults we had, it was always a fun event to be hiking, canoeing, or camping. We had the local police chief, the fire chief, two judges, a lawyer, two detectives, two firemen, and the rest of us who were either self-employed or working at local businesses. A few of those men have passed away over the years, but they are not forgotten. A few of the boys who were in the troop at the time have died early in life. One particular young man comes to mind. As a boy, his life can be described in the context of "good-natured." His smile and caring manner drew others to him. I wish to honor my friend by mentioning his name in this chapter. Harvey E. Forsyth, Jr. lived to be thirty-six years of age. Leukemia struck Harvey and took him from us all. His positive spirit and love of life touched his fellow scouts and made the many camping trips he participated in a bit more fun. A scout troop is made up of patrols. There are usually six to eight boys in a patrol, and each one had an adult to help them. Charles Cripps was the "patrol dad" for Harvey's patrol. Charlie was one of my good friends who passed on early in life also. I never heard Harvey use a curse word. He and his patrol members got along great. Much of this was because of Harvey and his good nature. His positive nature, his energy, and his outlook on life enriched those he spent time with and caused the boys with him to do the same. Respect and courtesy came natural to him. This reflects upon his mother and her example to him. I can remember one time when Harvey asked me to take him on a twenty-mile hike in order to finish his hiking merit badge. We were camping in the Pine Barrens of Southern New Jersey at the time. It was in February. The rest of the boys and adults were doing a ten-mile hike, so we stayed with them then set out to cover the other ten miles along the Batona Trail. We did it easily because Harvey never complained or asked, "How much farther?" In fact, he and I joked and talked so much the miles went by without us realizing how quickly we were finishing his requirement. Harvey was a runner, a lifeguard, a skilled swimmer, and a surfer. We surfed quite a few waves together before I had moved to Maine. I considered Harvey a true friend. We didn't spend much time together except for camping, canoeing, skiing, and surfing together, but I knew if I ever needed help with anything, he was the kind of person I could call. Harvey E Forsyth, Jr. is my example of a good-natured person. He is missed and remembered.

Every now and then, I will bump into one of the scouts or leaders from those days. The boys are adults now, and many have children of their own. Our discussions involve how much fun we had and how there never seemed to be any serious problems. That was due to the "nature" of how we all got along and acted together.

Surfing Friends

Because of writing and thinking about Harvey Forsyth, I just realized something. Most every person I spent time surfing with and hanging out at the beach after surfing have been people of good nature. I am thinking back over the years right now and picturing in my mind those who were my closest friends (not associates) because of surfing and hanging together. Jimmy Young and I surfed together during our grade school and high school years. Jimmy was my closest friend during those years. I met Jeff Walden because of surfing. I consider Jeff a friend for life even if we hardly see each other now. Earlier in this book, you read my poem, "Early Departure." It is because of surfing I met Michelle. Because of surfing, I met Sandy who was my soul mate. She did not surf, but she loved being on the beach and watching the ocean. I taught Ron Samartino how to surf. This part of *Pure Power* is dedicated to him. Troy Cawley and I surfed and snowskied together for quite a few years. I guess it is the same with skateboarders. You love the art, you associate with those who love the art, and you hang out together because of what you have in common. Every person I just mentioned is, or was, a person of good nature. I value the times spent with every one of those friends. They are true friends. Every one of them saw the value of appreciating the simple things in life. I can honestly say I never had a negative feeling or thought about any one of them. They all have enriched my life!

Now I am wondering, what is it about the surfing scene that fosters good-natured people? Is it the vast ocean and the waves it produces? Is it the sunshine and the saltwater? It is the natural high you get while riding the waves? Is it the excitement some feel by riding waves in the Great Lakes (fresh water and bordered by land)? Who knows? The good thing is my associations with these good people made me a better person. Thank you, Harvey, Jimmy, Jeff, Michele, Sandy, Ronnie, and Troy. God bless you all.

Negative

In order to have a positive, you need a negative to compare the two. It is like having good and bad. If we don't like to have a few bad days now and then, how can we appreciate the good days? We can understand what causes a good-natured person by understanding what causes grumpiness or peevishness. We simply look at the opposites and compare them. We all have times when it is difficult to be in good spirits. Things happen in life which causes us to feel down at times. Sometimes, we don't even realize we are being moody until someone tells us. It is natural for humans to have "off days," but it is up to us to make those times as short as possible. Catching oneself acting or thinking negatively then correcting oneself is a good thing. Sometimes, we need the help and advice of others to rid the negativity. Being of negative mind for long periods of time hurts our relationships with others and endangers our inner peace. So what are some of the things which cause us to be grumpy and peevish? Medications can cause changes in our attitudes, especially when a person is taking a number of medicines concurrently. Loss of a loved one can cause people to become short tempered or irritable. Abuse of alcohol affects people in different ways. Some over intoxicated people become abusive and violent while others become overly sociable. The use of drugs, which are basically chemicals, causes people to act, react, speak, and think unnaturally. Different drugs cause different reactions and mood swings. You could be "up" one minute then "down" the next minute. The abuse of either alcohol or drugs is certainly a negative when it comes to being a good-natured person. Do you wish to be a person of good nature? Do you want people to enjoy being around you? If you do, avoid the negatives daily and associate with positive thinking people who value having good clean fun. It may be easier said than done, but it is the truth, and it has been proven to work throughout society. Be true to yourself (no fakeness allowed). Have or be around people who enjoy good humor. Keep things simple and help out those having tough times. Remember, you cannot help others much unless you yourself are strong, so take care of yourself in order to help others. Identify the negatives in your life. This way, you are aware of what can hold you back and affect your nature.

Speech

How we speak to others or about others matters tremendously concerning our manner of socializing. Think about this example. You and your coworkers get together after work at a local restaurant for a meal. There are eight of you sitting together at a table with other patrons of the restaurant sitting at their tables near you. You have one person with you who just cannot talk without using profanity as he talks. Some of the words are not too mild. At work, this same person uses the *F* word frequently. But now you have others sitting near your group, and it makes you and others sitting in your group feel uncomfortable and embarrassed by the cursing. Does the use of profanity offend others? If you think it does offend others, then how could the use of curse words and profanity seem "cool" to a lot of people and many young people? A person who gives presentations to business groups or gives speeches at schools certainly does not want to use these words. Why?

Is gossip a negative or a positive? It can be either. When speaking about a person in a good way, even though it is talking about someone, you are speaking of them in a positive light. When the gossip is idle rumors dealing in derogatory talk about another person then of course it is a negative. To hurt someone's reputation or to demean their character by using unfounded rumors or untruthful conversation about them is definitely negative and opposite of being good natured. In fact, a good-natured person will not want to hear such talk because it goes against their nature. People who gossip regularly can get "carried away" with their talk. We need to correct them at times by asking the question. "Have you looked in the mirror lately?" We all become negative at times. It is human nature. We can catch ourselves becoming negative, or we can be corrected by someone. Usually, it is a spouse or a close friend who will correct us. We can keep ourselves in check by listening to ourselves. It is like the old saying, "Did you hear what you just said?" Some people give the advice to think before you speak. This is good advice. It can keep a person out of trouble at times, and it can help to keep a person more likeable. My grandparents had a saying, "It is sometimes better to say nothing than to speak of ill things." This also means something like, in order to keep the peace, you "bite your tongue" a bit. Or it may mean with somethings said we only do harm. My grandparents were very experienced in life and always had our best interests in mind.

How You Are Perceived

If it is important to you of how people describe you and of how they see you as a person, then I hope this chapter helps you to become better natured and to treat the people around you in good ways. Are you a boss? Do your employees like working for you? Working at a particular place is not simply about money. The atmosphere in the workplace is very important, and a good-natured boss will make productivity a stable asset. Are you a desk clerk at a hotel? Do repeat customers enjoy seeing you, or do they just conduct their business and go to their rooms? Do you manage a store? How many of your customers know you and talk with you when they come to purchase items? In New England (Vermont, New Hampshire, Maine), the old "General Store" was the social center of many small towns because of the atmosphere encouraged by the owner. It was the "nature" of doing business. Are you the captain of a party fishing boat? How do the fishermen and woman see you? Do they say you are knowledgeable about the sport of fishing? Do they come onto your boat because they like your telltales? Remember, fishing tales are very popular, but most are exaggerated. The fish always grows during the tale. During my younger years, I fished regularly on the party boats out of Cape May, New Jersey. The captain's demeanor had much to do with us returning to his boat time after time. With a captain who made us laugh and taught us a few tricks on how to hook fish more often, our fishing trips were times we looked forward to. How do most people perceive the captain? The captain is seen as the most important "part" of the boat. You can have a fancy boat with a lot of flair, but the people will still seek out the best captain. That also goes for the captain's mate who has the constant connection with the quests on board.

In general, people enjoy being seen favorably. If this is how you feel, then take the two words *good-natured* and become that person. You will be pleased at the results!

CHAPTER II

Loss

When thinking about loss, we consider the losing of something, someone, or a cherished pet. When a human dies, their body returns to nature because of decay or cremation, but their spirit lives on. Every human has a soul. The soul is the spirit which continues according to God's wishes. Imagine how many souls there are. Since the first man and woman until now, the number must be enormous. Loss is something we all deal with. We also deal with loss in different ways. When I wrote the chapter titled "Understanding Death," I did not realize my thoughts and my revelations would affect so many people. The most common letters I received from teens were letters concerning teenage suicide. The letters were of their own thoughts and survival. Letters concerning suicide outnumbered the letters concerning music, humor, or friendship. It pains me every time when I hear of someone taking their own life.

To many people the loss of a pet is like losing a family member. Sometimes, the loss of a pet is a child's first experience of what death is. To witness their pet motionless, still, and not breathing is a shock to all children. *It* is a lesson not easily learned about life. Whether it is their cat, dog, turtle, fish, etc., the child feels loss for the first time and needs someone to explain why their pet is gone. The tears on the child's cheeks are real because of the feelings and love they have. Many adults remember the first pet they lost and the mixed emotions they felt as a young person experiencing death for the first time. I have helped to bury several dogs and cats over the years for people who saw their pet as a family member. It isn't easy, but it is a reality.

Parents

Since I published *Pure Power* (parts I and II) and after my walking was done, both Mom and Dad have passed away and joined God in heaven. They had happy years together. They were married for fifty-three years, and they raised five of us. Mom was the best good-natured person you could ever meet. Not long before her death, she told me she would be "wearing her wings" and seeing Dad, her mom, dad, brother, and sisters again soon. It was clear blue sky that day and only a few puffy clouds. She pointed up to one of those clouds and said, "I'll land on that one." We laughed. She had a humor which is only explained by the term "old Irish humor." Her eyes, gestures, and manner of speaking were all part of her humor. I mention my father often within this book. He worked hard, put in over four years with other brave soldiers during World War II, he loved to fish and follow sports. His love of history and his knowledge of American history could have enabled him to be a history teacher. He dedicated his entire adult life to Mom and us five. The loss of Dad and then Mom is a true loss, but I rejoice in believing they are with God and His heavenly family. Someday, we will all know the answer to our afterlife. For now, it is a belief given to us from Jesus when he taught his apostles and his followers while He was here on earth.

Most everyone experiences loss during their lives, everyone except the millions of those aborted who never get a chance to experience life outside the womb. It is my belief their souls go right to heaven!

The ways people deal with losing a loved one, a close friend, or a relative varies. Some mourn for a while then get on with their lives. They do not forget the person who died, but their mourning turns to memories. This is how I am. Some people mourn for years or even the rest of their lives. I feel sorry for them because the person they mourn would probably not have wanted this. Eternal life is a celebration. Mourning is for the living. The most celebrated day for the Catholic Church is Easter because it is when Jesus was resurrected and proved to us that He is God's Son. The Friday before Easter Sunday is the day of mourning, but Easter is a time of great celebration. Christmas and Easter are the two most celebrated days of the Catholic Church. They both celebrate life!

When a person close to me dies, I remember all the good times, the experiences, the love shared, and the fun we had doing things together. I picture the person in my mind's eye. I do this every time I am reminded of the person who I lost. I do this as I write about those I mentioned in this book. I realize I could be joining them at any time, or it may be years from now. Only God knows. I have sorted through my photos while writing this book, and I have come across photos of those who have left us. I do not mourn when I see their photos. I remember them and what they were doing at the time the pictures were taken. We relive good times because of photos. They are missed, but they are also remembered! The toughest loss just has to be the loss of a son or a daughter, especially if they are children. I think only a parent who is torn apart by losing their child can tell you how tough it is to cope with the loss.

The tragedy which happened on September 11, 2001, shocked every American and many of good people across the globe. I want to remember all the innocent people who were killed that day in New York, Pennsylvania, and Washington DC. Also I wish to remember every American person of our military who have died overseas because they answered the call to fight against and prevent anymore terrorist attacks against our nation and our people. Their sacrifices keep us safer here at home and prevents terrorist from harming other innocent civilians. The attack to our nation on American soil was a wakeup call to how hateful and evil those people are who kill others because of what their fellow believers say. There is no justification for murdering children, women, and the elderly. God is their Judge. I feel no loss for the terrorist. The world is safer without them.

Degree of Loss

The loss of a love one, an associate, or of the aborted unborn child is of the highest degree of loss. The loss of a pet, especially a pet considered as family, is of a high degree of loss. We feel a degree of loss even when we don't know the person or persons who die in tragic ways or circumstances. This is exemplified by how we felt when we heard about the school shootings at Columbine, Virginia Tech, and Sandy Hook Elementary School in Newtown, Connecticut. I think back to the loss our nation felt when John F. Kennedy, our president and energetic leader, was assassinated or when Martin Luther King was assassinated early in his life. Most of us never met or were not near both of these great leaders, yet we felt the loss of not having them alive and well. President John F. Kennedy, his brother Robert Kennedy, and Martin Luther King were all shot and killed during the nineteen-sixties. It was a time of change within the American culture, and all three of these men were leaders of change. The changes they caused and spoke about were changes of good substance and thinking. The loss of their leadership, knowledge, courage, and dedication was, and is, a loss to the country. It was, and is, our loss. They went on to another life; the spiritual life in heaven, I believe.

Abortion is one of the most controversial issues in the United States. It should not be. The reason I say it should not be is because abortion is the cause of millions of lives being stopped just after life is begun. It is the loss of life! If a doctor has to sacrifice the life of an unborn baby to save the life of the mother, I see this as justified and the decision of the doctor, whose life is dedicated to saving lives and helping people within the medical world simply because a female does not want a child or cannot support a child is no reason to have the fetus killed. You are alive and reading this book because you were allowed to live. Shouldn't this same allowance be given to all others? The arguments on both sides of the abortion issue are many. I see it as choosing life over death. The problem is, the life at stake has no say about it. We can also ask, "What answer to this issue would God give us?" More American lives have been ended by abortions in the United States then by all the wars our country has fought. This is one serious loss! We need to elevate the importance of life to a much higher degree and to emphasize the loss of an unborn child is the loss of life. Think about the person you love the most. Then thank their mother for not aborting them. We should not cause death, even if it is an unborn life within the womb. Adoptions need to be encouraged more.

This may be a short chapter, but it is probably the most serious chapter in this book. It is also not an easy topic to talk about because loss affects every one of us, and sometimes, it brings back the tears. Because death is a reality and it is definite, I have done my best to explain it in my own way. Death is not the end because our souls live on! Our spirits stay alive with the people who loved us and remember us.

Chapter 12

Relaxation

The saying "All work and no play makes Bill a dull boy" is very true. We need to balance ourselves when it comes to work and relaxation. Feeling overstressed and tired out is the end result of working too much and not giving oneself time for relaxation. If you ask, "What is too much?" I can give you my opinion which has no scientific proof. It is simply based upon personal experience. It shocks some people when I tell them I like to work. In today's world, the word *work* is not very popular. People today look for many ways not to work, and most people actually count the years and days until retirement. What a poor reflection this is on the job they have. Today's culture of avoiding work creates a problem for the country because the nation needs to maintain stability and strength through productivity. A productive nation is a strong nation. Supplying energy, developing new technology, building the things needed for transportation, growing food, delivering the water and treating the waste, making the clothes, building the shelters and the numerous other necessities of a country are the jobs people have to do. Unless we have robots everywhere it is people who see that tasks are completed.

There are jobs I just do not enjoy doing. Whenever I have to do them, I get through it because sometimes we just have to do things out of necessity. One such necessity is proofing and editing my writings. I love to write. I do not see writing as work even though it is. I feel I am expressing an art by writing. But when it comes to having to correct my writings so those who read it can understand the writings in a clear manner, I get through it! I am relaxed when I write. I can write for four to six hours after working an eight-hour shift of doing maintenance work and not feel overworked. Putting my thoughts down on paper or telling stories by writing is actually a relaxation for me. Many of you who write journals, keep diaries, or write poems understand this. The chore comes when you have to organize everything. But it is a necessity if you want your writings produced into a book form.

Some of the ways in which we relax and relieve our everyday stresses are physically demanding. During most of my life, the three most favorite ways of relaxing have been surfing, learning, and teaching the art of karate and hiking through forested areas or up mountain trails to reach the summit. The physical tiredness which comes from surfing, karate, or hiking is a healthy thing. I call it a "good tired." These three hobbies helped me to keep my mind clean and my spirit good. Because of my back injuries, I had to change my ways of relaxing mentally. I still experience pain along my spine, but I live with it. I do not complain. I accept it for what it is, and I feel lucky because I can still do most everything I use to do. My forms of relaxation are now writing, doing work I enjoy doing, and resting my body with a daily nap after work. The goal I have of traveling around the country to promote this book and my other books will be another form of relaxation even though it will require a great deal of effort and earning money through book sales to keep the goal alive.

People with occupations that involve high degrees of mental stress tend to relax differently than those people who have physically demanding occupations. Years ago, I fished with an officer from our local police department. His form of relaxation was fishing at night when hardly anyone else were on the water in their boats. We fished the back bay area and inlet north of our island home. He told me several times that he needed to be away from the crowds and to be in a quiet, peaceful environment a few times a week. The spots we fished were just that. We were away from the crowds and drifting with the currents. He was a terrific person. He worked his way up to becoming the chief of police. He was also on the local Boy Scout troop committee. He spent four or five years helping the scouts. Sitting around the campfire telling stories, laughing at jokes, or simply staring into the fire was another form of relaxation for him. While his son was in scouts, he made almost every campout. I recall him telling us how important it was for him to be able to "unwind" and enjoy the atmosphere we had around our campfires. Police work is very stressful because they are mostly dealing with other people's problems. They deal with violent people, disoriented people, criminals, hateful people, ungrateful people, etc. Who do we call when we need help? Having Bill work with the scout troop was a good asset, and the boys who are now men in their forties all remember him. He gave the boys a good path to follow!

How do we relax? Have you ever thought on the ways different people relax? Do you keep a balance between being active and relaxing? Some people relax too much while others need to relax more often. Our financial situations determine plenty on how we can relax. Many people have to work two jobs just to pay their rent, mortgage, have enough food to eat, and/or support their children. People who work and live week to week financially are hit the hardest when our country's economy is bad. During times like this, relaxation is far down the list for people trying to survive financially. For the people who are lucky enough to be financially sound, relaxation is on the top of their list. Personally, I am with those who are living week to week. I live on what I make by working hard. The government does not help me, and I do not ever want to rely on the government. I do wish the government, on all levels, would not tax us so much. They tax us on everything they can. We could all relax a bit more if the government didn't have their hidden "taxes" on everything we use or buy. Have they taxed toilet paper yet?

Along the East Coast of the United States, there are tolls everywhere. There are tolls on roads, bridges, and tunnels. When you travel west away from the East Coast and northeast United States, the tolls dwindle in numbers and actually disappear the further west you go. California is highly populated, yet they do not have tolls. You can cross over the Hoover Dam and not have to pay a toll.

How to people who work at the toll booths relax after they finish a day of sitting and standing in a booth the size of a closet? I am guessing they take a walk, jog, or run a few miles or take a swim.

Maybe they go dancing. I hope they don't go and sit in a bar some-where. I doubt anyone suffers from claustrophobia is working at these toll booths. I could be wrong, but I just can't see it happening. They certainly would not be too relaxed while working. Maybe they are the ones who are frowning as you drive through and hand them your money. Well, it used to be your money. You paid a tax on the gas you bought, and now you are taxed again as you drive through the toll. Don't worry. Relax and let your big government keep growing. For those who do not get it, I am being cynical.

Where we live has an effect on how we relax. People living in the suburbs like to have barbecues. People living in the city like to sit out on their porches or "stoops" and watch the activities of the neighborhood. People living in the country like to ride horses, take their ATV (all-terrain vehicle) out for a ride, or go for a swim at a pond or lake. The one activity everyone has for relaxation is watching television or a movie on their entertainment center. Going to a movie at a theater used to be very popular and a common thing to do on the weekends. Because of the costs and because you can now see movies at home with your friends and family members, going to movie the-aters is more of a night out than the weekly ritual it was. Before the VCR and DVD or cable networks, going to a movie in your town was a common form of relaxation and socializing. With technology comes changes. I was in seventh grade when I had my first date. We met at the movie theater! During my school years (1960s to 1970s), we all met on Friday nights during the fall, winter, and spring at Hunts Theatre in Wildwood, New Jersey, to see whatever movie was playing. It was as much a social thing as it was watching a movie you could not see on television. Cable television did not come to Wildwood until 1975. The most common way of dating was either going to a movie or to a dance held at our school to benefit the PTA (parent-teachers association) or our Booster Club which supported our sport teams. You do not have to relax when you are a student. You just go out and have some fun!

People of different ages relax in different ways. The older person may relax by sitting and taking naps more often. A young person may relax by playing basketball with friends or even taking a kayak for a run on the rapids. A middle age person would do either, depending upon the individual. Our energy level, physical abilities, post injuries, medical situations, and our "frame of mind" determine how we relax as we age. It is normal to slow down after forty or fifty years of living. It is also normal for our desires to change while we age. At the age of twenty, you are looking ahead. At age of seventy, you start looking back. Reminiscing is a form of relaxation for many people who reach their seventies, eighties, and beyond. It is a good thing. To be able to remember the good times and the people who meant so much to you over the years is a blessing. With the reminiscing, there is usually laughter associated with the memories. Laughter is a relaxing activity for both the body and the spirit. The world needs more laughter and joy. There is too much of the opposite going on today. The people who have the gift of making others laugh is a positive thing. They cause people to relax and to enjoy the moment. I just had a thought! How does a mortician relax? I'll leave the humor up to you.

Relax on the Road

A problem which has been around for a while now is termed "road rage." It happens all over the country where traffic is heavy and people are in a rush. It is very common in the state I live in now. It's a matter of the lack of courtesy and patience. If drivers could be more considerate and be in less of a hurry to get to where they are going, road rage would not be common. It might surprise you who hits their horns the most and speeds around you. My experience has shown me it is young females or middle age men who do. I drive with courtesy. Many times, after speeding around me, I pull up behind that driver at the next red light. They were in such a hurry, yet here I am right behind them waiting for the light to change. I smile every time! Road rage is no way to relax. It causes problems. If you tend to get upset while operating a vehicle, keep in mind a few things: 1) the person you just gave an obscene gesture to might just be diving an unmarked police vehicle; 2) the person you just curse at might just be a person suffering with cancer and they are on the way to get chemotherapy treatments; 3) the people you just yelled at, hit your horn at, and sped by just might be gang members who will pursue you and maybe even hurt you. Calm down. Relax and stay alive longer.

Relaxation, like many things in life, is good when kept in balance. Over relaxation can cause boredom, gain of weight, relaxed muscles, or poor blood circulation. To relax after a good workout feels more rewarding than simply relaxing for the sake of relaxing. To take a short time to relax in between business meetings lets one gather their thoughts and ease the stress, if there is any. Whatever form of relaxation you choose, it helps your body, mind, and spirit to keep a balance. The result is positive. God tells us to relax and worship one day of the week. His command should show us how important relaxation is. We are instructed to "keep holy the Sabbath Day," which is the seventh day of the week. For the Jewish faith, this is Saturday. For the Christian faith, it is observed on Sundays. The point is, God instructs us to relax and worship on the seventh day. For other faiths, I am sure relaxation (to rest) is in their doctrines. Rest is for the body, the mind, and the spirit. Our lives after death will be our eternal rest.

This chapter concerning relaxation has a connection with the chapter concerning simplicity. Keep it simple. Relax. Many of you read books to relax. I can relate to that! Reading a good novel takes you into another world for a time. I think reading is still one of the most common forms of relaxation for people. Some people like studying. Some like history. Some like fiction while others like non-fiction. No matter what the desire, reading sure is good way to relax.

CHAPTER 13

Trivia

Because people have fun playing trivia with their friends or at small group gatherings, I have decided to include a collection of trivia questions I have written out over the years. Every now and then over the past twenty years, I have jotted down certain questions for a variety of age groups. The questions range from the first grade level up to a high school level. Most of all, the questions are general knowledge so we can get most of them right. I have not used any sources for information except may own memory from learning about things over the years. The answers are at the end of each group of trivia questions. Have fun!

1. What scandal caused President Nixon to resign as president?
2. Who became our president after Nixon?
3. What is a mass of polluted air hanging low over a city?
4. What room does a judge try cases in?
5. What is the first day of the week?
6. Is an oak tree a hardwood or softwood tree?
7. What commonly used book gives us the spelling and meaning of words?
8. What is the capital of Maine?
9. What sport involves a player, a puck, at stick, a goal net, and ice?
10. What is the neutral color?
11. What was the largest land mass purchase our country had?
12. Which US president began our space program?

13. What is 12 plus 13, minus 6, times 2, divided by 2 equals?
14. What does FBI stand for?
15. What is another name used for water moccasin snake?
16. Where does natural rubber come from?
17. What sport did American football develop from?
18. Is a whale a mammal?
19. Does a whale breathe air?
20. What is the joint between your hand and your forearm?

Answers

1. Watergate
2. Gerald Ford
3. Smog
4. Courtroom
5. Sunday
6. Hardwood
7. Dictionary
8. Augusta
9. Ice Hockey
10. White
11. Louisiana Purchase
12. John F. Kennedy
13. Nineteen
14. Federal Bureau of Investigation
15. Cotton Mouth
16. Sap of tropical plants
17. Rugby
18. Yes
19. Yes
20. Wrist

*****

1. What do we call a person who worries a lot?
2. Is a snake a reptile or a mammal?

3.   What is the capital of France?
4.   What southeastern state is a peninsula?
5.   Is the state of New Jersey a peninsula?
6.   What American state consists of islands?
7.   What do we call a horse of a small breed?
8.   Where does pork come from?
9.   Is a copperhead snake poisonous?
10. What do we call a young goat?
11. What is the sixth month of the year?
12. What do we call a rock wall built out into the ocean to protect a harbor or a beach?
13. What is our northern most state?
14. What river divides New Jersey from Pennsylvania?
15. What is the largest man-made dam in the United States?
16. What is the cup used by Jesus at the Last Supper referred to as?
17. What does XVIII equal to?
18. What is a group of war ships under one command?
19. Are the leaves of a dandelion plant (weed) edible?
20. What plant family is the clover of?

Answers

1.   Worrywart
2.   Reptile
3.   Paris
4.   Florida
5.   Yes
6.   Hawaii
7.   Pony
8.   A pig
9.   Yes
10. Kid
11. June
12. A Jetty
13. Alaska

14. Delaware River
15. Hoover Dam
16. The Holy Grail
17. Eighteen (roman numeral)
18. A fleet
19. Yes
20. The pea family

Quiz Time
Three

1. What does a cloud consist of?
2. What does 3 plus 6, divided by 3, times 10, minus 6 equals?
3. What president of the United States was a general and a commanding officer during WWII?
4. What is the common language of Austria?
5. Is a pickerel fish of salt water or fresh water?
6. What family does the leopard belong to?
7. How many days does Lent consist of?
8. When does leap year occur?
9. Where does lard come from?
10. Does a spruce tree have leaves?
11. Is an oak tree deciduous?
12. Who was the second king of Israel?
13. Is a pine tree a hardwood or a softwood tree?
14. What is the capital city of Alabama?
15. What is the capital of Italy?
16. What does YMCA stand for?
17. How many yards measure a football field?
18. Of what branch of government is the US president of?
19. How many branches of government does the US Government have?
20. What country began WWII in Europe?

Answers

1. Water
2. Twenty-four
3. Dwight D. Eisenhower
4. German
5. Freshwater fish
6. Cat family
7. Forty
8. Every four years
9. Hog's fat
10. No
11. Yes
12. King David
13. Softwood
14. Montgomery
15. Rome
16. Young Men's Christian Association
17. One hundred
18. Executive Branch
19. Three
20. Germany

The playing of trivia with others increases your general knowledge. It is a fun activity for millions of people. Teachers who use trivia questions inside the classrooms make learning fun when they put it into a game type forum. Trivia contests between students make them study various subjects, do extensive research, and expand their knowledge. This is another reason I have put a whole chapter on trivia. I hope our student's knowledge about our nation's history increases. American history is not taught in schools like it was in the past. The many facts (not opinions) about the United States and what makes our country unique is not taught regularly. As a result, you will have students who cannot answer simple questions about our nation's history or even its geography. Knowledge needs to be within a student's brain. They should not rely so heavily on getting their answers from electronic devices. A student going into the business world after graduation should be able to figure simple mathematics using their own brain if they wish to succeed in life. What if the electricity goes out? What if the Internet is out of service? Our brains are reliable, and they function because of our own energy levels. Our brain power travels with us wherever we go. The more knowledge we put into our brains the more benefits we receive in the long run. You can look at your brain as your personal, living computer which is vastly underused.

I am breaking down the trivia sheets into twenty questions and answers so you and your group can keep score if you wish. You can also design your own game plan and time schedule, as you choose. I hope you enjoy the average questions I have put together so that almost everyone can play along. For parents or grandparents, I have put a few very easy ones together for younger children. If I have any mistakes, I am sure I will hear about them. Before going to print, I have tried the various sheets with small groups of people to see if I have made any mistakes. So far so good!

Quiz Time
Four

1. What is the capital of the state of Montana?
2. What is enclosed within a pine cone?
3. What is the capital of the state of Pennsylvania?
4. Where does solar energy come from?
5. A world famous Weather Observatory Station is found atop what mountain of New Hampshire?
6. Is the wood from walnut trees used for making gunstocks?
7. What does a gypsy moth larvae feed on?
8. What is a major product of a wood pulp mill?
9. What is a mature female called concerning domesticated cattle?
10. What do we call a mature female elk?
11. What do we call the front part of a boat?
12. What is the back part of a boat?

13. What is the capital of Nebraska?
14. How many pints equal one quart?
15. What bay separates New Jersey from Delaware?
16. What famous store in Maine has no locks on its doors and is always open for business?
17. What bay does the Potomac River flow into?
18. Which two states border Washington DC?
19. Where does sugar come from?
20. Does cotton come from a plant?

Answers

1. Helena
2. Seeds
3. Harrisburg
4. The sun
5. Mount Washington
6. Yes
7. Tree leaves
8. Paper
9. Cow
10. A cow elk
11. Bow
12. Stern
13. Lincoln
14. Two
15. Delaware Bay
16. L.L. Bean
17. Chesapeake Bay
18. Maryland and Virginia
19. Sugarcane and maple trees
20. Yes

Quiz Time
Five

1. What body of water borders Florida to its west?
2. Is a maple tree a softwood tree?
3. What region of the United States is sage bush commonly found?
4. What do we call the right-hand side of a ship or boat?
5. In what country did the sport of baseball originate?
6. What does 3 plus 3, minus 2, times 6, divided by 8 equals?
7. What two territories were admitted as states to the United States in 1959?
8. What body of water separates Alaska from Russia?
9. What is the capital of Massachusetts?
10. How many Great Lakes are there in the Northeastern United States?
11. Which river separates New York state from Canada?
12. Which officer commands a naval fleet?
13. American football developed from which game?
14. Is the nut of a Beech Tree edible?
15. Of what color is the American songbird Cardinal?
16. From where do cashew nuts come from?
17. Which state borders Montana on its west side?
18. How many states does the Pacific Ocean border?
19. What is the outside covering of a tree?
20. What is the common term used to describe an unmarried man?

Answers

1. Gulf of Mexico
2. No
3. Western
4. Starboard
5. United States
6. Three

7. Alaska and Hawaii
8. Bering Sea
9. Boston
10. Five
11. Saint Lawrence River
12. An admiral
13. Rugby
14. Yes (Beech Nut)
15. Bright red
16. A tropical tree
17. Idaho
18. Five
19. Bark
20. Bachelor

Quiz Time
Six

1. From which cultural folk line does the leprechaun originate?
2. The side of a mountain away from prevailing winds is called what?
3. The nickname of a person who favors their left hand is what?
4. What part of a building is a penthouse located?
5. How many states make up the United States of American?
6. What do the Roman numerals XV equal to?
7. What ship can operate under water?
8. What is the left side of a ship or boat called?
9. Where is the keel of a boat located?
10. What do the Florida Keys consist of?
11. How many sides does a rectangle have?
12. What does six times six, minus four, plus eighteen, divided by five equal to?
13. How many states have borders with the Atlantic Ocean?
14. What survey line divides the North and South in the eastern US states?

15. Which island of the Hawaiian Islands is the largest?
16. How many states border Nebraska?
17. Which state borders Texas on its western side?
18. What do we call a house where Catholic priests live?
19. In what country did the D-day Invasion of WWII take place?
20. What does the Japanese word KARATE mean in English?

Answers

1. Old Irish
2. Leeward Side
3. Lefty
4. Top
5. Fifty
6. Fifteen
7. Submarine
8. Port
9. Bottom length
10. Islands
11. Four
12. Ten
13. Fourteen
14. Mason-Dixie Line
15. Hawaii
16. Six
17. New Mexico
18. A Rectory
19. France
20. Empty hand

Quiz Time
Seven

1. Who was the first pope of the Roman Catholic Church?
2. How many quarts equal a gallon?

3. How many degrees of longitude equal twenty-four hours?
4. What is the capital of the United Kingdom?
5. What do we call a wood boring worm which destructs wooden structures?
6. What elements make up the center core of a pencil?
7. What is the common term used to describe a basketball rim?
8. Is the juice from a honeysuckle plant flower edible?
9. What river would you cross to go from Mississippi to Arkansas?
10. What river flows along the Texas/Mexico border?
11. The Great Salt Lake is in which state?
12. During the Revolutionary War between the Colonialists and the British how did the colonialist describe the British soldiers?
13. The group of islands stemming out from Alaska Peninsula are named what?
14. How many feet equal one mile?
15. Is a potato a vegetable or fruit?
16. What part of the asparagus plant is used to eat with our meals?
17. What are the two common colors of a lilac bush or shrub?
18. On a compass, which degree shows us south?
19. After WWII, what Bill was passed by the government to help our military people returning from war get restarted in civilian life?
20. What country shares the largest border with the United States?

Answers

1. Saint Peter the apostle
2. Four
3. 360
4. London
5. A termite

6. Graphite containing lead
7. Hoop ("through the hoop")
8. Yes
9. Mississippi River
10. The Rio Grande River
11. Utah
12. The Redcoats
13. Aleutian Islands
14. 5280 feet
15. Vegetable
16. The Shoot
17. Blueish or light purple
18. 180
19. The GI Bill
20. Canada

Quiz Time for Children

1. What does four plus four equal to?
2. What is the fourth letter of the alphabet?
3. What kind of water does the ocean have?
4. What is the common color of a clear sky?
5. What ocean borders the Californian Coast?
6. What do we call a zippered bag used to sleep in while camping?
7. Who was the first president of the United States?
8. What does three plus four equal to?
9. What is the common color of grass?
10. Who is the person usually in charge of a boat or ship?
11. What do we call a boy who helps the priest during the Mass?
12. What is the ninth letter of the alphabet?
13. Who is the executive leader of our country?
14. What causes gravity on earth?
15. How many hours are in one day?
16. If you have no shoes or socks on your feet, you are what?

17. How many states does the United States have?
18. What part of our body allows us to smell?
19. What can you fly in the sky by holding it on string?
20. What building on a farm do the horses live in?

Answers

1. Eight
2. D
3. Saltwater
4. Blue
5. Pacific Ocean
6. Sleeping bag
7. George Washington
8. Seven
9. Green
10. The captain
11. Altar boy
12. I
13. The president
14. The earth's rotation
15. Twenty-four
16. Barefooted
17. Fifty
18. Our nose
19. A kite
20. A barn or stable

Quiz Time
Nine

1. What does 7 plus 6, minus 5, times 12, divided by 3 equal to?
2. What is a horse's fastest gait?
3. How so we refer to a teacher or spiritual advisor of Hinduism?
4. What is the Japanese term we use for a teacher of Karate?
5. Do oranges grow on trees or shrubs?

6. If you went to New York state to see a massive waterfall, where would you go?
7. What do we call a male deer?
8. Of what family of plants is the strawberry?
9. Do tulips multiply through seeds or bulbs?
10. During WWII which country in Europe became an ally of Germany?
11. What is the common outside covering of a surfboard?
12. What is the name of the London Police Headquarters?
13. What body of water divides the state of Michigan into two parts?
14. Is the color red a primary color or a combination of colors mixed?
15. Which pheasant has the most brilliant colors, the male or the female?
16. Are badgers fur covered animals?
17. On which Great Lakes does the state of Pennsylvania have a coastline on?
18. The centerpiece (or strings) of a surfboard is of what substance?
19. Does the lettuce plant grow from seeds or tubular bulbs?
20. During the Vietnam War what country backed and supported the North Vietnamese?

Answers

1. Thirty-two
2. A gallop
3. Guru
4. Sensei
5. Trees
6. Niagara Falls
7. A buck
8. Rose family
9. Bulbs
10. Italy

11. Fiberglass
12. Scotland Yard
13. Michigan Lake
14. Primary color
15. Male
16. Yes
17. Lake Erie
18. Lightweight wood
19. Seeds
20. China

Quiz Time for Children
Eight

1. What does eight plus two equal to?
2. How many letters are in the alphabet?
3. In what direction does the sun set?
4. What is the opposite of black?
5. How many inches equal one foot?
6. What does zero equal to?
7. How many days are in a week?
8. What is a young sheep called?
9. What is a young goat called?
10. What does six plus four equal to?
11. What is opposite of left?
12. Where does the light come from which reflects off the moon?
13. What does BSA stand for?
14. What is the fourth month of the year?
15. Which state borders New Brunswick, Canada?
16. What force keeps us from floating while standing on earth?
17. What does a moving ship leave behind it in the water?
18. Before learning to walk, what does a baby do to move across the room?
19. What is the color of growing grass?
20. What is a young bear called?

Answers

1. Ten
2. Twenty-six
3. West
4. White
5. Twelve
6. Nothing
7. Seven
8. A lamb
9. A kid
10. Ten
11. Right
12. Sun
13. Boy Scouts of America
14. April
15. Maine
16. Gravity
17. Wake
18. Crawl
19. Green
20. A cub

Quiz Time for Children
Eleven

1. What is the Earth's nearest neighbor?
2. Who was the first Disney character?
3. What is a young dog called?
4. What do we call the king's wife?
5. What does two plus three equal to?
6. What star heats the earth?
7. What parts of your body enable you to hear?
8. What letter is the eighth letter of the alphabet?
9. How many pennies equal one dime?
10. Where does wood come from?

11. Where does paper come from?
12. How do fish breathe?
13. What is a baby elephant called?
14. What do nine minus three equal to?
15. What part of the body keeps your blood moving?
16. How many people make a dozen?
17. What is at the top of the earth?
18. What is opposite of north?
19. What protects and covers our body?
20. What is water frozen by cold called?

Answers

1. Moon
2. Mickey Mouse
3. Puppy
4. Queen
5. Five
6. Sun
7. Ears
8. H
9. Ten
10. Trees
11. Trees
12. Through their gills
13. Calf
14. Six
15. Heart
16. Twelve
17. North Pole
18. South
19. Skin
20. Ice

CHAPTER 14

Whatever Your Belief or Religion

Because of our Nation's Constitution, I am able to write about a variety of topics, express my beliefs, and relate my opinions without being concerned about government censorship. I am a citizen of the United States of America, and I am protected by our Bill of Rights, and I have freedoms many people around the world do not have. I can write about religious beliefs and be comfortable listening to others expressing their religious beliefs. Our Founding Fathers were mainly Christians, yet they saw the value of having religious freedom within our nation so no one is persecuted for their beliefs. When you visit a city in the United States, you will see churches, synagogues, mosques, temples, and other buildings of worship spread throughout the city; it is a very common thing, and they coexist peacefully. Libraries have books and texts on most every religion or belief. Even atheism is covered. Atheism is a belief that there is no God. I am explaining this because readers who live in countries where their government censors contain books or even dialogue concerning religion or belief can know we are free to worship and express our beliefs.

Within the United States, we are slowing falling into a certain degree of censorship within our school systems. Because this book has a Christian theme and I mention Jesus Christ, I am prevented from speaking at most every public school if I mention God's name and speak about some of the things I write about. This is because Christianity is under attack within our country even though our country is founded on Christian/Judeo beliefs and principles. The majority of citizens of the United States are of the Christian belief, yet our public schools shun even the mentioning of God's name. Many parents are sending their children to private schools, charter schools, and even homeschooling their children because of the censorship public schools in American are participating in. The learning about any religion is educational. Because you learn about a particular religion does not mean your beliefs change. I went to Wildwood Catholic High School. We learned about other religions in our religion class. We were educated about the different religions around the world and of how their followers believed. It did not change my beliefs. It only strengthened my beliefs more.

As I am writing this, we have just celebrated the Christmas of 2012. Christmas is a national holiday in the United States. Unfortunately, it has become more of an economic season than a celebration of the birth of Jesus Christ. Remember? The original meaning of Christmas is because of a special baby being born in Bethlehem. The Wise men brought gifts, but that was after Jesus was born. Santa Claus came much later. It is a great season for the children, but I think we could cut back on the economic side quite a bit. The stories, the music, and the fun should all stay strong. The very calendar most of the world goes by is based upon the birth of Jesus. You have BC (before Christ) and AD (after Christ).

Knowledge is hard to suppress with having the Internet available in most every country around the globe. The Holocaust may not have happened or the number of Jews in Europe killed by the Nazis of Germany during WWII would have been considerably less if the Internet and cell phone technology was around then. Secrecy is how dictators, leaders with absolute power, and kings who are tyrants control their people. There are powerful leaders, even today, who censor religious worship and try to impose certain beliefs by using law. Most of the terrorism happening now is because of religious beliefs taken to an extreme level and used as an excuse for violence and control. Throughout history, this has happened. The system and the culture of the United States of America put religious freedom as a priority of its people. Many of the very first colonialists who came from Europe and settled in "the New Land," which is now America, came because they were escaping religious persecutions in their homelands. The desire to have freedom of worship caused entire families to cross the Atlantic Ocean during the era of navigational uncertainties and boats powered by wind. Along with our freedom to worship comes the respect for others to worship in their own ways. Governments should not dictate how people pray or have faith in God or their gods. The God I believe in is the Supreme Being which most major religions have as their core belief. There is only one God. That is why we use a capital G when writing His name. The Romans and Greeks during the time of Jesus had many gods. Jesus spoke of only one God and referred to Him as the Father. Jesus taught us the prayer, the Our Father, which is referred to as the Lord's Prayer. The Roman Empire was a theocracy because the emperor ruled as a god. We, in America, and in many other countries will not allow a theocracy to happen because God comes before government and government here is of the people, for the people, and by the people. Since the people worship in different ways and have different beliefs, the people will protect diversity.

There is God's Law, and there is religion law. The Ten Commandments are God's Law, and the Bible is the Word of God. Remember, I am speaking and writing as a Catholic person. Religion law is of human origin and can be changed by humans as it has been done in the past. No human can change God's Law because it is absolute and of divine origin. The differences in religions are what causes wars and terrorism. It is the human origin of religion law which is fought over, argued, and causes conflict. Debating is a healthy thing as long as emotions and human desires are kept in check. We have continuous debates about religion beliefs, yet the "control" of other's beliefs are not considered because of our freedom, as I have written about. We have extremists. They are a small (very small) percentage of the population. Our government officials are of various religions backgrounds and of every ethnic background. Diversity is what makes American special and at the same time united. My ancestors are from England and Ireland. My two grandmothers and one grandfather came from Ireland. My Grandfather Wilson was English. I consider myself American. I am of the American culture. I consider myself lucky and blessed because of the rights and freedoms we enjoy here in the United States. Many Americans have given their lives or limbs to protect the rights and liberty we have. From the Revolutionary War to the Korean War, we have battled tyranny. America does not have to engage itself in conflicts around the world unless our security as a nation and the security of our people are at stake. We do not need to shed America blood over political battles or ideologies. We do need to protect ourselves from terrorism which is a whole new kind of war and it has its base with religion. Communication, education, knowledge, and trade will help to combat terrorism, but it will continue because of extremism and hate. There are many Americans who are of the Muslim religion. These Americans practice their faith openly and are protected by the same rights I enjoy. I am sure many Muslims will read this book. The extremists will not like my writings and probably hate me. Most American Muslims will not hate me but will look at this book as an educational text because it shows how an average Catholic American thinks, lives, ponders, explains, and believes. I am only one American out of nearly four hundred million, but I am considered an average and typical citizen. The reason I write about Muslims here in the United States is because of the terrorists who hijacked the planes and flew them into the World Trade Center, the Pentagon, and into a field in Pennsylvania on September 11, 2001. They were of Islam faith. They murdered innocent people; women, men, and children of various faiths. They were following Bin Laden's plan of attacking Americans and killing Americans. These murderers were extremists, and our nation took the offensive against their fellow extremists because our national security is at risk and the citizens of the United States do not tolerate terrorists. We have people in our military who are Muslins. They are Americans just like me. They are ready to shed their blood or give their lives to protect our country. They do not fight because of religion. They fight to protect our nation, its people, and its sovereignty. We are a sovereign nation because we are independent and we govern ourselves. These men and women of the military have enlisted to keep it that way.

Mark my words! What happened on 9/11/01 will never be forgotten. It is not about capitalism. It is about innocent Americans being killed! It is about our national security being breached and our freedom being attacked. The American public woke up. A sleeping giant was awakened and put on the offensive. Our intelligence department has been strengthened, and we citizens are more watchful now. The sleeping giant is a metaphor for the people of America. We are not called the United States of America for nothing. When tragedy strikes, our people *unite* as one.

My chapter title, "Whatever Your Belief or Religion," is so worded to let you, the reader, know that I am not preaching to anyone. I am expressing my thoughts, my own philosophy, my outlook upon things, and my beliefs. My college degree comes from the College of Hard Knocks. This is a saying that comes from my dad. It deals with knowledge gained through experience and mistakes. Reading and studying is good for everyone. It develops your brain and adds to your knowledge. The Bible gives me knowledge about Jewish history and my Christian faith. It teaches me and gives me a direction to follow even if I "take the wrong path" at times. We all do that! Take a moment and think about all the people who have been killed because of their religious beliefs. Now think about the many nations of today which allow people to worship freely. Follow your thinking with how many (and which) nations of today put censorships on worships or expressing your beliefs in public.

What is the most common theme found in all the major religious? Despite all the wars fought over religious beliefs throughout history, the most common theme found in every major religion is the theme of peace. Isn't it ironic? God bless the United States of America!

Chapter 15

Addiction

Before sitting down and writing this chapter, I put considerable time into thinking of how to approach this serious subject involving habits which become addictions. I have decided not to be heavily sociological, philosophical, or to appear as one who is an expert on the subject. I will put down my thoughts to open up avenues of thought by groups or individuals. I have been encouraged by various people to write on this subject. The most requests have come from Alcoholics Anonymous members (AA). I bow to their wishes, and I hope I can develop a worthy chapter.

Types of Addiction

When we hear the word *addiction*, what habits first come to mind? I presume it is alcohol and drug addictions. Is alcoholism a disease or simply a habit? I believe it is a habit first formed by excessive drinking, then it develops into a disease and overtakes the brain cells as the years of drinking progress. In younger people, I believe the excessive drinking is due to other problems in their life. Being intoxicated is more of an escape then a disease. We have millions of social drinkers who know how to control their alcohol intake and can substitute other drinks like soda, iced tea, or flavored water when needed. The alcohol itself is not the need. The socialization is the important thing. Since the age of twenty-five, my taste buds do not like the taste of alcohol, so in a way, I am lucky. When I socialize, I drink soda mostly. I have saved a lot of expense over the years, and I can drive anytime I want.

Thousands upon thousands of books have been written about alcoholism and its effect on society. I will be brief on the subject, but being brief does not diminish its seriousness. I am sure every reader has a family member or associate who drinks excessively. I wish to cover of variety of addictions. What I write about with other habits will have similarities with most all addictions.

The use of "social" drugs explodes during the nineteen-sixties and continued throughout the nineteen-seventies. Before the cultural change of the sixties, drinking alcohol was the "accepted" pastime and "thing" to do. Marijuana and chemicals such as LSD became very popular within the younger generation during the sixties and seventies. LSD is psychedelic drug and was also referred to as "acid" back then. Marijuana is a plant and grows very easily as a weed. This is probably where the term "weed" came from by its users. It was mostly referred to as "pot" during that time. The smoking of marijuana did not become an addiction for the majority of people who "tried" it or used it occasionally. Many people did become addicted to it because of euphoric feelings they experienced while smoking pot. The addiction (in my thinking) is more psychological than anything else. The current medical use of it helps a person deal with pain. The use of marijuana has grown since the era of our cultural change. The use of LSD did not escalate because other chemical drugs entered the scene and people tried them. Some are addictive after the first use. Some of these new drugs have controlled the user's life from day one, and the addiction is tremendous because of the chemical used. It often amazes me that the generation which protests chemicals fouling the environment and ruining our water is the same generation who participates the most with injecting, swallowing, or snorting chemicals into their bodies. Think about it! The use of illegal drugs during the sixties and seventies involved mostly the younger people. Today (2013), the use of illegal drugs spans all ages and is much more common that it was forty or fifty years ago. For that matter, legal drugs are used much more freely by the medical industry also. To give you one example, when I was born, the doctor gave my mom a few aspirins. That was the extent of her medications. And the cost of the aspirins was ten cents. I know this because Dad saved the hospital bill and gave it to me when I turned twenty-one. The entire cost of the doctor, the aspirin, and an overnight stay in the hospital was just under ninety dollars. This included the nurses and the person who wrote up the bill. Near the end of most senior citizens' lives, they are on so many prescription drugs they need a chart to keep track of them and when to take them. We have become an over medicated society. For those who have become addicted to pain killers, you know what I am saying here. When I broke my back, I used meditation to deal with my pain and only used the prescribed drug during the first two weeks of healing. There are times when you just need the medicine!

I will admit, I have a coffee habit. I am definitely not alone. The consumption of coffee in the United States is second only to drinking water. I believe this is a fact, but I could be wrong. I don't think any other fluid comes close to how many people drink coffee each day. I think this is a perfect example of how some habits are not bad habits. How many of you start your day with a cup of coffee? How come most jobs allow employees to have a coffee break? Some South American countries have prospered because of our "addition" to coffee. This is also true for the US dollars traveling south because of illegal drug use. The difference being is that coffee sales help the economy and illegal drug markets help spur criminal activities which involve violence and control of territories. Back to the topic of coffee. Think about how much effort it takes to get you that cup of coffee. The next time you are sitting at a diner counter with a cup of hot coffee in front of you, take a look at the coffee, and think about what it took to get it there. First, you have the coffee farmers. The bean pickers and the sorters are the first in the process. Then you have the transportation of the product, the exporters, the importers, the ships used, the warehouse storage, the truck driver, the salespeople involved, government inspectors, and the various company packaging involved even before the product gets to the diner. Because of our coffee habit, we support a large chain of economic activity. The final link in the chain is the waitress who pours you the cup of coffee. It doesn't really end there. When you finish your coffee and leave the diner, a busboy cleans your table, then a dishwasher washes your cup. Wow! I wonder if the coffee picker ever realizes how far that coffee bean travels or of how many people are involved to support our habit and taste buds. I have left out the two products we use along with coffee. If you add milk or creamer to your coffee, we are talking about a whole new market. Milk might surpass coffee as the leading fluid consumed in the United States. I am guessing they are both up there at the top. The second product associated with coffee drinkers is sugar. Sugar cane is grown in the United States and its market is huge. When you read ingredient labels on things you eat or drink, sugar is usually on added ingredient. As for our coffee habit, adding cream or sugar is up to each one's choice of taste. The coffee itself is the primary reason for our wanting a cup or two each day. I have enjoyed my coffee breaks for some forty years now without going a day or two without it. It is not a bad habit, and I could do without it, so I do not see it as an addiction. It is more of an everyday enjoyment similar to how most people enjoy watching their television shows every night.

Here is something most Americans cannot do without. It is made from cacao through the process of roasting and grinding. It is chocolate! What would Valentine's Day be without chocolate? What would Easter Sunday be without chocolate bunnies? In my case, it would be white chocolate. No matter how you prefer your chocolate or your chocolate-covered items, the very mention of the word *chocolate* causes our mouths to water. If you are making up survival packages of food items in caste of long periods without fresh foods, you better make sure your chocolate bars are included. If a disaster hits and you need to rely on canned foods, freeze dried fruits and vegetables, crackers, peanut butter, and other things, your chocolate bars will probably be the most prized items in your packages. I am not saying it is the most nutritious item or the most filling item, but when it comes to satisfying your tastes buds, chocolate is at the top of the list. Is the eating of chocolate addictive? With some people, it is. It is a problem some people deal with daily. The problem with eating too much chocolate is due to the calories taken into our system and the sugar intake which sometimes is at harmful levels. A person addicted to eating chocolate and chocolate-covered snacks is at risk to having serious health problems because of their sugar intake. I am not a doctor, but I am guessing that a person could risk getting diabetes if addicted to eating chocolates and gives in to their addiction. This could be a good topic for a high school class to discuss after doing some research on the disease. I realize a diabetic has a deficiency of insulin within their system, but I would guess a chocolate addict could develop a disease such as diabetes if their habit is not curtailed. Here is a subject for you students to explore and debate. Do your research and go to it! Maybe your teacher can supply the chocolates for everyone to sample?

A newer and more modern addiction is the habitual use of relying on electronic devices. If the terrorists were to strike at our electrical, communicative, or even our satellite sources, our country would be at a standstill. Most people today do not know how to survive without their new technologies functioning. Most everything is run by the new technology which needs electric or battery operation. Hand-operated tools are hardly used today. Are you a twenty-year-old carpenter? Have you ever cut a two by four or two by ten with a handsaw? I only give this as one more example of relying on electric power to do things. The addiction of electronic devices involves the use of computers, the surfing of the Internet, the communicating with other people via the Internet on a continual basis when most of your time is spent awake is involved. Because of your personal computer, you can sit at home and view things or communicate with others privately. It does cause a lack of socializing with the "real" community which is your neighborhood or the town you live in. The habitual use of a computer diminishes your social contact with people. We all need to have social contact with real people in real settings. It is a human need. We need to see, hear, smell, feel, and speak to others so we can experience things and other people as nature expects us to. We dehumanize ourselves by not interacting with others on a natural basis. The new technologies are tremendous and a great improvement to society. But without a balance, even the best things can be harmful. Our lives need balance just as our bodies do.

We need to balance our physical needs, our mental needs, and our spiritual needs. There are twenty-four hours in a day. We generally sleep about eight of those hours. What we do during the other sixteen hours is a matter of balancing our day. We take time to eat, shower, dress, travel, work, or take care of our children. The many other things we do take time. Some days, we shop or have our vehicle repaired. There are times we see the doctor, dentist, or optometrist. To live a balance life, we cannot spend most of our time sitting at home in front of a computer unless that time spent is our work and produces an income as a result. The addiction I am referring to involves playing games, viewing websites, etc. for personal enjoyment. This addiction cuts into people's sleeping hours and other time needed for a balanced day.

Here is an idea for a CEO of a company which is involved primarily in electronic technology. Take some of your key people and managers to an outdoor resort, ranch, or camp for five nights and four days. They can eat well, live comfortably, and enjoy each other's company. The requirements is that for those five nights and four days, they must partake in things which do not require any modern technology. No electronic devices are allowed. No cell phones are allowed to be turned on unless of an emergency. They must rely on writing with a pencil, pen, and paper. No television or radio is allowed; only a daily newspaper or magazine is allowed. Have the manager of the place you stay at set up activities for your people to do during the day. Have a daily meeting where everyone discusses how they feel and what they are experiencing. In essence, your key people and managers will experience life without electronic devices for the first time in their adult lives. Or for that matter, maybe their entire lives. It is an idea which could strengthen your company's skills at a later date because these people will realize what life is like without modern technology. Because of their ages, they may not know how it was before the age of modern technology. If they are over forty years of age, then they will remember about doing things differently. Things were done slower, and our brains were required to store the knowledge we gained by studying books or paging through our encyclopedias. We could not have a computer do our research. Visits to a local library were common because most students would do their researching there. It was also a place to meet and hang out awhile with friends. Most parents didn't know about that type of research their teens were doing.

If you ask most teenagers or people in their twenties if they could do without their cell phones, their computers at home, or their games boards, you will usually get a no for an answer. They will probably ask you, "Why?" Or they may say, "What in the world would I do?" They may consider you "old fashion" for simply asking the question. If you are a parent, you know the financial burden all the new devices have put on you. There is an answer: have your child work for any new items. Set up an allowance system for the chores they do or have your older children work after school and weekends at a local store or market. This might just curb their addiction a bit, and they will take better care of the things they have to toil for. It is not a bad thing for young people to learn about the financial world while they are still in school. Look at how many young entrepreneurs have become very successful before the age of thirty because they started working on their dreams (or desires) while still in school. I think they looked at what they are doing with technology as an art, a challenge, or making a dream become reality. I would not call that an addiction. I call it imagination.

Most of the use on the Internet is of business-oriented or of very innocent personal use. An addiction which has grown to dangerous levels on the Internet is sexual addiction because of the entire world being able to post sites, share photos and information, exploit children from all corners of the globe, show the most explicit deviant sexual acts, etc. People within your communities who you would never expect or imagine to be viewing or even contributing to these activities can do so because it is mostly done within the privacy of their homes or apartments. In the past, people had to order and receive sexual material through the mail or go to a certain section within a city to partake in live viewings. Their materials came packaged in the plain brown paper wrappings so that no one could identify the contents. Their material now comes onto their computer screens. Live action, real people (mostly I guess) every act imaginable, both genders, all ages, and anything else which can feed the sexual addiction of people willing to pay the providers who are raking in billions of dollars is available through the net. The sad thing about this addiction and the easy availability to feed this addiction is that innocent children are being used and abused to facilitate other's sexual wants. Young women and young men are being enslaved because of this. For the providers, it is extremely profitable. For the viewers, it is, only they know! Here we are in the year 2013, and we have slavery going on (sex slavery). I guess it doesn't matter how far we progress with technology. We will always have evil. I hope by writing about this sort of addiction, it can prevent someone or even a few people from going that path.

Since I do not have, use, or know how to use a computer, I apologize for any technical errors about the computer world. Despite my lack of knowledge, I am very aware of what goes on in the world because of reading newspapers and listening to radio programs on a daily basis. I do not even own one because my time is spent writing. The idea of writing about the modern technological devices and Internet came from one of the readers of *Pure Power*. I thank you, Eric, for your suggestion. Enjoy your coffee!

Most of the things we do on a daily basis are good. The most common thing I do comes naturally to me. I think constantly. No matter where I am or of what activity I am doing, I think about things. I accredit my deep-thinking abilities as a gift from God. Every one of us has a certain gift which God has bestowed on us. Mine is to be able to think and then write upon it.

Take a moment and think of what your common likes are and what activities you do because you enjoy doing them. I'll write about a few to help you or your group create a discussion. One of the more popular activities is golf. Talk with any member of a golf club or golf course, and they will verify this. A very healthy and enjoyable activity is horseback riding. Whether it is riding for miles in open country or riding and jumping in smaller areas, the people who do this love horses and take great care of them. Have you ever done any kayaking? The kayaking I have enjoyed is exploring calm and remote waterways. It is a great way to see a variety of wildlife because you are quiet and low to the surface of the water. If you are adventurous, then you can take your kayak onto the fast-moving rivers and streams. Learn first from an expert because it can be very dangerous at times. Here is a very popular activity—shopping! With some people, this can be an addiction. With most people, it is a fun way to spend a day. The guys will be in the hardware stores, fishing and hunting stores or automotive stores, and the women will be anywhere a store is. Am I right?

There used to be a bowling alley in every town. I would say there is at least one in every county now. Bowling is still a fun activity, and the sport still has a fairly large following but not like it was during the fifties and sixties. If you have never bowled, take some of your friends and try it out. It is fun, and you don't have to be good at it. During our grade school days, we all hung out on Saturday mornings at our local bowling alley because they had a bowling league for us to play in at a very low cost. To show you how my thought patterns sometimes work, I am going from bowling to dogsledding. Have you ever met a team of dogs and their trainer? What an incredible experience! When I was living in Eustis, Maine, I got to meet one such team and their dedicated trainer who gave dogsled rides during the winter season along the trails which were groomed for cross-country skiers and/or snowmobilers. It is not an addiction; it is a joy!

Twenty years ago and before that, millions of Americans had a hobby which benefitted them financially. They put together coins and stamps into an organized collection. Most of their coins were from the era when the coins were made of silver. Their stamp collections were bound in plastic sheets and put into large binders. I don't think as many people collect coins and stamps today because of the economy. Many people have had to sell their collections as a matter of survival. The wealthy and the rich have built up their collections because they have the money to spend. During the hard times, the average Americans see a decrease in their saving and assets while those with money to invest see increases. It is just the way it is.

During the nineteen-fifties and sixties, every young boy and teenager had a baseball card collection. We traded our cards, flipped our cards, and threw our cards. Flipping involved putting a card into your hand and with a twist of your hand let it go spinning to the ground. You had two boys doing this at the same time. You called heads or tails just like with a coin. Heads was the baseball player's picture. The boy who won took both cards. If you tied, then you did it again. Throwing your cards meant you needed to get a "leaner" against a wall. This could involve a whole group of boys. The cards stayed on the ground until someone got their card to lean against the wall. This boy collected all the cards and had a big smile. Of course, you didn't throw your Mickey Mantle, Ted Williams, Lou Gehrick, Yogi Beara, or other valuable cards. But this was how you picked up extra cards in order to trade. Back then, a Mickey Mantle card would trade for a least twenty-five other player cards. The baseball cards (new) were bought at a local store. In our area, we mostly got the Philadelphia Phillies, the Boston Red Sox, the New York Yankees, and the Chicago Cubs cards. Our average card collection was about five hundred cards which your kept stacked in shoeboxes. It was a fun hobby, and I don't remember anyone being addicted to saving their cards. My cards all disappeared one day. Someone took them! I was a young teen then.

Habits or hobbies that do not develop into addictions are simply things we do in life. They do not control us. They do not disturb our life. They add to our lives in a good way because they keep us busy. The most widespread addictions and maybe the most harmful are the first two I wrote about: alcoholism and drug abuse. The addictions will always be with societies. They are not going away. But we can try not to fall into their traps. I do not believe sex addiction will ever go away either because it seems that so many are involved in it no matter what age they are. Unfortunately, a lot of violence comes along with some of the addictions. The violence is usually done against the young and the females. How many rapes occur in our country every day? How many children or teens have died because of sexual predators? How many lives have been ruined? The answer is, too many. Do not become one of them please.

I encourage students to discuss addiction among their peers. The more you know about a subject, the more you can prevent yourself from falling into a bad habit or of becoming a victim. Many students around the country are "street wise." Those who live in the cities usually are, and they see much more then children who live in rural areas or small communities. My advice is to stay clear of the gangs and their activities. Be your own person. A gang will not strengthen you. It will only make you a part of a group you will rely on. The gang will force you to do things. This is not freedom! Walk your own line. Be free to choose what you want to do. Be strong physically, mentally, and spiritually. If you want to join a gang, then join the toughest gang there is in the world; join the United States Marines! You will get all the action you can handle. If you don't want to fight, then join the medical corps. There are not too many gang members who grow old unless they are in prison or have left the gangs. That should tell you where gang membership will get you. There are a few big celebrities out there who left the gangs and went into the entertainment industry. Listen to their message to see what they think.

I will end this chapter on a light note. I did not write about our addictions to eating snacks because that is all I did while writing this week. Tonight, I wrote the last three pages while finishing a bag a Cracker Jacks, half a bag of Tastykake mini donuts, two packs of premium saltines, and a half gallon of water. My stomach is full, and my brain is tried. Eating snacks is not an addiction for me; it is simply something I enjoy now and then. This week was a snack week. I will walk it off, don't worry.

CHAPTER 16

Closing Thoughts

In chapter 3 of part 1, I wrote, "Dream about things, but don't stop there! Put them into action and make your dreams a reality." This is what I have done by completing this book. Even while writing part 2, I know I would not be completing my dream of putting together a book which would satisfy the dream (or goal) floating around in my mind. I now feel I have completed my dream, and these writings will remain long after I leave this earth. Also by writing about "Journey for Peace," people will know about my attempt to promote personal peace and peace in schools. We set goals, work to complete them, but sometimes, things just do not work out. It is the trying that counts! I am glad I have the opportunity to mention people throughout this book. It is good because a lot of people do good deeds without ever getting recognition for their work, their charity, their writings (reporters), or their positive effects on others. You may have noticed how many people I named in the chapter about my walks. I tried to recognize as many as I could, and I apologize to those whom I have left out. It is not intentional.

By using my own experiences, thoughts, and feelings, I believe it communicates to you, the reader, in a more personal way and an honest way. I do not profess to be a professional writer. I write more for the art of writing then for fame or fortune which many strive for. Purpose is its own fame and good effect upon others is its own fortune. The writings in this book began way back in the late nineteen-eighties. It is now 2015 as I complete proofing and editing part 3. For those who gave me encouragement to keep writing, I thank in spirit because some have passed away during the years since putting out *Pure Power*. Mom, Dad, Ron Samartino, William Wienberger, Harvey Forsyth, and Jimmy Young are the true friends I lost. My brother John left us also. He is truly missed! Jack (as we called him) and I had plenty of good times together, God bless him. This is life! This is reality! One day, I will leave also, as we all do. God has His plan. It is His will. "Thy will be done, on earth as it is in heaven" (from the Lord's Prayer).

I know there are repetitive thoughts recorded in this book, but I do not edit myself because of the way I write. I meditate on much of what I write, as I write. So to eliminate certain repetitions, I feel it would take away from the meanings I wish to project at that particular time of thought. So be it; it isn't conventional. Three of my other books are not too conventional either. I write to please the readers, not the professors or the scholars. Unless, of course, they enjoy how I write. The three other books are:

> *Surfers' Love Story*
> *Secret Tales of the American Wealthy*
> *Surfers' Love Story II* (manuscript form)

They are fiction with a base of nonfiction disguised within the stories. I am also working on a murder/adventure which I am writing in a Mark Twain style of storytelling. Who knows when I will complete it? It is something different for me because I am making everything up from pure imagination. The characters came to life in my head, but they are still purely fictional. It is actually fun to create this story from my imagination.

For the young people who are thinking about writing for a career, I suggest you take the appropriate courses at a college or university. With a degree, you will be accepted more readily when seeking work. Without a degree, it is extremely hard to land a good paying job writing for a newspaper, magazine, or other publications. I do not have a degree in literature. The degree I have earned in the martial arts allows me to write with knowledge concerning the subjects involved in the art. I retired from teaching after breaking my back, but it has not retired me as a writer. I retired as Renshi (expert teacher) Fourth Degree Black Belt, USA-GOJU KARATE. A Fourth Degree Black Belt is equal to receiving a master's degree. I taught nonprofit, but if I make a profit from writing, that is fine with me. I will travel the country promoting and selling my books. We all need to eat and be comfortable! The smartest businesspeople say we should choose our occupations within the field of work we enjoy most. This is what I intend to do the rest of my life, God willing. If you are a student, think about what the smart businesspeople are telling us. Contemplate on what you enjoy doing and what careers you can purse to match it. You may as well be happy with your work because working for a living is hard enough. If you choose a physically hard career, keep in mind that certain injuries can change things overnight. After my fall and because of the injuries to my back and leg, my financial situation changed drastically. I thank God I can still work and get around fairly well. My advice is to prepare yourself as a boss and have employees in case you are injured. Being self-employed is a good thing. Small businesses are the backbone of our nation. Math and science careers are probably the most important careers of the future. My thinking is the medical field will always have the most needed careers no matter what our economy situation is. People are born, they get hurt, they get sick, some get old, and we all die. It is a fact of life, and it has always been so. Have you ever met a poor undertaker?

Choice of Themes

Part III of this book varied a little from my other themes because of several factors. First, it is because I listened to what people who read *Pure Power* said to me. Numerous people asked me to write about my adventures and elaborate in better detail about them. I hope I have. The trivia questions were not planned for this book until a group of people encouraged me to include them near the end of my book. I did not realize trivia was so popular with so many people until I began asking various associates what their thoughts were concerning trivia. It seemed overwhelmingly popular, so I included them. Now that I did, I am happy there is a chapter with them in this book.

I did the chapter about the United States of America because I know people will be reading this book in other countries. With eBooks becoming popular and more inexpensive to purchase, this book, like others, will reach a global market. I also want to give an American view to those readers which reflects one (me) American's perspective on the nation he was born and raised in. If chapter 7 of part 3 can cause people to discuss the United States and my writings about America, then the time spent was worthwhile and has good purpose. When the peoples of other countries can get perspectives of an average American and not from the media which tends to be "politically correct" or biased, then the "average" citizens of other countries might understand our nation better. Look at our relation with the Russian people now. Our countries were once divided and aiming nuclear missiles at each other. Because the people of our country and of Russia understand each other better and communicate freely now, we are friends and have exchange student programs. Hundreds of students from Russia come every summer to work in the resort town I live in. They learn about us, and we learn about them. We are not very different! They blend in very well with their own age groups. They work, party, and shop just like the American kids do! With the people of different nations knowing each other on personal levels and understanding the cultural differences on personal levels, peace is bolstered. Again, it is the average people (not the political leaders, dictators, or kings) who need to share ideas, fashions, sports, music, and dialogue. Hopefully, this book will reach a world market so people can read how one American thinks, questions, writes, and reflects upon life. This can give them a different perspective about us Americans since there is too much propaganda going on throughout the world. Also because the media outlets tend to sensualize stories and dwell upon the negatives, this book can enlighten people outside of our borders. One of the constant themes of this book concerns peace. Peace starts with individual, spreads because of people's desire to feel comfortable and safe, then spreads to take hold in nations and between nations. It is like building a mountain with stones. You start with one and keep adding more until the mountain becomes high.

I wrote this poem, which could be to music, while recovering from my back injury. Someday, a good songwriter might refine it and have it put to music.

Nature's Peace

Can you feel it?
Can you see it?
It's in the air.
Chores—it's everywhere.
Peace is now and here to stay.
Peace is now and here to stay.
An eagle circles the mountain summit.

Song:

A fawn plays in a field of wildflowers.
The harvest moon rests upon a calm ocean.
Use your eyes and see peace in motion.
Peace has no boundaries; no fences.
Feel the obvious; use your senses.
A rainbow guards a plush green valley.
A brook rambles through a quiet forest.
A buoys light filters through the fog.
A white heron stands, watching the meadow.
Can you hear the birds sing at dawn?
Do you smell the scent of a fresh cut lawn?
A pond reflects a puffy white cloud.
The flowers spread their soft pedals.
Oh, the smell of honeysuckle is so sweet.
A farmer looks out over his field sunrise.
Peace is there; in a young child's smile.
Peace is there; during a fiery sunrise.
A bee goes from rose to rose.

How can peace have any foes?
Evil is out!
Peace is in!
Think about it.
God has the ultimate clout.

Some of the themes and a few of the chapters in part 3 concern things which are not too philosophical, yet they are included to entertain. We need not be serous all the time. If I was better at humor, I would have had a chapter of jokes! I will leave that to comedians to do.

It is a fine thing to be on the positive side of humanity, but I am compelled to question some of our negatives. Wars, terrorism, and the harming of innocent people will always be with us. It is the battle between good and evil. Why do humans constantly battle each other? Is it because evil is always with us? I think, yes. The good side of society wants peace and wants its people to live happily. This is always disrupted because of evil. We are constantly engaged in this battle. We cannot ignore the negatives, yet we cannot ignore the positives which cut away on the negatives. Take for example the issue of hunger and thirst. Hunger, malnutrition, and lack of clean drinking water kill millions of humans every year. Hunger is a negative. It is also a sad way to die since our world has the knowledge and capabilities to grow plenty of food, transport it, and preserve it. Groups are involved everywhere to fight hunger, yet we still see millions of people suffering from the lack of nutritious food. Hunger, like war, will always be around and will continue to kill most vulnerable people who are usually children and the elderly. You and I can help in small ways to limit hunger. I encourage students to research the causes of hunger and to see where the problems lie. In the United States, we have people suffering from hunger and malnutrition in every state. Why? Education about nutrition is probably the best way to fight hunger in an advanced country like ours. We have enough water, and we grow enough food for every citizen and every visitor within the United States. Our nation can end hunger within its borders if our leaders would simply deal with the real issues of hunger and stop playing politics with it! Here is a fact of the "streets." The government issues millions of people food stamps as a solution to hunger. Many, many people receive their food stamps or buy food with their vouchers and sell the food to other people so they can use the cash to buy alcohol, drugs, cell phones, and other items. The people who buy the stamps or food products get a discount, but they really do not need assistance. Do the people receiving the assistance really need assistance? If they were hungry, they would buy food. Have you ever been hungry? That is one thing. Have you ever suffered from hunger? That is very different from simply feeling hungry. A really hungry person will eat almost anything. Government assistance is needed, but government "handouts" are not needed. Better methods are needed to see that the needy are provided with food, and the "not so needy" are weeded out of the system.

Here is my take on charities today. Do not just give money to charities. Research the charity first. See where the money goes and how much of the money goes to salaries, founders, and administrative costs. The charity industry (yes, industry) is big business. Believe me. I have learned this over the years. I did my homework, and I was surprised at the things I learned about why so many people get involved running charities. I would not want to do any walks for the charities who had high administration costs, high salaries for their executives, or (with some) questionable accounting practices. This is one part of the education on hunger you can partake in. I call it "doing your homework." Keep an eye on those who would use charity to gain a profit for themselves. Any charity you intend to help should be scrutinized first. Hunger charities are just a fraction of the charity industry. There seems to be a charity for every cause out there. Do you agree? Charity is a good thing! But let us keep our eye on the need more than money. Do not allow sympathetic feelings to shadow reality. In my mind, an example of a good, solid charity is the charity doing the work they are meant to do on a regular basis. One example: every time we have a disaster in the United States, who is there? It is the American Red Cross. It is the Salvation Army. We really do not need our government to be involved in every need to our citizens because there are too many people using the government to carry them through life and it has created an unproductive society within a society. Both of our political parties are at fault here. The government does need to monitor their programs a lot more than they have been doing. The more programs that are in place requires more government employees who are paid through the "peoples" money. We simply need stronger, trusted, and more localized charities to ease the burden. Whether it be food, clothing, or shelter (the three basic needs), local charitable groups can do a better job than the government because the charities don't just hand out money. They give actual food, actual clothes, and screen people very closely when it involves long term shelter. People, themselves, must be more responsible for their own lives. Our schools should be teaching our young the importance of social responsibility. It is important because it makes for a strong and free society which has made the United States stand out among the other countries of the world. Do some research to see just how many countries of the world receive foreign aid from the United States every year. The amounts are in the billions of dollars! Where does the money come from? It comes from the American people, not the government agencies. We are the government.

In order for an individual to be able to help others, the individual needs to be secure first. It is not very easy to rescue a drowning person if you cannot swim. Being secure first transcends to our communities. A community that is secure can take care of its people. The churches, charities within the community, the volunteers, the food banks, and the local businesses are all very important to the welfare of those who live there. Look at your own town or city. How many volunteers are active? How many local charities are functioning? How many churches, synagogues, temples, and lodges are reaching out to the needy? Quite a few, I would guess. This is all done because of compassion and humanitarian responsibility; two virtues we need not to lose. Their work comes from caring, not control. Their work produces hope, not dependency. This is good. This is freedom. It is local so many, if not all, of the people know each other. The government agencies know us as a number or an applicant. Our communities are the backbone of the nation. They are the cornerstones of each state. Think about this when you are ready to volunteer or donate.

Last Thought

I see this book as a completion of a major goal. I have been working on, meditating on, praying on, and writing part 3 for a long time now. I have proofed and edited all these chapters three times. Within a short time, I will get to see my efforts reach others in the form a book. I will look forward to your feedback and opinions, good or bad. This is a major purpose for me. I hope students everywhere will get a chance to read this book. I encourage teachers to use this book as a teaching tool. There are plenty of topics to pick from! If you know a student, please let them know about this book and encourage them to read it from page one to the end. You will be helping them because the schools skip over a lot of real-life values and have their own agendas. Thank you for reading this book!

I can now rest with the knowledge that *Life Going Forward* is completed. God bless you all. Maybe I will see some of you while I am on my tour promoting and selling this book. Peace!

Bill Flynn

About the Author

Bill Flynn has been writing for nearly forty years. This is book number 5 for him. He puts purpose as his priority when writing non-fictional works—as you will see by reading this book—by using his own life experiences, deep thoughts, and reflections. The American culture is described and exemplified in a simple manner.

Bill Flynn spent twenty-eight years training, learning, then teaching the traditional martial art of karate. He is a fourth-degree black belter with the given title of RENSHI. Certified by Master Edward Veryken USA—GOJU KARATE. Author Bill Flynn is often referred to as an ordinary person who has done extraordinary things. He sees writing as art and a way to teach young people about life.

CPSIA information can be obtained
at www.ICGtesting.com
Printed in the USA
LVHW011323061020
668069LV00003B/248

9 781098 044671